Edna M. Swigart

1103 E. Huron St.

SEVENTH EDITION

THE

HOMOPHONIC FORMS

OF

MUSICAL COMPOSITION

AN EXHAUSTIVE TREATISE ON THE STRUCTURE AND DEVELOPMENT OF MUSICAL FORMS FROM THE SIMPLE PHRASE TO THE SONG-FORM WITH "TRIO"

FOR THE USE OF

General and Special Students of Musical Structure

BY

PERCY GOETSCHIUS, Mus. Doc.

(Royal Württemberg Professor)

AUTHOR OF

"THE MATERIAL USED IN MUSICAL COMPOSITION"
"THE THEORY AND PRACTICE OF TONE-RELATIONS"
"MODELS OF THE PRINCIPAL MUSICAL FORMS," etc.

NEW YORK:
G. SCHIRMER
1913

13710

To

Mrs. H. H. A. Beach

AS A CORDIAL TRIBUTE

TO AN EMINENT WOMAN-COMPOSER

OF

AMERICA

PREFACE.

I.

This book undertakes no more than the systematic enumeration and exhaustive explanation of all the formal designs and methods of structural treatment in the homophonic domain of musical composition, as revealed in classical or standard writings. The student who aims to acquire the Science of composition, is expected to imitate these designs and methods, and to look for additional illustrations and confirmations in general musical literature. This will develop skill and facility, will induce correct habits of musical thought, will enrich the mind with a fund of resources, and stimulate the imagination to increased responsiveness and activity.

But, further than this, the book lays no claim to furnishing clues to the subtle Art of composition. In converting his theoretical knowledge into successful practice,—into a *means to an end*,—the student can appeal to no other authority than that of his own fancy, good taste, and natural or acquired judgment.

II.

The examples given for reference *must be inspected*,—if not totally, at least in great part. No student should hope to be entirely successful and efficient as a composer without possessing quite extensive acquaintance with the products and processes of successful writers. Therefore, the pupil must regard the conscientious examination of these carefully selected quotations, as a *very significant and distinctly essential* part of his study. This applies more especially to the works cited in Divisions I, II and III.

Some of the works,—those to which constant or frequent reference is made,—he must endeavor to own; for example:

The Pianoforte Sonatas of Beethoven, Haydn, Mozart and Schubert;
The Symphonies (arr. for 2 hands) of Beethoven and Haydn;
The Bagatelles of Beethoven;

The "Songs without Words" of MENDELSSOHN;
The Mazurkas, Nocturnes and Preludes of CHOPIN;
The Pfte. works of SCHUMANN (op. 12, 15, 68, 82, 99, 124), and of BRAHMS (op. 10, 76, 79, 116, 117, 118, 119);
And some of the Songs of SCHUBERT and SCHUMANN.

III.

The author hopes and expects that the book will prove quite as necessary and useful to the *general music-student*, as to the prospective composer; a knowledge of homophonic musical structure being, undeniably, of equal importance to *all* musical artists, reproductive as well as productive.

The general student, while studying and analyzing with the same thoroughness as the special student of composition, will simply omit all the prescribed Exercises.

PERCY GOETSCHIUS. Mus. Doc.

Boston, Mass., December, 1897.

TABLE OF CONTENTS.

(Figures in parentheses refer to paragraphs.)

CHAP. III. THE DEVELOPMENT OR EXTENSION OF THE PHRASE:

CHAP. XII. THE ORDINARY COMPLETE THREE-PART SONG-FORM:

CHAP. XIII. ADDITIONAL DETAILS OF THE SONG-FORMS:

DIVISION 3.

DIVISION 4.

CONVENTIONAL STYLES OF COMPOSITION.

INTRODUCTORY.

The four most important requisites of successful musical composition are: 1stly, ample comprehension and command of the relations and associations of tone; 2ndly, an active and fertile imagination; 3rdly, a strong and well-balanced intellect; and 4thly, the life-breathing attribute of emotional passion.

Of these four, the last-mentioned cannot be acquired; it must be innately present in the disposition of the individual; and, consequently, it will not, and cannot, be a subject of consideration in this treatise upon Composition. On the contrary, the second condition, Imagination (with the no less important faculty of Discrimination), can evidently be cultivated and developed to a large extent; and one of the chief aims of the following pages will therefore be, to point out every possible means of arousing and stimulating this imaginative faculty.

The first-named condition, finally, skilful technical manipulation of the tone-material and its resources, is very largely indeed a matter of study, and may be acquired by any ordinarily intelligent student, to an extent proportionate to his application and patience. Though not the most significant, it is the most indispensable—the first and fundamental, requirement. Therefore, the mastery of the principal details of Tone-relation (Harmony) is expected of the student before he undertakes the study of composition proper. Adopting the view that much facility (probably the greatest and best) is to be acquired through the *application* of this fundamental knowledge to the construction of musical designs, rather than through its exercise as an independent object of study, the present author demands no more preparatory harmonic and contrapuntal knowledge than will have been acquired by the faithful and exhaustive study of "The Material used in Musical Composition" *,

* Latest (4th) ed. G. Schirmer, New York. 1895.

or "The Theory and Practice of Tone-relations" * (with the supplementary exercise indicated in its preface), or any other standard treatise upon Harmony.

The Harmonic Fundament.

The broadest principles of Harmony are herewith recapitulated; not for the information of the beginner, who would learn nothing of value from such a summary review, but in order to afford the advanced student of Harmony a bird's-eye view of the entire domain of Tone-association, such as will facilitate his choice and use of the material in the execution of the given musical designs:

1. The source and material basis of all music, of whatsoever character and style it may be, is the Chord—i.e., a structure of from three to five tones, arranged in *contiguous intervals of the* (*major or minor*) *third*. Of these chord-structures, there are three of fundamental rank, erected upon the Tonic, Dominant and Second-dominant (or Subdominant) of the chosen key. The nature of every Chord is determined by the key, which latter resolves itself into a Scale of conjunct tones, constituting the Platform of musical operations.

2. The movement from one chord into another, whereby all harmonic vitality is generated, seems to be dictated largely (if not mainly) by the simple choice between a whole-step progression and a half-step progression, either of which is invariably feasible in one or another, or all, of the respective tone-lines (parts or voices), which describe or delineate the figures of the musical design.

These chord-changes are Regular when the distinction of whole-step or of half-step progression is not determined by option, but by the strict harmonic conditions of the key; they are Irregular (not necessarily "wrong") when the choice is arbitrarily made, giving rise to more or less frequent changes of key.

This sweeping option (of leading the respective parts upward or downward a whole step or a half-step) discloses one of the most comprehensive and inexhaustible sources of harmonic and melodic motion, including, as it does, every conceivable chord-progression, regular or irregular. But at the same time it is so vague and seductive, that the student should not adopt it as a rule for the

* New Engl. Conservatory, Boston, Mass. 1894.

determination of his harmonic conduct. He must regard it rather as a *result* (e. g., of some thematic or formal design) than as a *cause;* and must accept it chiefly as a proof that there can never be an excuse for harmonic monotony or apathy. It is obvious, furthermore, that the free exercise of this option can be conceded only to those who have first become firmly grounded in all the principles of *regular* harmonic progression. The following random successions illustrate the point in question:

*1) Up to this point all the chord-successions are regular, because, in each separate case, both chords belong to the same key, and are connected according to the natural law of chord-progression.

*2) These two successions are irregular, because not in conformity with the rules of diatonic chord-movement.

*3) And this succession (in common with all chromatics) is irregular, because a mixture of keys takes place.

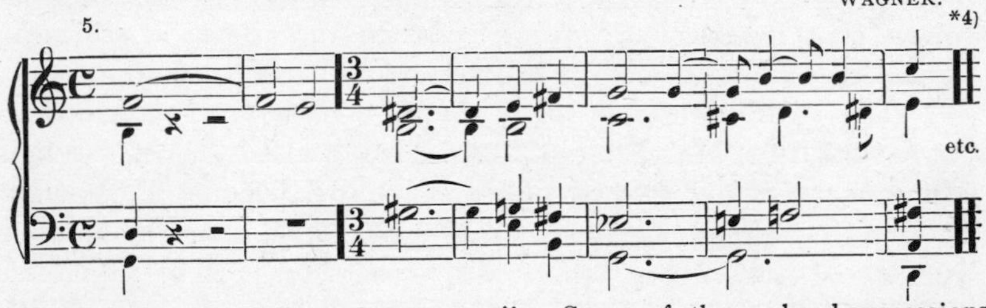

*4) From the "Götterdämmerung". Some of these chord-successions can be accounted for in no other way than as a purely optional choice of whole- or half-step part-progression.

*5) This unique cluster of half-step movements may be demonstrated as passing-notes upon a *regular* chord-basis.

3. The tones which form a chord constitute the harmonic nucleus of the phrase; but, while they may, and frequently do, appear in their primary condition (see Ex. 10; Ex. 27), they are often ornamented with those other scale-tones which lie immediately above or below the individual chord-tones (as Neighboring-notes); sometimes so richly, that a very simple and otherwise perhaps monotonous measure assumes a more unique and elaborate shape, and is transformed from the character of rugged or stolid simplicity into one of greater grace or deeper passion. For illustration (chord-tones in large type):

4. Furthermore, the chord-tones (possibly in connection with their auxiliary neighbors) are not always presented in one simultaneous bulk, but frequently so separated (dispersed or "broken") as to produce an animated rhythmic and melodic effect, and to extend into other, higher or lower, registers than the common and convenient tone-locality corresponding to the compass of the human voices. Thus:

These fundamental varieties of tone-combination, supplemented by a large number of inferior distinctions which will be pointed out in their proper place and order, constitute the MATERIAL out of which the composer develops his artistic creation.

The processes to be pursued in this act : the draughting of the design, the execution of the details, and the modes of manipulating the natural material—these it is the province of a treatise upon "Musical Form" to expound.

THE DIVISIONS OF MUSICAL FORM.

The entire range of musical forms is divided into three grand classes :

1stly, THE HOMOPHONIC FORMS; embracing the majority of smaller designs, and a number of the larger ones, and characterized by the predomination of the simpler styles of harmony, and the element of SINGLE MELODY.

2ndly, THE POLYPHONIC FORMS; embracing the Invention, Fugue and Canon, and characterized by the CONSTANT ASSOCIATION OF TWO OR MORE INDIVIDUAL MELODIES.

3rdly, THE HIGHER OR COMPLEX FORMS; embracing the majority of larger designs, and characterized by the union of the homophonic and polyphonic principles of treatment, and also by greater logical continuity and closer affinity between the component members of the design. The matter under treatment in the present volume is that of the first of these classes :

THE HOMOPHONIC FORMS.

THE HOMOPHONIC FORMS.

DIVISION ONE.

THE PHRASE-FORMS.

CHAPTER I.

THE PHRASE.

1. The Phrase is the structural basis of all musical forms. It is a series of chords in uninterrupted succession, extending (when regular) through *four ordinary measures* in ordinary moderate tempo.

When the tempo is slow (Adagio — Larghetto), or the measures large (6/8—9/8—12/8), the Phrase may extend through only two measures; and, inversely, in rapid tempi, or when the measures are of a smaller denomination, the Phrase may contain eight measures. Any other, larger or smaller, number of measures (3, 5, 6, 7, 9, etc.) must constitute an irregular design, the causes and purposes of which will be seen in due time (par. 33).

2a. The simple Phrase begins with the tonic chord; or, in exceptional cases, with the dominant (see Ex. 14, No. 1), or with some other harmony of preliminary effect. The first tone of the Phrase-melody may appear upon any beat or fraction of the measure.

In case it begins upon any *unaccented* beat, or fraction of a beat, it is evident that the first (apparent) measure will be an incomplete one, and it must be distinctly understood that such an incomplete measure is merely preliminary and is *never to be counted as first measure*, no matter how little it may lack of being an entire measure. (This must be borne constantly in mind in counting the measures in all given references. The *first* measure in a Phrase, or composition of any design, is the first *full* measure!) The preliminary beats or fractions are in reality a borrowed portion of the *final* measure, and will be deducted from the latter, as a rule. See Ex. 5; Ex. 10 (beginning upon first accent). Ex. 6; Ex. 7b; Ex. 12 (beginning on last beat of preliminary measure). Ex. 13, No. 2; Ex. 14, No. 2 (beginning one beat and a half before first accent); Ex. 14, No. 1; Ex. 23, No. 6 (beginning on secondary accent of preliminary measure); Ex. 7; Ex. 13, No. 1; Ex. 22, No. 5 (beginning four beats before first accent); Ex. 41, No. 1; Ex. 45, No. 1; Ex. 66, measure 4.

(b) The Phrase closes with a Cadence; if a simple Phrase, independent of associates, or the final one of a series of Phrases, it closes with the so-called PERFECT CADENCE; otherwise with a semi-cadence (explained in par. 36).

A cadence is an interruption of the harmonic and (particularly) the melodic current, — a check, or pause, — a point of repose, which marks the conclusion of some melodic line, — but without affecting the fundamental rhythmic pulse. Cadences are distinguished, and their employment determined, by the force and extent of this interruption.

3. Of the perfect cadence there is only one harmonic form, namely: the Tonic triad, with its root in both outer parts, on an accented beat, and preceded by a fundamental form of the Dominant harmony (whose rhythmic location and extent is, however, optional). Thus, in the skeleton of a 4-measure Phrase:

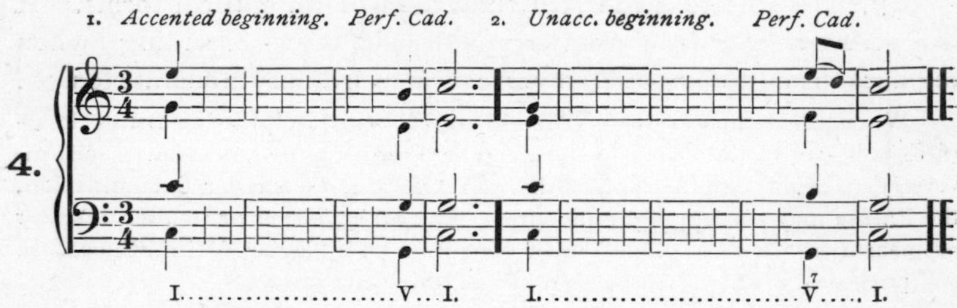

4. But this unalterable *harmonic* form is, nevertheless, subject to a *rhythmic* modification, which consists in projecting the final tonic chord a beat or more beyond its proper cadence-accent, by holding over the preceding dominant harmony (or parts of it) in any of the manifold Suspension-forms. Thus:

*1) The V at the accent of this cadence-measure is merely a Suspension of the Dominant which appears in the comparatively unaccented third measure. This *unaccented* impression of the Dominant must always be preserved, in order to sustain the comparative rhythmic superiority (accent) of the cadence-tonic.

The object of the rhythmic modification is, to avoid abruptness, or to diminish the power of the cadence. As a rule, the cadence-tonic may be thus deferred to any extent (even beyond the cadence-measure); but it is generally objectionable for it to appear upon any pulse beyond the final *accent* (in case it is compound time, with more than one accent to a measure), or beyond the last *full beat* in 2/4, 3/4, and other simple measures. In the Polonaise, and certain other styles of composition, this belated cadence-tonic is characteristic. For example:

See also Ex. 63,—Cadence on the second 8th-note, in 2/4 time.

5. Viewed in its HARMONIC aspect, the Phrase will contain a certain number of different chords between the initial Tonic and the perfect Cadence, but their number and choice cannot be reduced to any rule. In general, it appears wise to use AS FEW CHORDS AS POSSIBLE (better only one chord for an entire measure, than a different one for each beat), because the purest and strongest melodies arise from the simplest and quietest harmonic source. Still, it is just as necessary to observe the principle of variety with regard to chord-durations in a Phrase, as with regard to the tone-durations in the rhythmic structure of a melody. The following example illustrates the two extremes of harmonic repose and harmonic activity in the chord-design of a Phrase:

(a) One chord only, from beginning up to Cadence.

(b) Different chord to each beat (rapid tempo).

The pupil should scan a large number of the Phrases given in this book (and such others as he may encounter in examining classical music literature), and closely observe the harmonic structure, i. e., the number and choice of chords upon which the Phrase is based. See Exs. 61, 62, 64, 73, 74, 76, 83, 89, 91, 94, 96, and others.

6. The part of the Phrase where the harmonic arrangement appears to assume a certain degree of regularity (neither by accident nor tradition, but for perfectly natural reasons), is the *approach to the cadence.*

The final cadence-basstone is the *Tonic* note, and this is preceded (in Bass) by the *Dominant* note of the scale, as has been seen. The former is accented; but the rhythmic location and extent of the penultimate basstone (Dominant) is optional. It usually appears twice, at least; the first time often as $\frac{6}{4}$ chord of the tonic (I_2).

The basstone most naturally chosen to precede this penultimate Dominant, is its *lower neighbor*, not only because of its tonal importance as Subdominant of the scale, but because of its convenient proximity,—conjunct melodic progression being generally preferable to disjunct. The location, extent, and harmonic character of this antepenultimate basstone is also optional; and it may, furthermore, be either the *legitimate* 4th scale-step, or may be *raised* (as Altered tone). For illustration:

8.

Sometimes the *upper* neighbor of the Dominant is chosen to precede the latter, as antepenultimate basstone; either as legitimate 6th scale-step, or lowered.

Or, *both* neighbors precede the Dominant basstone, in either order. Thus (Bass part alone):

7. This is the harmonic "highway" to the perfect cadence, as marked by the lowermost part; and it will be traversed in such modes, such varieties of style, and in such degrees of speed and forms of rhythm, as the fancy of the composer (who is not limited to copying or imitating what others have done, if he will simply exercise the faculty of original combination) may discover. In the following instance (an 8-measure Phrase, with an unusual harmonic outset—II^{7} instead of Tonic), the three basstones shown in Example 8 underlie the entire Phrase, from beginning to end:

8. Viewed in its MELODIC aspect, the Phrase (or, more exactly, the melody of the Phrase) will be found to consist of a certain number of sections, called Phrase-members or melodic Members, or Motives, or (if very brief) Figures. They are more or less distinctly separated from each other by slight interruptions—corresponding to the "Cadences" which separate entire Phrases from

each other, but differing from these "Cadences" in being so transient as to subdivide the *melodic* line only, without severing the harmonic continuity of the Phrase. (Some writers call these spaces between the members "Quarter-cadences".)

This element of "Phrase-syntax" is obviously the most important one in homophonic phrase-construction, for the entire purpose and signification of the Phrase is concentrated in its principal melodic line, i. e., its Melody (the "Air" or "Tune", as it is more popularly called). The Melody *is* the Phrase, and all the other structural and technical factors subserve the melody.

But the author would reiterate his belief that melody, to a very large extent (if not altogether), is primarily a Product. THE MUSICAL SOURCE IS THE HARMONY, i. e., THE CHORDS; AND THE MELODY IS THE PRODUCT OUT OF THIS SOURCE, just as leaf, flower and fruit are the product out of soil, root and branch. Hence, the student will do wisely, at least as beginner, to bear in mind the rules of rational chord-succession, and evolve his melodic motives out of this consciousness. The pages of our strongest classical literature abound in proofs of *direct* eduction of melody out of the chord. Examine the harmonic origin of the melodic motives in Ex. 2, No. 2; Ex. 7, a; Ex. 34, No. 2; Ex. 35, No. 1; Ex. 46, No. 3; Ex. 74; and others.

At the same time, inasmuch as the melodic extract from one and the same chord or chord-series may assume a multitude of different shapes (precisely as one and the same melody may generally be constrained into agreement with different accompanying harmonies), it is plain that the *choice* of shape will be dictated by other conditions altogether, namely: those of *thematic* relation, agreement, or contrast, and other structural considerations. Therefore, it is not only possible, but even necessary, to design a Phrase largely from the standpoint of its Melody alone, without running the risk of any serious violations of the harmonic laws which must, by this time, be almost a second nature to the student. *Review paragraphs 5, 6, and 7, the principles of which must never be neglected or ignored.*

9. In rare cases, there is no perceptible break in the Phrase-melody; in other words, the Phrase consists of *one single member*, in which, at most, a vague subdivision into Figures may be traced.

Usually, however, there is at least one melodic interruption, as a rule exactly in the middle of the Phrase, dividing the latter into

two equal members (the pupil may first glance over par. 10). For illustration :

Also Ex. 61, meas. 1–4; Ex. 70, meas. 1–4.

Additional interruptions are most likely to occur exactly in the center of either the first half, or (rarely) second half of the Phrase; or in the center of both halves. Thus :

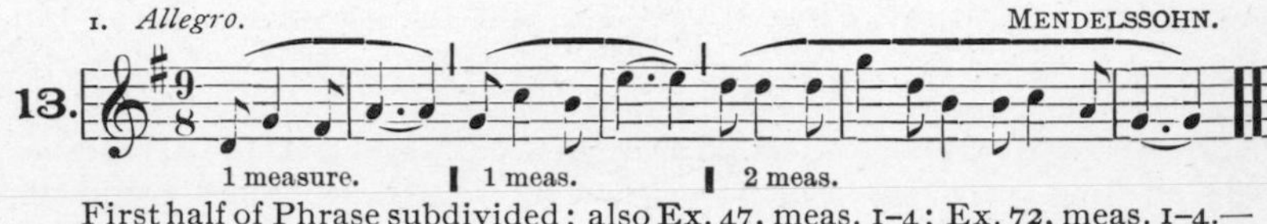

First half of Phrase subdivided; also Ex. 47, meas. 1–4; Ex. 72, meas. 1–4.—

Second half of Phrase subdivided; also Ex. 15; Ex. 29.—

Both halves of Phrase subdivided; also Ex. 60, meas. 1–4; Ex. 66, meas. 1–4; Ex. 74.—

In this process of division (or, more properly, the synthetic process of compounding figures and members into a complete Phrase) the principle of *regularity* naturally prevails; but there are occasional cases of irregular metrical association, as follows :

10. The means of marking (or of locating) the "spaces" between the members of a Phrase-melody, are numerous, but often so vague that the student will frequently have to depend more upon instinct than upon rule; different analyses of the same melody are often possible, and, in fact, the performer may (to a certain degree) place an arbitrary construction upon the syntax of the Phrase.

This is simply because the distinctions between the inferior grades of "Cadence" (in the sense that every interruption, however slight, is a "Cadence"), like those of punctuation, are necessarily subtile; and, therefore, it is not always possible to define with accuracy the various degrees of cadential interruption corresponding respectively to the space between Figures, between Members, or even between Phrases themselves. See par. 11.

The most reliable methods of marking *the limits of a melodic member*, are:

1stly, to introduce a Rest (sufficiently emphatic not to be confounded with mere *staccato*); this is seen in Example 12, Example 13, No. 3, and Example 14, No. 1.

2ndly, to dwell upon the final tone, thus giving it *comparatively longer duration* than its associates, as in Example 13, No. 1, and Example 14, No. 2. That this rule cannot hold good for *every* heavy note, is demonstrated by the 𝅗𝅥 at the beginning of measure 4 in Ex. 12, and by the first note in Ex. 3—neither of which marks the *end* of a melodic member. The heavy tone must stand in the proper place, and must impart a cadential (closing, concluding) impression. Ex. 13, No. 1; Ex. 14, No. 2.

3rdly, the trait which is more convincingly indicative of melodic division than any other, is that of *Repetition* or *Sequence*, or, in a word, the *recurrence of any sufficiently striking melodic or rhythmic figure*. See Ex. 13, No. 1, members 1 and 2; Ex. 13, No. 2, members 2 and 3; Ex. 13, No. 3, members 1 and 3, 2 and 4, Ex. 14, No. 2, members 1 and 3; Ex. 17; Ex. 18; and the following, in which the characteristic repetition of the first tone unmistakably marks the beginning of each following member:

15. 

The only danger of error, in this method of analysis, is that of accepting too many "spaces", and thus confounding the smaller particles of the Phrase (the Figures, or subdivisions of the Members) with the Members themselves. Further:

11. The smallest musical particle is the single TONE,—corresponding to the single letter in orthography. The *uninterrupted* association of two or more tones (in melodic succession) constitutes the FIGURE.

The association of two or more figures (separated by very slight interruptions) generally constitutes the PHRASE-MEMBER or MOTIVE,—corresponding to the words, small and large, in a sentence.

The association of two or more members (separated, as above shown, by "quarter-cadences", corresponding approximately to the spaces between the words of a printed sentence) generally constitutes the complete PHRASE or sentence.

The usual (but not invariable) subdivision of the melodic member into its figures, and the consequent distinction between these factors, is shown by the double system of slurs in the following illustrations (upper slurs for Members, lower ones for Figures):

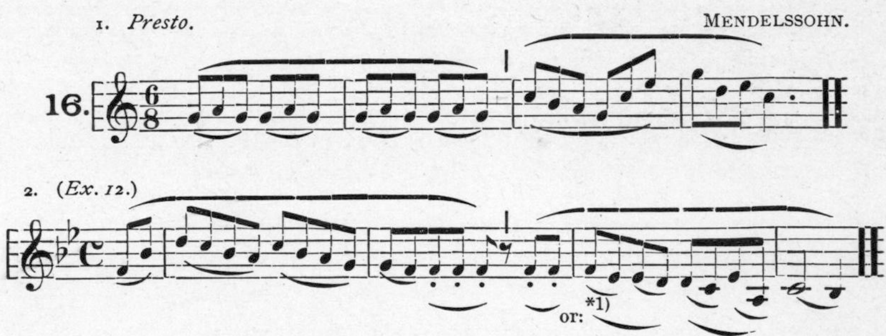

*1) These possible variations in the analyses of Phrase-syntax need give the student no concern. Review the first few lines of paragraphs 8 and 10; and examine the given examples with regard only to such of their divisions and subdivisions as are *plainly* definable.

12. In the composition of a Phrase-melody, some attention must be paid to the melodic and metric relations between the members; and while there will appear to be no system, nor any limit to the possibilities, still, each individual possibility is a *suggestion* to the alert student, and consequently becomes a definite stimulus to his imagination.

As concerns the *metric* relation, it has already been seen, in Examples 12, 13, and 14, that the Phrase-members may be either similar or dissimilar in length.

And with regard to their *melodic* (or thematic) comparison, both similarity (Ex. 13, No. 3) and difference (Ex. 14, No. 2) have been observed.

In Examples 12 and 13, similarity of *rhythmic* character prevails, while in Example 14 there is striking rhythmic diversity.

There is probably a slight preference in favor of regularity and similarity, in all of these respects.

Total thematic agreement (Repetition) is illustrated in the following:

See also Ex. 30, No. 1, meas. 1–2; Ex. 35, No. 1, meas. 1–3; Ex. 46, No. 3; Ex. 71, meas. 1–4.

Comparative thematic agreement (by Sequence) prevails in the following; (N. B. A Sequence is the reproduction of a melodic figure or member *upon other*, *higher or lower*, *steps*):

See also Ex. 27, meas. 1–3; Ex. 34, No. 1, meas. 1–3; Ex. 37, meas. 1–3; Ex. 52, meas. 3–5.

Frequently, actual thematic agreement is cleverly disguised, or modified, as follows:

See also Ex. 30, No. 1, meas. 2–3; Ex. 79, meas. 1–2, and 5–6.

After carefully and repeatedly reviewing all the conditions of Phrase-construction given in the preceding paragraphs, the pupil may venture to apply them in the invention of original examples of Phrase-melody, according to the following directions:

EXERCISE I.

Invent a number of instrumental *Phrase-melodies* of diversified character and design, principally four measures in length,—a *very few* of two and eight measures.

Alternate regularly between the major and minor modes in successive examples; employ the different varieties of duple and triple time impartially; and employ the various grades of tempo (from *Adagio* to *Allegro*). Exemplify the principal forms of phrase-syntax (Exs. 11, 12, 13), and thematic relation (Exs. 17, 18, 19).

The harmonic basis must be borne in mind constantly (par. 5, 6, 7), but is not to be written down; THE MELODY ALONE constitutes the object of this first exercise.

CHAPTER II.

THE HARMONIC EQUIPMENT OF THE PHRASE-MELODY.

13. The general principles governing the harmonization of a given melody having been acquired in the course of "harmonic" study, it only remains to add a few directions here in reference to the various *styles* of harmonic accompaniment. These will be dictated, most naturally, by the character and tempo of the melody; but they may be chosen according to the particular effect desired.

14a. In those cases where the melody in itself exhibits its harmonic source with sufficient distinctness, or where it is to appear in impressive isolation, the harmonic accompaniment is apt to be omitted altogether, during one or more members, or perhaps during the entire Phrase; the melody appears as SOLITARY PART, or tone-line (unison), or is simply doubled in one or more octaves. For example:

See also Ex. 38, No. 6 (also 4 and 5); Ex. 52; Ex. 81, meas. 1–2; Ex. 84, meas. 1; Ex. 94.

(b) Or, the Phrase-melody is supported by ONE ADDITIONAL PART or tone-line, which either assumes a coördinate melodic character (Nos. 1 and 2), or becomes, as figural part, the arpeggiated representative of the entire chord-basis (Nos. 3 and 4). Thus:

See also Ex. 32, No. 3; Ex. 64; 68; 69; 77; 78; 97.

(c) The addition of two accompanying tone-lines (3-VOICE STYLE) secures a complete harmonic effect without bulkiness, and, for this reason, the 3-voiced style must be regarded as *generally preferable and most commendable.*

Here, again, the parts may be similarly melodious, as in the vocal style (though dictated by the rules of *chord*-structure);

Or one of the tone-lines may be a figural part,—a choice which is more common and appropriate in instrumental (or keyboard) music, and especially suitable for the HOMOPHONIC forms.

In this harmonic style the device of *duplication in thirds or sixths* is both convenient and effective (see particularly Ex. 22, Nos. 4 and 5; and observe how the parts are related in Ex. 62).

For illustration:

See also Ex. 26; 28; 49; 56; 58; 59; 66; 75; 89.

(d) The 4-VOICE STYLE is often necessary for greater harmonic breadth and fullness. It usually resembles the vocal (or choral) style very closely (Ex. 27), although one or more of the four tone-lines may be a figural part. It will be most appropriate for melodies of a comparatively serious and stately character, but less desirable for graceful or rapid melodies. Illustrations of this style will be found in Examples 7*a* and *b*, and in the second half of Example 5; to which may be added the following varied specimens of its treatment:

See also Ex. 25; Ex. 27; 36; 51, No. 1; 54; 72; 74; 96.

15. By simply duplicating one or more of these fundamental tone-lines (or single chord-intervals) in upper or lower octave-registers, the harmonic volume may be increased to any desired extent, and copious, rich, powerful or pompous effects achieved. Such voluminous harmonies are seldom sustained very long; and it is very important to observe that, in general, (only excepting in strict vocal writing,) *it is neither necessary nor wise to adhere rigidly to any number of tone-lines.* That is to say, the volume of harmony may be increased or decreased during certain members or figures, or even at single points, for the sake of dynamic and harmonic variety. But the principle of "coherent tone-lines" (the most vital in music) must never be violated; at least *two* lines (the uppermost, or Melody proper, and lowermost, or Bass) must always be conducted with strict regard to melodic law; and usually one inner part also. These quantitative fluctuations in harmonic volume should, therefore, plainly appear to be transient duplications, or omissions, of a portion of the original bulk, which do not disturb the effect of the fundamental lines ("Material of Mus. Comp.", par. 413, 414).

For illustrations of this species of harmonic accompaniment, and also those explained in par. 14, the pupil is referred to the pages of standard literature, (Mozart, Beethoven, Mendelssohn, Chopin, Schumann, Brahms), which he is urged to examine with special reference to this point. See Ex. 2, Nos. 2 and 3: Ex. 5; Ex. 6; Ex. 10; Ex. 20, No. 3; and the following:

See also Ex. 38, No. 3; Ex. 40, No. 4; Ex. 47; 61; 67; 83; 91; 95.

MISCELLANEOUS EXAMPLES OF THE SIMPLE 4-MEASURE PHRASE.

SCHUBERT, Songs: "Die schöne Müllerin", first four measures of Nos. 1, 4, 6, 8, 10, 14, 20; "Winterreise", first four measures of Nos. 9, 11, 14, 22, 23.

MENDELSSOHN, "Songs without Words", No. 4, meas. 5–9; No. 28, meas. 1–4; No. 41, meas. 1–4; No. 44, meas. 1–4.

Also Ex. 62, meas. 1–4; Ex. 66, meas. 5–8; Ex. 73, meas. 5–8; Ex. 74, meas. 1–4; Ex. 76, meas. 1–4; Ex. 78, last four measures; Ex. 92, meas. 1–4; Ex. 96, meas. 1–4.

EXERCISE 2.

Add the harmonic accompaniment to some, or all, of the Phrase-melodies invented as Exercise 1. As a very general rule, the pupil is expected to adopt the *pianoforte-style*, at least for a time; though he is at liberty to write occasionally for any other instrument or *ensemble* with which he may be familiar (Organ, String-quartet, Trio, Duo, etc.). He is warned not to overstep the purpose of the Exercise, which in this case is limited to the simple regular PHRASE.

Though it is by far the most common habit to place the Phrase-melody in the uppermost part, the pupil is urged to assign it now and then to an *inner* part, or to the *lowermost* one. See Ex. 22, No. 3; Ex. 28; Ex. 91, last seven measures.

Review paragraphs 5, 6 and 7, and avoid overloading the phrase. THE FEWER CHORDS, THE BETTER. Avoid the faulty habit of harmonizing *each individual melody-tone* with a separate chord; that is, harmonize as many successive melody-tones as convenient with the same chord; taking care, however, to change the harmony at the *stronger* accents, i. e., the *first* accent in a compound measure, and, analogously, the first accent of all measures which, in the regular alternations of heavy and light pulses throughout the Phrase, represent the heavier units.

Very positive preference must be given to the 3-voice style.

CHAPTER III.

THE DEVELOPMENT OR EXTENSION OF THE PHRASE.

16. Musical composition involves two distinct mental processes: that of Conception and that of Manipulation.

The process of conception comes first, and dominates during the creation of the thematic germ, the Motive or Phrase. The process of manipulation is maintained more or less steadily the rest of the way, even though it be in such close interaction with the imaginative and conceptive faculties that the limits cannot always be defined in the writer's consciousness; upon this latter process depends most largely the success of the product. Composition is not an *aggregation* (merely the collecting and associating of a quantity of kindred, or, worse still, heterogeneous musical fragments, without regard to structural design, logical arrangement, or unity); it is the result of *evolution* and logical deduction,—an unfolding of one phase after another out of the thematic germ, until the growth is consummated.

Of this fact, the pupil should encourage the most absolute conviction, for any other conception will prove an effectual obstacle to his aspirations in the classical avenues of serious and enduring musical composition.

17. The "Phrase" having been conceived, the next step, then, is its enlargement or development. This is not yet to be effectuated by the addition of other Phrases, for that would overstep the limits of the present purpose, which is: the development of the resources embraced within a single germinal Phrase, upon a correspondingly narrow scale of structural design.

The principal means employed in the Development or Extension of a Phrase (or thematic germ of any kind) are those of Repetition, Sequence (i. e., the reproduction of a figure or member bodily, a certain interval-distance higher or lower), and Expansion. Their application may be classified in a fourfold manner, namely:

(1) The Repetition of the entire Phrase;
(2) The Extension at the End,
(3) The Extension at the Beginning, and
(4) The Extension in the Course of the Phrase.

1. Phrase-repetition.

18. When the whole Phrase is to be repeated, it is customary (though not absolutely necessary) to fill out the measure allotted to the perfect Cadence, *by continuing the rhythmic pulse* in some form or other, so as to "bridge over" the space between the end of the Phrase and the beginning of its repetition, and thus partly *conceal* the Cadence. This is more or less desirable, according to the width of the intervening space.

It is not to be an "*Evasion*" of the perfect Cadence, and therefore the harmonic form and the cadential effect of the latter *must be preserved*.

The final Tonic chord must be retained; but it may be embellished;

And the chord-third, or even the chord-fifth, may be substituted for the Root in Soprano, or (rarely) in Bass.

The rhythmic pulse should be maintained within the tones of the Tonic harmony; still, smooth harmonic progressions (through other chords) may be ventured, if made in so cautious a manner as not to cancel the cadential impression (i. e., not until the tonic effect is established). See par. 21 and 25*a*. For example:

*1) Correct perfect Cadence, omitted because of the coming repetition.

*2) Concealed form of perfect Cadence: compare with final measure. The rhythmic pulse is actually more rapid during this measure (16th-notes) than anywhere else in the Phrase; and the uppermost part has the chord-fifth (e) for a time, instead of the root (a), as at the end. The cadential impression is, however, preserved by the cessation (rests) in the lower parts. For other illustrations of cadence-bridging, see Exs. 26, 27, 28; Ex. 46, No. 1, meas. 4; Ex. 50, meas. 8; Ex. 66, meas. 4; Ex. 73, meas. 8; Ex. 78, meas. 12; Ex. 89, meas. 8; Ex 92, No. 2, meas. 8.

19. The Phrase may be repeated *literally*, without any changes whatever, excepting those involved by concealing the perfect Cadence. See Ex. 25.

Also BEETHOVEN, Pfte. Sonata, op. 27, No. 1, first movement, first, second, and third Phrases (repetition-marks); Pfte. Sonata, op. 28, Finale, meas. 1–8; 9–16 (slightly embellished).—SCHUMANN, "Album-Blätter", op. 124, No. 2; No. 7; No. 9; No. 15; No. 17—*first eight measures of each.*—CHOPIN, Prel. op. 28, No. 15, meas. 1–8.

But it is far more usual and desirable, as conducive to thematic development, to introduce *unessential alterations*, or variations, during the repetition. (See par. 40.) By "unessential" is meant unimportant—not affecting any characteristic or *essential* element of the Phrase. These unessential modifications of the repetition may be classified as follows:

(a) Unessential embellishment of the Melody:

*1) In this concealed form of the perfect Cadence, the cadential impression is preserved by every prescribed condition (par. 3) excepting the pause or check in the melodic current; the rhythmic movement is here again (as in Ex. 25) accelerated, and thus maintained during the melodically ornamented repetition. See also: CHOPIN, Mazurka No. 2 (op. 6, No. 2), first 8 measures.

(b) Changes in the harmony and modulation:

See also Ex. 51, No. 1, meas. 1–8.—Ex. 62, meas. 9–18.

To this class of modifications would belong, also, a repetition in the opposite mode of the same keynote (i. e., transformed from major to minor, or vice versa); returning, perhaps, to the original mode at the final Cadence.

See CHOPIN, Nocturne 17, meas. 14–6 from the end; CHOPIN, Mazurka 20, meas. 17–24; also last nine measures; BEETHOVEN, String-quartet, op. 18, No. 6, first movement, meas. 45–52. Ex. 89, Part II, meas. 1–8.

(c) Shifting the Phrase-melody upward or downward to a different register, or different part; either bodily (i. e., the entire Phrase), or in sections:

MENDELSSOHN.

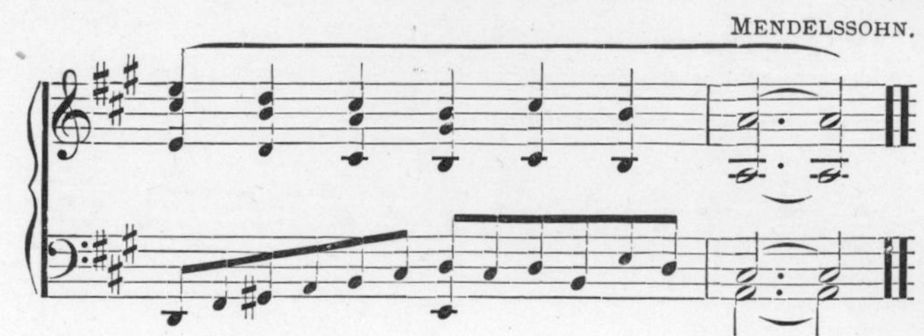

*1) The melody is shifted bodily upward one and two octaves, from "Tenor" into "Alto and Soprano" registers. See also Exs. 29; 30, No. 1; 31. BEETHOVEN, Bagatelle, op. 33, No. 6, meas. 1–8.

(d) Changes in character and style of accompaniment:

29.

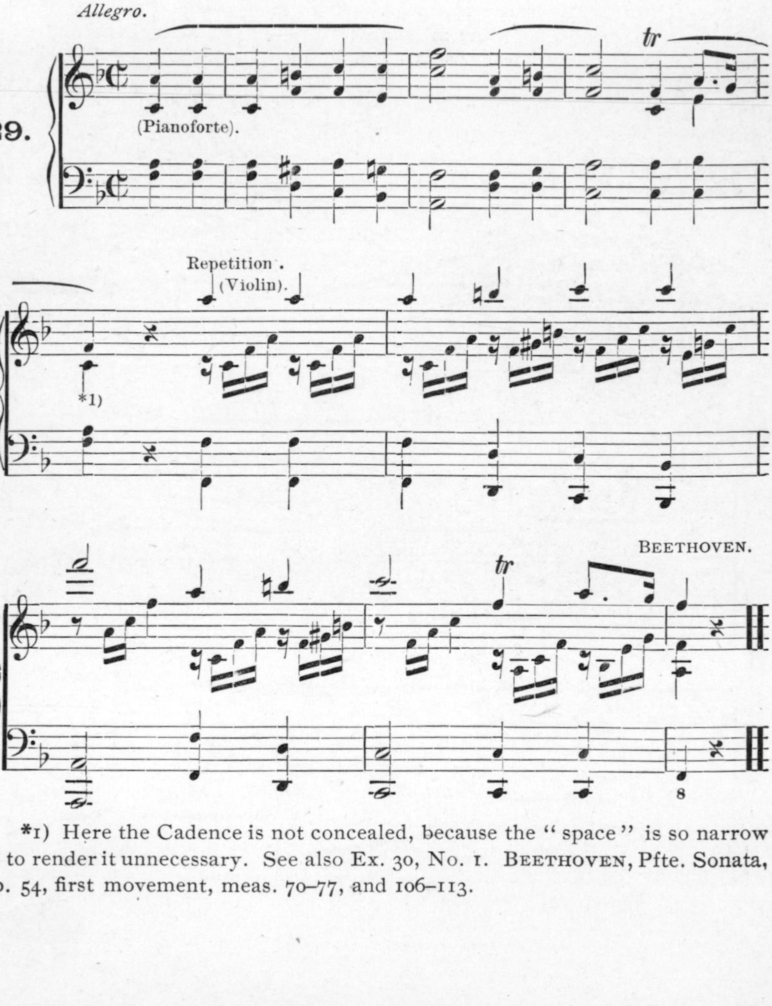
Allegro.
(Pianoforte).
Repetition.
(Violin).
*1)
tr
BEETHOVEN.
8

*1) Here the Cadence is not concealed, because the "space" is so narrow as to render it unnecessary. See also Ex. 30, No. 1. BEETHOVEN, Pfte. Sonata, op. 54, first movement, meas. 70–77, and 106–113.

(e) More complete and radical changes in the *course* of the Phrase-melody (not, however, affecting the beginning, or the end, or destroying general resemblance) :

30.

*1) This Cadence is not concealed, before the repetition, because there is no space left at all. See par. 4.

*2) The second member of the Phrase is entirely changed; but the Cadence is preserved. See also Ex. 51, No. 1, last eight measures.

20. In rare cases, the bridging-over of the perfect Cadence. before repetition, is extended into a brief Interlude, or transitional passage, of one or more (superfluous) measures; but it must be kept so inferior in character and contents *as to appear unessential and extraneous.* For illustration, the 8-measure Phrase given in Example 10, is continued and repeated as follows:

31.

*1) This measure is kept subordinate by reduction to one part, and by the suppression of the accompaniment.

*2) Compare this repetition with Example 10; it illustrates the change of register (19*c*), not entire, but *in sections.*

See also MENDELSSOHN, "Songs without Words", No. 46, meas. 3–12.

Nothing more than such a distinctly unessential interlude could intervene between a Phrase and its "repetition", without transforming the structural trait of "repetition" into that of "recurrence". A repetition is a (practically) *immediate* reproduction. See par. 81 *a* and *b*.

21. Reverting to par. 18 (which review), it must be distinctly understood that *no essential change of the harmonic form of the Cadence* is permissible in the case of entire repetitions. This preservation of the cadence-harmony is the inviolable condition upon which the assumption of "repetition" depends.

The Cadence is the "aim" of the Phrase; and it is only when the original harmonic aim is retained, that the Phrase may be said to have been "repeated". Any essential alteration of the harmonic aim (the Cadence-chords) would resolve an otherwise apparent "repetition" into two separate Phrases, with independent direction and aim. See notes and context to Ex. 46. The distinction between apparent repetition and actual repetition (depending upon whether the Cadences are *essentially different* or not) is of the utmost importance, because *genuine* repetition, whether variated or not, never constitutes any change or actual advance in the formal design of the composition; whereas, an *apparent* repetition, which proves ultimately to have been thwarted by a real change of cadence, contributes, as new member, to the progressive enlargement or evolution of the design.

22. Two, or even more, repetitions may occur in succession, somewhat like a series of simple Variations (e. g., the Ciaccona for solo violin, by BACH; the Chaconnes of HÄNDEL, for Harpsichord; the thirty-two C-minor Variations of BEETHOVEN, etc.); each repetition being differently modified, possibly in a certain systematic progression. See BEETHOVEN, Bagatelles, op. 33, No. 6, meas. 31–46. BRAHMS, op. 118, No. 5, second tempo (Phrase with 5 repetitions).

23. The OBJECT of Phrase-repetition, and of repetition in general, is:

To establish unity of thematic design by direct corroboration;

To give additional emphasis to the Phrase or member, and to define its contents more clearly;

And, finally, to obtain greater simplicity and repose of elementary character than would result from a succession of constantly changing Phrases or members. The repetition will, therefore, be most desirable when the Phrase is of a somewhat abstruse or complex nature; or of unusual length; or when interesting and important enough to tempt the desire for (and justify) a second hearing.

EXERCISE 3.

Select a number of the Phrases invented in Exercise 2, or invent new ones, and *add a repetition* to each, illustrating the five principal varieties of modification given in paragraph 19. All five modes may be applied successively to one and the same Phrase (22); or single repetition may be applied to each of five different Phrases, with that variety of modification which appears to be respectively most appropriate.

2. The Extensions at the End of a Phrase.

24. The extensions at the end are of a two-fold nature, consisting, 1stly, of such as lie *within* the Cadence, and 2ndly, of such as lie *beyond* the Cadence.

25. To the first class (inside) belong:

(a) The repetition of the second half of the Phrase; possibly exact, but usually modified.

This involves, as a rule, a more or less complete "*Evasion of the perfect Cadence*,—an act which differs from the simple concealment of the Cadence (shown in par. 18), in being a more pronounced deviation from the latter, and often consisting in a different form of harmony altogether. The *approach* to the Cadence is usually not affected by the prospective evasion, as the latter does not begin until the Tonic element of the Cadence is due, or has been felt, upon its proper beat. The evasion is then effected:

By substituting an Inversion for the fundamental form of the Tonic chord (i. e., 3rd or 5th in Bass);

By substituting the VI for the I (Ex. 33, No. 1);

Or by substituting any other chord, even of another key, which contains the original Tonic note in sufficient prominence to preserve the cadential impression.

In any case, the rhythmic pulse is sustained in one or more of the parts; and the melody and harmony are so conducted as to lead smoothly into the desired repetition.

The difference between "concealing" and "evading" the Cadence will become amply apparent upon carefully comparing the details enumerated in these last few lines, with those given in paragraph 18.

For illustration:

MENDELSSOHN.
Cadence.
*1)
Extension
2. Andante.
evaded Cad. *2)
exten-
(e V I)
sion.
MENDELSSOHN.
*3)
3. Andante.
evad.
MOZART.
Cad. *4)

*1) The expected Cadence is evaded in this case by placing the chord-third in the Bass, and the chord-fifth (leading downward to the Root) in Soprano. Compare with correct form, two measures later; and observe the modification in the treatment of second Phrase-half, when repeated.

*2) This peculiar evasion of the expected Cadence will be best understood by comparing it with the correct form, four measures later. It even affects the *approach* to the Cadence, but the cadential relation is preserved by clinging to the key-note (e) in the Soprano.

*3) In this example, there are *two* repetitions of the second half of Phrase; the first time with the same form of evaded Cadence, and the second time with the correct perfect Cadence.

*4) Also a peculiar mode of Cadence-evasion, sometimes called "Intercepted Cadence". It answers sufficiently well for the expected Cadence, as the accented chord (the IV_1—b, d, f) actually contains the Tonic-note. The repetition covers a little more than half the Phrase, reaching back abruptly to the beginning of the 2nd measure.

See also MENDELSSOHN, "Songs without Words", No. 11, meas. 9–3 from the end. BEETHOVEN, Bagatelle, op. 33, No. 1, last nine and one-half measures. SCHUBERT, Song, "Haiden-Röslein", meas. 5–10.

(b) The repetition, or (more rarely) the sequence, of the last member of the Phrase; possibly a single repetition, but usually twice in succession.

This generally refers to the last quarter of the Phrase, or a trifle more; and the evasion of the Cadence is necessary, because, in this case, the original (expected) Cadence is *not* to be included in the extension. For example:

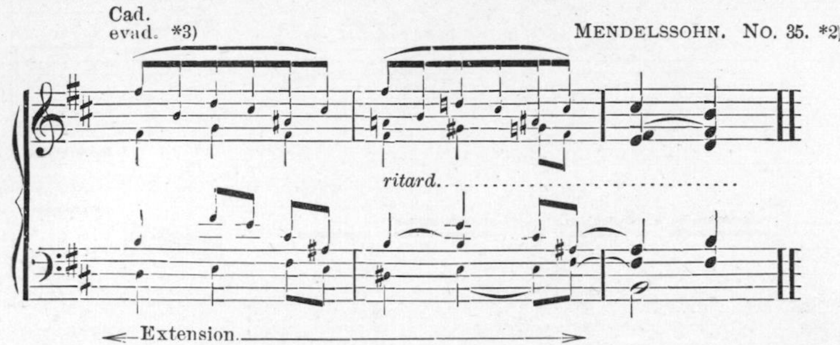

*1) The expected perfect Cadence is evaded by substituting the VI for the I. The three notes in Soprano, which immediately follow, *are included in the evaded Cadence*, and serve: 1stly, to sustain the rhythmic pulse; 2ndly, to lead smoothly into the first tone (b) of the member to be reproduced. The reproduction of the last member, which then follows, occurs *twice*, each time in a modified melodic and rhythmic form (the harmony remaining the same).

*2) The numbers after Mendelssohn's name invariably refer to his "Songs without Words".

*3) The perfect Cadence is completely evaded by turning back abruptly one measure, where, on the first beat, a Tonic chord occurs in the very form suitable for evasion (chord-fifth in Soprano, and chord-third in Bass; see Ex. 32, No. 1, meas. 4). The extension consists in repeating this third measure twice, the first time exactly, and the second time with altered harmonization.

26. To the second class (outside of, or beyond, the Cadence) belong:

(a) The Repetition of the entire Cadence-group (of chords), usually at least twice, and possibly modified.

This will usually embrace the last three or four chords, inclusive of the original Cadence; and *no evasion* of the latter will be necessary or even practicable, because the Cadence, as it stands, is to be included in the extension. The rhythmic pulse may, or may not, be sustained. For example:

*1) This is a Semicadence (par. 36) instead of a perfect Cadence; but that makes no difference, as this principle applies to every variety of Cadence. The rhythmic pulse is not marked, contrary to common usage. The repetition of the Cadence-member occurs in this instance no less than eight times, including one change of register, an acceleration (diminution) of the rhythm, and a series of rhythmic shifts which alter the location of the figure in the measure.

*2) The five 16th-notes which follow the Cadence merely serve to sustain the rhythmic movement (compare Ex. 33, note *1)).—*3) Original melodic form of Cadence, transferred to next higher octave.—*4) Embellished form of the same.—*5) Half-measure sequences of foregoing figure.

See also Ex. 41, No. 4, note *7). And MENDELSSOHN, "Songs without Words", No. 20, meas. 12–5 from the end.

(b) The repetition of the two Cadence-chords (V and I); usually at least twice, and either in the same form, or with *any rhythmic or melodic modification of the form.*

This species of extension will often be found to differ but slightly from (a), cited above; though it is generally more fragmentary than the latter. For example:

*1)
MENDELSSOHN.
Cad. Extension.
V V I V V I V V I
2. Allegretto.
V
Cad. Extension.
*2)
MENDELSSOHN. No. 42.
I (V I) V I (V I) V I
3. Allegro.
V
*3)
HAYDN.
Cadence. Extension.
I...... V...... I...... V...... I V I V I

*1) Two exact repetitions of the last three (Cadence-) chords.

*2) Four repetitions of the two Cadence-chords, as continuation of the accompaniment. The first and third repetitions are slightly altered in form, and sound parenthetical, because the melody pauses meanwhile upon its Cadence-tone. The second and fourth repetitions are an exact reproduction of the Cadence, including the Soprano.

*3) The Cadence is concealed by the quicker rhythm in the Soprano (borrowed from the Bass of the first measure).

See also: MENDELSSOHN, "Songs without Words", No. 16, first three measures, and last four measures.

(c) The reiteration of the final Tonic chord, to an optional extent, and in optional rhythmic and melodic form.

The extent (number) of these reiterations can hardly be determined by rule, as this extension usually represents the last oscillations of the swinging harmony, the "dying out" of which will depend upon the peculiar circumstances embodied in the Phrase. Instinct will be the best guide. As a rule, the Cadence-tonic, in this case, must fall upon the *first* accent of the measure. For example:

See also: MENDELSSOHN, "Songs without Words", No. 4, first five measures (compare with last five measures); No. 6, last six measures; No. 8, last eight measures; No. 12, last twelve measures (4-measure Phrase, repeated and extended); No. 27, last twelve measures (illustration given in Ex. 32, No. 2, with reiterations of last chord); No. 31, last five measures; No. 42, last eleven measures (illustration given in Ex. 35, No. 2, with reiterations of final

Tonic-chord, and one additional final announcement of the perfect-Cadence chords, V–I).

(d) A plagal cadence, of more or less elaborate character, during the prolongation of the final Tonic note in Soprano, or in both outer parts. For illustration:

37.

See CHOPIN, Nocturne 11 (op. 37, No. 1), last five measures; during the plagal extension, the major Cadence is substituted for the original minor. Nocturne 7 (op. 27, No. 1), last eight measures; a two-measure Phrase, repeated, and extended by a somewhat elaborate plagal ending.

These various extensions are often applied successively to one and the same Phrase: see BEETHOVEN, Pfte. Sonata, op. 53, Finale (Rondo), measures 191 to 220:—(an 8-measure phrase), beginning:

27. The OBJECT of extensions at the end of a Phrase is, to prevent the movement of harmony and rhythm from breaking off too abruptly; and the degree of momentum which the sentence may have acquired, must determine the propriety and *extent* of their use. Furthermore, they also serve, of course, to develop their portion of the resources of the Phrase, and are for this reason generally permissible.

EXERCISE 4.

A number of former Phrases, or new ones, with extensions at the end, according to the modes of treatment described in par. 25*a* and 25*b*.

EXERCISE 5.

The same, according to the modes of treatment described in par. 26, *a*, *b*, *c*, and *d*.

3. The Extensions at the Beginning of a Phrase.

28. An extension of the Phrase at its beginning will necessarily assume the nature of an introduction; i. e., some form of harmony and melody which suggests (or prepares for) the initial member of the Phrase, and leads smoothly into it.

The chief difficulty is, to keep such an introductory extension so *inferior and unessential* in character, that it will not be mistaken for the real beginning of the Phrase.

The necessary inferiority will be ensured if either the element of definite melodic or definite harmonic progression be absent, or obscure, during the introductory passage.

Hence, the best form of introduction is that which is limited to the figure of the accompaniment, which may anticipate the announcement of the melody proper, either with or without changes of harmony.

It may, however, also consist in an anticipation of the first figure of the melody, without accompaniment;

Or, in a brief one-part "Cadenza", leading into the latter, (see Ex. 31, meas. 2 and 3);

Or, in one or more simple annunciations of the key-note (or Tonic harmony), or possibly both Tonic and Dominant tones, or chords, without definite melodic form.

The length of the introduction is largely optional, but it will rarely exceed half the length of its Phrase. For example:

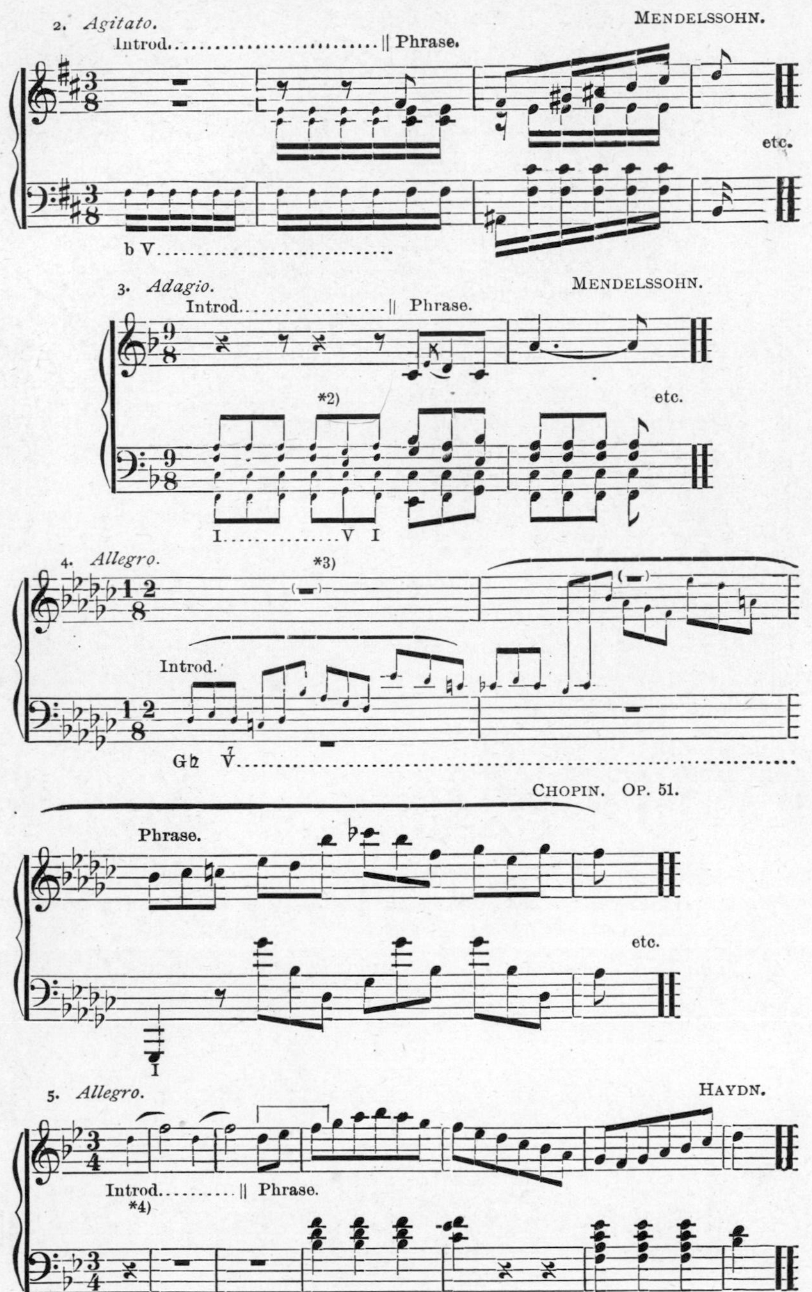
2. Agitato.
MENDELSSOHN.
Introd.............................|| Phrase.
etc.
b V.............................
3. Adagio.
MENDELSSOHN.
Introd....................|| Phrase.
*2)
etc.
I...............V I
4. Allegro.
*3)
Introd.
G♭ V...
CHOPIN. Op. 51.
Phrase.
etc.
I
5. Allegro.
HAYDN.
Introd..........|| Phrase.
*4)

*1) In the first and second examples, the accompaniment precedes the Phrase-melody by a few beats, without harmonic change.

*2) Here there is an actual chord-succession in the introduction; but it is derived from the accompaniment, and the entrance of the melody is conspicuous enough to mark the beginning of the Phrase proper.

See also MENDELSSOHN, No. 35, first measure; No. 1, first two measures; No. 24, first two measures; No. 26, first three measures; No. 34, first two measures; No. 36, first three measures. The passage at the beginning of Nos. 19, 29, and 46 is too long to be called an introduction to the first Phrase. (See par. 44.)

*3) The upper rests in this measure and the next one are only imaginary; while the introductory passage surely does not belong to the "Melody", as such, it is, nevertheless, the same tone-line, and leads uninterruptedly into the latter.

*4) A tentative anticipation of the first figure of the Phrase-melody.

See also BEETHOVEN, Symphony No. 1, Finale, first ten measures; BRAHMS, Serenade in A, op. 16, Finale, first six measures; SCHUBERT, Pfte. Sonata No. 6 (op. 147), Finale, first six measures.

4. The Extensions in the Course of a Phrase.

29. These represent probably the most important class of Phrase-extensions, as they conduce more directly than those at the end or at the beginning, to the coherent development and growth of the thematic substance of the Phrase as a whole. They consist:

(a) In one or more repetitions (exact or variated) of any *well-defined* member of the Phrase, anterior to the Cadence-member.

It is manifest that all extensions of a Phrase will simply create confusion and lead to a misapprehension of the writer's intention, unless *they are recognizable as "extensions" which merely add to the sum of beats and measures without entirely destroying the outlines of the original (regular) Phrase*, or cancelling the impression of a "regular design" as fixed basis of the irregularly inflated result. And, for this reason, this more misleading class of extensions, in the *course* of a Phrase, can be safely undertaken only in those phrases which contain strongly marked members or figures, *with well-defined extremities*.

At any such well-defined "joint", the Phrase may be—figuratively speaking—pried apart to admit of the insertion of a repetition, sequence, or extension of any kind (and of almost any extent); and, if sufficiently marked in character, the foregoing member will be readily recognized as the origin of the interpolated reproduction.

For illustration:

*1) Repetition of first member (first half) of Phrase, in slightly modified form. This class of repeated Phrase-members must not be confounded with the illustrations of symmetrical phrase-formation given in Ex. 13, No. 2, and Ex. 17. There they are *essential*, and contribute to the 4-measure design; while here they are *unessential*, inasmuch as they constitute *extra measures*, beyond the 4-measure design.

*2) This extension consists in a three-fold repetition of the first figure, in alternating upper and lower registers.

*3) A sequence of the second figure, as in Ex. 40. If these two extensions be cut out, a perfectly coherent 2-measure Phrase (the original design) will remain. This is sometimes the case, but *not necessarily so*.

*4) A curiously modified version of the first Phrase-member. This extension, also, might be eliminated, leaving a regular 4-measure design.

(b) In one or more sequences (exact or modified) of any *well-defined* member of the Phrase. For example:

2. Allegro.
Extension.
MENDELSSOHN.
*2)
3. Presto.
Extension.
Exten-
*3)
*4)
sion.
HAYDN.
4. Allegro.
(Violin.)
Extension.
*5)
(Orch.)
Extension.
BRAHMS.
*6)

*1) A sequence of the second measure (figure) of the Phrase.

*2) A sequence of the second Phrase-member (or figure) in slightly modified form.

*3) A sequence of the first member.

*4) Sequence of the second member. As already intimated (Ex. 39, notes *3) and *4)), these extensions are often so adjusted to the line of development, that the members of the original 4-measure Phrase may be discovered in coherent form without them. This, however, is by no means necessary; it is somewhat more likely that the interlined extensions will involve alterations of the original melodic design; or, better still, they will be so naturally interwoven with the texture of the Phrase as to affect, and even direct (apparently) its current. But see the remark following 29*a*.

*5) Two sequences of the first member (five beats in length, and, therefore, recurring in shifted measure)

*6) Two sequences of the second member (three beats) in modified rhythmic form.

The number of sequences or repetitions thus introduced in the course of a Phrase depends upon circumstances, and can scarcely be determined by rule. Smaller members or figures are usually reproduced a greater number of times than larger ones; and sequences may, without risk of monotony, be multiplied oftener than repetitions.

More than one single *exact* repetition is hardly permissible; in the event of two repetitions, the last one (the third version of the member) *must* be modified.

As a general rule, more than three successive sequences are considered weak; still, series of four (and even many more) sequences may be found in works of eminent rank; especially when consisting of smaller figures or members.

The student must appeal to his instinct and sense of proportion and balance, and carefully avoid Monotony on the one hand and Irregularity or Unevenness on the other.

(c) In the expansion of any prominent chord; or of any important (prominent) melody-tone; or melodic figure (of two or three tones).

This is probably most frequently and most extensively applied to the *Tonic* $^6_4$ *chord* (I_2) which almost always appears directly before the two Perfect-cadence chords, usually on a strong accent (see par. 6). This special example of chord-expansion as extension in the course of a simple Phrase, becomes the prototype of the more or less elaborate "Cadenza" in Concerto-movements. The conduct of the upper parts (especially that of the melody proper) during the prolongation of the chord, is largely optional; but it is obvious that it should be in strict thematic (or, at least, organic) agreement with the rest of the Phrase, and not create the impression of a foreign link. The rhythm may be treated with great freedom.

Frequently the *basstone alone* of the I_2 is prolonged as organ-point, while the upper tone-lines sway about in optional harmonic succession, either returning to the I_2 or passing into the V of the Cadence. In this case the I_2 should appear on a strong accent.

But the expansion may also be applied to the *Dominant* chord which precedes the final Tonic as first of the two Perfect-cadence chords.

And it is furthermore applicable to *any other* chord, or chords, in the Phrase, if they be of sufficient value and prominence to warrant the expansion. For illustration:

41.

MENDELSSOHN. No. 42.
*3)
7
V expanded
I
3. Andante.
MENDELSSOHN. No. 19.
*4)
V expanded
I
4. Allegro.
*5)
*6)
I2 expanded

*1) The expansion of the Tonic $^6_4$ chord enlarges the Phrase from its original four measures to five.

*2) It is left to the student to discover how ingeniously this long expansion of the Dominant-note in bass (as I_2) is interwoven, in the upper parts, with the thematic structure of the 4-measure Phrase.

*3) An expansion of the Cadence Dominant chord, which serves to counterbalance the foregoing expansion.

*4) A long expansion of the Cadence Dominant chord. See also MENDELSSOHN, "Songs without Words", No. 2, last ten measures; No. 33, last five-and-one-half measures; No. 31, last eleven measures (particularly meas. 9–6 from the end); and also Ex. 59, meas. 11–12.

*5) This exquisite example of BRAHMS (op. 79, No. 1) contains several of the above-mentioned extensions: at first, a sequence of the first Phrase-member. At *6) an expansion of the Tonic $^6_4$, with richly modified melodic repetitions (three measures). At *7) the Cadence is due; it is concealed by continuing the rhythmic pulse in the inner part (imitating the Cadence-member in soprano); and is followed by two repetitions of the Cadence-member. At *8) the final Cadence-chord is reiterated.

*9) The expansion of this melody-tone extends the 4-measure Phrase to five measures.

*10) The melody-tone *a* is expanded from a half-measure to a whole one. See Ex. 62, note *3). A remarkable illustration of chord-expansion will be found in BEETHOVEN, Pfte. Sonata, op. 57, meas. 17–24 (beginning, as usual, to count at the first *complete* measure). **BEETH. Bagat. op. 33, No. 5, last 19 m.**

See also: CHOPIN, Pfte. Sonata B♭-minor, Trio of Scherzo, first, second, and third Phrases (expansion of final melody-tone); CHOPIN, Prel., op. 28, No. 2, first and second Phrases (ditto). CHOPIN, Prel., op. 28, No. 12, meas. 49–65 (expanded II^7, meas. 57–63). Also Ex. 42, meas. 3 and 4.

N. B. It is scarcely possible to overestimate the significance of "Expansion" as a factor of composition. The principle of expansion lies, in a certain broad sense, at the very root of the entire art-growth, which carries along the germinal thought and enlarges the raw harmonic material from one stage on into another and higher stage, until the broadest development of the original idea has been consummated. The larger (i.e., longer) forms which are to follow the Phrase, will be found to be not altogether the results of *addition*, but also of *deduction* and *evolution;* not a multiplication of the chords contained in the smaller design, but these same chord-progressions *expanded* or magnified into broader dimensions. Thus, the primary succession I, IV, V, I, which might be the simple *beats* in a 4/4 measure, could become the four successive *measures* of a Phrase; or they might be expanded into four successive *sections* (at least in a general sense) of a still larger design; and so on. An illustration of this is found in Example 5, in which the harmonic basis of the four measures is, approximately, the very chords I, IV, V, I suggested above. See also Example 10, where the harmonic basis of eight measures is limited to no more than three chord-elements; and Example 7*a*, embracing only I, V, I;

and Example 74, the eight measures of which contain no other chord-progressions than I | V | I | V, I ‖ V | V | V, I | IV, V, I‖ (the last four approximated). This emphasizes the importance of the advice given in par. 5, and in Exercise 2, " to use as few chords as possible".

(d) In the substitution of a new Cadence-member for the original one, or the *addition* of a new Cadence-member, when involved by foregoing extensions.

After such extensions, in the course of the Phrase, as may diverge widely from the original thematic line, or lead quite away from the original (or expected) approach to the Cadence, it is often necessary to invent an entirely *new Cadence-member*. Its extent will depend upon where the ultimate cadential impression is required, irrespective of the aggregate number of measures.

It is evident that, while new, it must, nevertheless, be strictly coherent, and thematically homogeneous. For illustration :

*1) These two measures are an expansion of the chord c-e-g-b; the Soprano is thematically related to the *c* at the beginning of the 5th measure, of which it is an anticipatory expansion. *2) The two half-notes are expanded quarter-notes (half-measure expanded to whole measure). *3) The perfect Cadence is due on this beat (see two measures later); it is evaded by a Sequence of the foregoing measure. *4) The "new Cadence-member". It cannot be called a new "Phrase", not only because of its brevity, but because *no actual Cadence* has preceded it, to terminate the current Phrase. It is "new", however, inasmuch as it differs almost entirely from the original Cadence-member (in meas. 5–6). *5) The digression begins with this *c*♯, which enharmonically represents the original *d*♭. The three following measures are a repetition and expansion of the first melodic figure in measure 3.

*6) The "new Cadence-member"; see note *4).

*7) A curious suppression of the Cadence-tonic in the highest part. Its place is filled by the keynote in Bass.

30. The extension of a Phrase during its course, as above shown, is rarely, if ever, undertaken at the very beginning of a composition (i. e., with the *first* Phrase or upon the *first appear-*

ance of a Phrase). It is often very appropriately applied to the *repetition* of a Phrase, as a means of modifying the second version (see 19); and it may be introduced in any of the *later* phrases of a section of the form. It is of peculiar value in the construction of transitional passages and Phrases, as will be seen in due time.

EXERCISE 6.

Former Phrases, or new ones, with extensions at the beginning (par. 28);

And in the course, according to 29 *a* and *b*. In the latter case the Phrase is first to be written out (at least the Melody) in its original regular form, and then extended (about as in Ex. 42, No. 2).

EXERCISE 7.

Extensions in the course, according to par. 29*c* and *d*. The Phrases are first to be written out in regular form, and then extended.

CHAPTER IV.

THE CHAIN-PHRASE. MELODY-EXPANSION. IRREGULAR PHRASE-FORMATION.

31. The extensions in the course of the Phrase, particularly the repetitions and *sequences* (par. 29 *a* and *b*) *of small* motives and figures, are sometimes multiplied in such a manner and to such a degree as to give rise to an irregular design, for which the term "Chain-phrase" may most appropriately be adopted, inasmuch as the successive members assume the character of continuous small links, in a chain of arbitrary form and extent. It can scarcely be regarded as a legitimate design, for it is the type of formlessness, and is, therefore, beset with dangers for the beginner. But, if coherently developed, it is justifiable, and is often extremely effective in the service of necessary climaxes; and also in transitional sections, which tend persistently during many measures toward a desired point, in uninterrupted career.

The impression of a Cadence must be scrupulously avoided, as it would separate the "chain" of thematic links into a "group" of distinct Phrases.

And a certain reasonable limit must, of course, be observed. For illustration :

*1) The original 4-measure Phrase extends to this beat. The thirteen or fourteen measures which follow are all forged, like so many "links", out of the second half of the Phrase, chiefly out of the figure contained in its third measure.

*2) The "links" of the Chain-phrase are here derived from the second and third notes of the second measure of the original Phrase, and are reproduced sequentially, at first in groups of three, and finally in progressive ascending succession.

*3) This measure corresponds exactly to the original second measure.

*4) This example embraces no less than twenty measures (including the original Phrase and its repetition), all developed out of a brief 4-measure Phrase, and so interlocked as to avoid a cadential impression at any point in the course of the Chain-phrase.

See also Ex. 56, first thirteen measures. Ex. 85, meas. 9–19.

See also: Mendelssohn, "Songs without Words", No. 2, meas. 35–20 from the end; No. 14, last ten measures; No. 17, end of meas. 28 to meas. 35; *No. 23, meas. 21–10 from the end;* No. 45, meas. 24–12 from the end. Beethoven, Pfte. Sonata, op. 31, No. 3, first movement, meas. 34–19 from the end. Beethoven, Pfte. Sonata, op. 28, first movement, meas. 57–94 from the double-bar (thirty-eight measures long, and preceded by a similar Chain-phrase of sixteen measures). Schubert, Pfte. Sonata No. 7, (op. 164) first movement, meas. 16–27; Finale, meas. 71–94. Brahms, op. 119, No. 3, last 22 measures.

Melody-expansion.

32. A simple brief Phrase, or Phrase-member, may be utilized as a thematic germ, and be developed, by means of *repetition* and *tone-expansion*, into a melodic thread of considerable length. This process differs from that employed for the Chain-phrase, in that, as a rule, it does not involve the "sequence", nor the necessity of avoiding slight cadence-impressions in the course of the entire expansion. It is most commonly, though by no means exclusively, encountered in the closing sections (Codettas, see par. 51) of larger forms, where the gradual enlargement of a foregoing thematic member accords well with the gradual relaxation of the rhythmic and harmonic momentum. It is cited here more by way of illustrating a resource of great future value, than for special exercise by the student, at this point. For example:

*1) The pupil is expected to refer to each "Song without Words" indicated by number, and to examine, carefully, the entire harmonic equipment (which is of very great importance), and the general surroundings. The extracts given will all be easily found, near the end of the number.

*2) These three tones are apparently a gratuitous insertion, but they relate, as a kind of sequential anticipation, to the figure marked "a".

*3) Third Symphony, *andante* movement, near the end. The relation of figure "c" to figure "a" must not be overlooked.

Irregular Phrase–formation.

33. It is sufficiently obvious that the modes of extension and development explained in par. 24–32 are liable to impart an irregular metric design to the original regular 4-measure Phrase (as regards the aggregate number of measures).

But it is also possible that the *original conception* of a Phrase may assume an irregular dimension, namely: a length of 3, 5, 6, 7, 9 measures; and examples of this kind are by no means rare.

The irregularity results either from reaching the Cadence a measure too soon, and then simply omitting the following (legitimate Cadence-) measure, in order to relieve the Cadence of unnecessary weight; this accounts for the majority of 3-measure and 7-measure Phrases;

Or the irregularity results from an unequal association of melodic members. For illustration:

*1) This is a somewhat unusual specimen of a Phrase of three large measures in *slow tempo*. The 3-measure *Phrase* is quite frequently merely a magnified example of the triple-*measure*, each beat corresponding to an entire measure; and when this is the case it is most common and most intelligible in *rapid tempo*, and generally appears in groups of at least two or more Phrases. See BEETHOVEN, Symphony No. 9, second movement, twenty-seven measures from the first repeat (*ritmo di tre battute*). MENDELSSOHN, "Songs without Words", No. 9, first three measures; No. 16, first three measures. SCHUBERT, "Winterreise", No. 18, first three measures.

*2) 3-measure Phrase in more animated rhythm, and followed by a sequence. Compare Note *1).

*3) This 5-measure Phrase results from the union of one 2-measure with one 3-measure member.

*4) The 5-measure dimension might be accounted for, in this case, as the result of a modified repetition of the first measure,—i. e., regarding the second measure as superfluous; compare with Ex. 39, note *1), in which there is no doubt about the *unessential* nature of the extra measures. It appears probable, however, that this second measure is *essential*. See also BEETHOVEN, Pfte. Sonata, op. 27, No. 2, first five measures. SCHUBERT, "Winterreise", first five measures of Nos. 15, 19, 20.

*5) A 6-measure Phrase, consisting of three members of two measures each. See "God Save the King", first six measures.

*6) Two members of three measures each. See also BEETHOVEN, Pfte. Sonata, op. 26, last movement, first six measures.

*7) This Phrase aggregates only seven measures, simply because the Cadence-tonic falls prematurely (in the seventh measure) and is not held throughout the eighth measure. Compare with meas. 15–22 of the same "Song without Words"; and see "Song without Words", No. 6, first seven measures.

MISCELLANEOUS EXAMPLES OF PHRASE-EXTENSION.

BEETHOVEN, Pfte. Sonata, op. 31, No. 1, *Adagio*, last twelve measures (2-measure Phrase).

BEETHOVEN, Pfte. Sonata, op. 28, *Finale*, last eighteen measures (4-measure Phrase).

BEETHOVEN, Pfte. Sonata, op. 28, *Finale*, meas. 29–43 (Phrase repeated and extended).

BEETHOVEN, Pfte. Sonata, op. 2, No. 2, *Largo*, meas. 13–19.

HAYDN, Pfte. Sonata, No. 14 (Cotta ed.), *Adagio*, last fifteen measures.
" " " No. 17 (" "), first eight-and-one-quarter measures.

BEETHOVEN, Pfte. Sonata, op. 10, No. 3, *Largo*, meas. 17–26 (Phrase repeated and extended).

BEETHOVEN, Pfte. Sonata, op. 14, No. 2, *Finale*, last eighteen measures.
" " " op. 26, *Finale*, meas. 32½–48 (4-measure Phrase, *each half* several times repeated).

BEETHOVEN, Pfte. Sonata, op. 101, *Finale*, last fifteen measures.

EXERCISE 8.

Former Phrases of 4-measures, with a *repetition* expanded into Chain-phrase form. A few experiments in the process of Melody-expansion and in Irregular Phrase-formation may also be made.

CHAPTER V.

THE PERIOD-FORM.

34. The Period consists in the union of TWO PHRASES, extending consequently, when regular, through *eight ordinary measures* in ordinary moderate tempo. But see par. 1.

35. The first of the two Phrases, called the ANTECEDENT Phrase, begins with the Tonic chord, as a rule;

But it does not end with the perfect Cadence like the simple Phrase, because such a Cadence would completely finish the Phrase, and render the addition of a companion-phrase, in coherent (unbroken) succession, not only impracticable but unnecessary. (See par. 2*b*.)

The Cadence of the Antecedent Phrase must, therefore, be made in such a manner as only partially to check the harmonic and melodic current. Such comparatively lighter interruptions are called SEMICADENCES.

36. The harmonic form of the Semicadence may be best defined negatively, as "any chord-association (with cadential effect) which is *not* the perfect Cadence" (see par. 3).

The most common and natural Semicadence for an Antecedent Phrase is obtained by resting, at the prescribed accent, upon some *Dominant* chord, usually as concord, but occasionally in one of its discord-forms; this Cadence-dominant may be approached through *any* convenient chord (see Ex. 46, Nos. 1 and 3; Ex. 47, Nos. 2 and 3).

But the Semicadence may also fall upon a Tonic chord, on condition that its root does not appear in either outer part in such prominence as to suggest the *perfect* Cadence (especially when the Tonic is preceded by a Dominant chord);

Or, more rarely, upon the triad VI, the Relative of the I (see Ex. 48, Nos. 2 and 3; Ex. 60).

Or it may fall upon a Subdominant chord (IV or II), though this is rarely the case (Ex. 46, No. 2).

Or the Antecedent Phrase may *modulate*, so as to end upon some chord (usually the I) of a next-related key, in the following order of preference:

Upon the I of the Dominant key;
Upon the I or V of the Relative key;
Upon the I of the Dominant-relative key;
Upon the I (rarely the V) of the Subdominant-relative key;

More rarely upon the I of the Subdominant key. (Ex. 47, No. 1; Ex. 48, No. 1; Ex. 59; Ex. 68,—first Cadence of each.)

As regards the *location* and *rhythmic treatment* of the Semicadence, see par. 3 and 4; and Ex. 46, note *1).

37. The harmonic and melodic character of an Antecedent Phrase, while necessarily conforming to the directions given in paragraphs 5, 8–12, will naturally be influenced to a certain extent by the altered condition of the Cadence; and, as a rule, the choice of Semicadence-chord should be more or less definitely determined beforehand, as the aim toward which the current of the Phrase will tend.

It is at least certain that the less decisive nature of a semicadence imparts a corresponding unfinished (conditional or interrogative) character to the Antecedent Phrase, and renders it dependent upon its following companion for completion and counterbalance. It is a *thesis*, dependent upon its *antithesis;* a *Question*, awaiting its *Answer*.

38. The second of the two Phrases in the Period-form is called the CONSEQUENT Phrase. It begins with *any* chord, or key, which is reasonably adjustable to the preceding semicadence-chord; and it ends with the perfect Cadence, in the manner described in paragraphs 3, 4, 6.

Viewed in its metric aspect, the Consequent Phrase is, when regular, exactly similar in length to its Antecedent; and both its beginning and its cadence usually correspond (as to their location in the measure) to beginning and cadence of the Antecedent Phrase.

39. Viewed in its MELODIC aspect, the Consequent Phrase must, obviously, preserve close relationship with its Antecedent, though absolute corroboration is not obligatory.

The Period-form may (and doubtless should) be regarded as a *magnified Phrase*, whereby the "figures" have grown into "members", and the "members" into complete "Phrases"; and the "quarter-cadence" (par. 8) between the phrase-members has developed into a "semicadence". From this point of view, the metric conditions illustrated in Examples 12 and 13, and emphasized in paragraph 12, also apply, though in a broader sense, to the simple Period-form.

The following distinctions influence, and possibly govern, the melodic structure of the Consequent Phrase:

(a) THE PARALLEL CONSTRUCTION.

In this form, the melody of the Consequent-phrase more or less exactly corresponds to that of the Antecedent; sometimes so closely that it is prevented from being actual Phrase-repetition (the form out of which the "parallel Period" is evolved) only by the necessary distinction in the formation of the two Cadences, namely, the *Semicadence* of the Antecedent, and the *perfect Cadence* of the Consequent, which, of course, must *essentially differ* from each other, in order to constitute the Period-relation. Compare paragraph 21. This is the primary and most natural variety of the Period-designs.

Usually, however, the similarity between Antecedent and Consequent is less pronounced, and often only a general resemblance exists.

In some cases the parallelism is established by constructing the Consequent Phrase as sequence (partial or entire) of the Antecedent. For illustration:

1. Allegretto.
46.
Antecedent Phrase.

Semi cad.
*1)
Consequent Phrase.
V..........

BEETHOVEN.
Perfect Cad.
*2)
V
I

2. Allegretto.
Antecedent Phrase.
*3)
segue
Ab IV

*1) The Semicadence rests upon the Dominant concord, which falls upon the first beat of the Cadence-measure, and is projected into the second beat. The *rhythmic pulse is continued*, exactly in conformity with the principles which govern the "concealed cadence" (par. 18, which see). The necessity of thus "bridging over" the cadence-space between the two Phrases, is owing chiefly to the momentum of the accompanying figuration—a factor which never ceases its motion during any transient cadence, and usually impels itself even beyond the final perfect Cadence. But it is generally desirable, even in the absence of a figural part, to connect the Phrases as closely as is compatible with a *perfectly unmistakable cadence-impression*. After this latter condition has been fulfilled, it is not even necessary to remain any longer within the semicadence-chord. This is illustrated by the notes in small type which occupy the last fractions of the 2nd beat.

*2) The Consequent Phrase is a literal reproduction of the Antecedent, only excepting the *very last chord*, which, being the Tonic, constitutes a perfect cadence, and establishes the indispensable condition of opposition to the Antecedent Phrase. See again par. 21.

*3) This Period begins upon the Subdominant harmony, in consequence of occurring in the course of a larger composition.

*4) The Semicadence also rests upon the Subdominant, and, therefore, leads over very smoothly into the Consequent Phrase, which is identical with the Antecedent (excepting changes in register and rhythm) up to the penultimate chord.

*5) The Semicadence rests upon the Dominant harmony, and the rhythm is completely checked, as is most customary and appropriate in music of such a simple character. For further examples of the Period of *preponderantly parallel construction*, see MENDELSSOHN, "Songs Without Words," No. 28, meas. 5–12, and meas. 13–20 (imperfect Cadence); No. 29, meas. 5–12; No. 35, meas. 6–13; No. 22, meas. 10–17 (imperfect Cadence). Ex. 49 (of this book), first four measures; Ex. 55; Ex. 72, first eight measures; Ex. 73, meas. 1–8; Ex. 75, meas. 1–8; Ex. 84, meas. 1–8; Ex. 85, meas. 1–8.

Furthermore, BEETHOVEN, Rondo, op. 51, No. 1, meas. 1–8;
BEETHOVEN, Pfte. Sonata, op. 27, No. 1, *Finale*, meas. 1–8;
BEETHOVEN, Pfte. Sonata, op. 10, No. 3, *Menuetto*, meas. 1–16;
BRAHMS, Symphony I, last movement (*Allegro*), meas. 1–8.
SCHUMANN, Jugend-Album, op. 68, No. 23 ("Reiterstück"), first 8 measures; prevented from being a "repeated Phrase" by very last tone only.

(b) THE OPPOSITE CONSTRUCTION.

In this variety of the Period-form, the melody of the Consequent Phrase pursues largely or entirely the *direction opposite* to the melodic progressions of the Antecedent.

It can scarcely be claimed that this is a natural or spontaneous mode of construction, for it is based upon a process which is largely mechanical, and may result, when applied too strictly, in constrained and unmelodious tone-lines. But it represents the same resource of thematic development as the "*Imitation in Contrary motion*" in the Polyphonic forms, and is of value to the student because of its suggestiveness. In Homophonic composition its occurrence is rare.

Occasionally the delineation of the Antecedent Phrase is almost, or quite, literally thus inverted in the Consequent; but usually only the general melodic drift, or a few of the more striking members, reappear in the opposite direction. For example:

*1) The Semicadence rests upon the I of the Dominant key (with major 3rd, i. e., the "modulatory Stride"). The Consequent Phrase-melody is (intentionally) the *literal* contrary direction of the Antecedent melody, from beginning to end.

*2) This is by far the best and most common of all the forms of the Semi-cadence, viz.: the V, preceded by the accented I in $\frac{6}{4}$ inversion. The latter (the I_2) precedes the actual Cadence-chord (V) as embellishment ("appoggiatura"), and fulfils chiefly the important purpose of "bridging over" the cadence-space (Ex. 46, note *1)).

*3) The opposite direction of the Antecedent melody is maintained through about one-half of the Consequent Phrase, only excepting the preliminary tones.

*4) Here the *general drift* of the Antecedent (more especially of the accompanying harmonies) is reversed in the Consequent. This is also the case in Mendelssohn, No. 45, first eight measures. See also Ex. 54.

See also: Hummel, Pfte. Sonata, op. 13, *Adagio*, first eight measures; and *Finale*, first eight measures.

(c) The Contrasting Construction.

This variety of the Period-form is characterized by the *absence* of such parallel traits (in the same, or in the opposite, direction) as those explained above. The principle of "contrast" prevails, though not necessarily to the utter exclusion of parallel figures.

As has already been intimated, these three distinctions are to be accepted and applied more in a general sense, than in strict detail. The Consequent Phrase of a Period may reveal traces of all three varieties of construction, without belonging distinctly to either class; and probably the majority of Periods will be defined as "contrasting" construction, merely because sufficient evidence of parallel or opposite construction is wanting.

The "contrast" is generally limited to the melody (i. e., the THEMATIC element), and is rarely extended to the style, rhythm and general character (i. e., the FORMATIVE elements).

Hence the rule, for comparatively small forms, that while *thematic* contrast is permissible and necessary to a certain degree, *formative* relation must be preserved. For illustration:

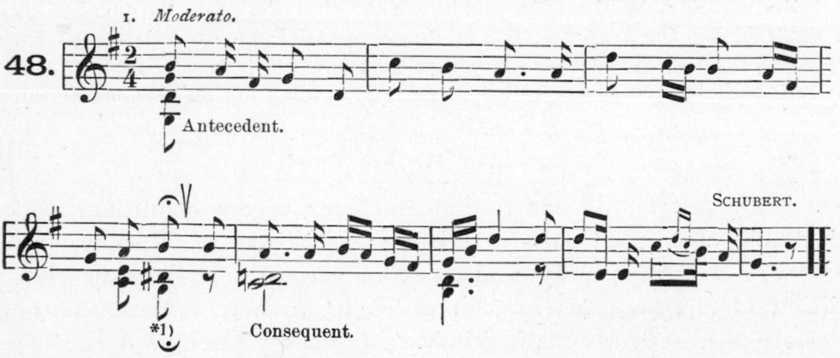

*1 The Semicadence rests upon the Dominant of the relative key, and obtains its cadential effect through the purely artificial pause (𝄐), which marks the otherwise vague point of rest. There is not a single point of melodic resemblance between the two Phrases. And the Consequent begins (*unlike* the Antecedent) upon a preliminary beat.

*2) Semicadence rests upon the Tonic triad, but with its Fifth in Soprano. The contrast between the two Phrases is here unusually marked.

*3) Tonic Semicadence, with Third in Soprano. The contrast is distinct, though traces of parallelism exist.

See also Ex. 44, No. 2 (probably a 4-measure Period); Ex. 52; Ex. 53, meas. 1–8; Ex. 60, meas. 1–8; Ex. 61, meas. 1–8; Ex. 71, each Part; Ex. 89, meas. 1–8. MENDELSSOHN, "Songs without Words", No. 9, meas. 3 (2d half)–7; No. 48, meas. 1–4. BEETHOVEN, Symphony IV, *Adagio*, meas. 2–9.

VARIETY AND UNITY.

40. Among the most vital and ever urgent conditions and demands of perfect artistic creation are those of Variety and Unity,— variety in unity, and unity in variety. Though the condition of unity appeals first in order to our consciousness, that of variety is of at least equal (ultimately of even greater) importance;

and each asserts its claims with equal emphasis. These two opposing forces are therefore incessantly at work in every creative process, and the skill of the master is displayed in so directing them that the most just balance is preserved between them.

The condition of UNITY dictates all the methods by which fundamental regularity, concentration, agreement and corroboration are obtained; these methods are:

The metrical arrangement of equal beats in equal measures and sums of measures;

The adherence to a central tonality;

The usual agreement of component members (Exs. 17 and 18; par. 38, 39*a* and *b*);

All repetitions, sequences and imitations (par. 19).

The condition of VARIETY dictates all the methods by which this fundamental regularity is divested of its monotony and fatiguing effect, and by which a judicious degree of grace and contrast may be gained; these methods are:

The modification of the rhythmic measure by use of longer and shorter tones;

The modulatory movements around the tonal center;

The alterations of register (par. 19*c*),— of style (19*d*),— of dynamic effect, within the same regular harmonic limits;

The sequence itself (as distinguished from exact repetition);

All unessential modifications (Ex. 19; Exs. 26–30), which sustain interest without jeopardizing the condition of unity, by too effectually disguising the necessary thematic and formative agreement.

The impossibility of formulating accurate rules for obtaining this "Variety in Unity" is clearly manifest. It is simply to be *borne in mind* by the student, and will thus exert a moulding influence upon his musical views and habits.

EXERCISE 9.

Invent a number of Periods, of diversified character and design, chiefly 8 measures in length. Alternate regularly between the major and the minor modes; employ the different varieties of duple and triple time, and the different grades of tempo (from *Adagio* to *Presto*). Exemplify the various forms of construction (parallel, opposite, contrasting).

Work toward the Cadence during each Phrase, and *from Cadence to Cadence*. Make both Semicadence and perfect Cadence sufficiently distinct; avoid, as beginner, vague forms of all cadences; all concealing or bridging-over of the Semicadence must be effected with strict consideration of a *perfectly definite cadential impression.*

Endeavor to preserve distinct *melodic character;* let there be a strong, prominent and continuous *melodic line* in some part or other (chiefly in Soprano) always.

In other words, the "tune" ("air", "cantilena") should always be conspicuously the dominating purpose, no matter what the style or tempo is.

Next in importance to this is the leading of the *Bass part,* which should be as smooth and melodious as possible, and should be sketched against the Melody *alone* before the inner parts are added. See also the N. B. on page 52.

CHAPTER VI.

THE DEVELOPMENT OR EXTENSION OF THE PERIOD-FORM.

41. The modes of extension explained in Chapter III are applied to the Period in the same general manner as to the Phrase, though on a correspondingly broader scale.

As usual, the principal factor is that of *repetition,* which may be applied to the entire Period bodily, or to either or both of its Phrases separately.

1. THE REPETITION OF THE ENTIRE PERIOD-FORM.

The Period may be repeated *literally,* without any other changes than those involved by concealing or bridging-over the perfect Cadence, before repetition. See pars. 18 and 21.

But here again it is far more usual and desirable to introduce *unessential modifications,* during the repetition, corresponding to the modes of manipulation described in paragraph 19*a*, *b*, *c*, *d*, *e*—which review. For illustration :

49.

*1) Neither Semicadence nor perfect Cadence requires any bridging-over, in this instance, because the "space" is reduced by the beginning of each Phrase three beats in advance of the primary accent.

*2) The modifications during the repetition consist in shifting the melody down an octave, and altering the style of the accompaniment; (also in the dynamic change from *pp* to *p*; and a change in orchestration—see later).

See also: Mendelssohn, "Songs without Words", No. 9, meas. 3 (2nd half)–11; No. 27, meas. 5–20; No. 29, meas. 4 (2nd half)–21,—one measure of interlude between Period and its repetition, as in Ex. 31.

Beethoven, Symphony IV, *Adagio*, meas. 2–17; Pfte. Sonata, op. 13, *Adagio*, meas. 1–16. Pfte. Sonata, op. 28, *Scherzo*, first thirty-two measures (large 16-measure Period, repeated).

Chopin, Prel. op. 28, No. 19, meas. 23–7 from the end. Prel. op. 28, No. 21, meas. 17–32.

Schubert, Impromptu, op. 90, No. 2, first twenty-four measures (two repetitions).

2. The repetition of the Consequent Phrase.

42. In case either of the two Phrases of the Period-form is to be repeated *alone*, it is much more likely to be the Consequent than the Antecedent. This corresponds to the repetition of the second half of a Phrase, defined in paragraph 25*a*.

The repetition may be, as usual, exact or modified,— generally the latter (par. 19).

The treatment of the perfect Cadence, before the repetition of the Consequent, must conform precisely to the conditions explained in 18 and 21, which review; i. e., the Cadence may be bridged over, but *must not be completely evaded*, by any *essential* change of harmony. For illustration:

*1) The perfect Cadence, due at this accent, is concealed by passing on chromatically in Soprano into the chord-Third; and the space is bridged over by continuing the chromatic succession directly into the first tone of the (repeated) Consequent.

*2) Compare this measure with measure 7, and observe how the very same melodic figure is here manipulated, in order to obtain an earlier and stronger cadence-impression.

See also: MENDELSSOHN, "Songs without Words", No. 14, meas. 17–28 from first double-bar; No. 19, meas. 24 (2nd half)–30.

BEETHOVEN, Pfte. Sonata, op. 2, No. 3, first twelve (13) measures (slightly expanded cadence).

CHOPIN, Prel. op. 28, No. 20, entire.

3. The repetition of the Antecedent Phrase, or of both Antecedent and Consequent.

43. As already stated, the repeated Antecedent is of far more rare occurrence than the repeated Consequent. It is most likely to appear in connection with the latter, i. e., *each* Phrase separately repeated.

The treatment of the Cadences must conform, here again, to the rules given in paragraph 21. For example:

*1) The Semicadence, here, corresponds *exactly* to the first one, four measures back.

*2) The perfect Cadence is slightly modified (concealed) by placing the chord-third in Soprano. Otherwise it agrees with its repetition, four measures later.

*3) The Melody is considerably changed, during this repetition, though not essentially so. It belongs partly, for that reason, to the "Group"-forms, explained in paragraphs 54–55.

*4) The Antecedent and its repetition close with precisely the same Semicadence (on the Tonic chord). It will be observed that this example begins with a Dominant chord; that is because it occurs in the course of a larger form. The same is true of the preceding illustration.

*5) The Consequent Phrase contains *eight* measures (twice the length of its Antecedent), owing to chain-phrase extension (par. 31).

*6)6) The harmonic alterations during the repetition (a persistent inclination into the Subdominant keys) are noteworthy. *See the original* ("Songs without Words", No. 21, thirty-eight measures from the end).

MOZART, Pfte. Sonata, No. 11 (Cotta ed.), first movement, meas. 29–8 from the end. BEETHOVEN, String-quartet, op. 18, No. 3, "Minore" of third movement, first twelve measures.

EXERCISE 10.

Former Periods, or new ones, with complete repetition (according to par. 41). The repetitions *must* be variated by means of unessential modifications, care being taken, however, to preserve the original harmonic form of the Cadences.

EXERCISE 11.

87

The same, with repetition of the Consequent Phrase (par. 42).

The same, with repetition of the Antecedent Phrase, or both Antecedent and Consequent Phrases (par. 43).

The repetitions must, here again, be unessentially modified.

4. THE EXTENSIONS AT THE BEGINNING OF EITHER PHRASE, OR OF BOTH PHRASES.

44. An extension at the beginning is, naturally, more likely to be applied to the *Antecedent* Phrase than to the Consequent.

As usual, it will assume the character of an Introduction, as explained in paragraph 28, which review. But in serving, as it may, as an introduction to the *entire* Period, it can be somewhat longer, and, at the same time, a trifle more individual in character than the introduction to a single Phrase.

This is the case, to a moderate degree, with the passage at the beginning of MENDELSSOHN'S "Songs without Words", No. 29, and No. 46; and, more strikingly, in No. 12, No. 15, and No. 32. In each of the last three of these examples, the preliminary passage might be called an "Introductory Phrase"; for, on account of its length and importance, it appears to fulfil a more independent mission than that of an extension at the beginning of the first Period only, and refers, properly, to the whole piece. But the style is, nevertheless, kept so subordinate that no doubts can arise as to the actual beginning of the Period-melody; and, moreover, it is inseparably connected with its Period by ending upon the *Dominant* harmony.

See also: CHOPIN, Mazurkas Nos. 9, 34, 13, 15, 17, 20, 21; more pronounced, Nos. 7, 31, 2.

45. When such an introductory passage is conducted into a complete Tonic Cadence, and thus *separated* from the following Period, it ceases to be an "Introduction", in the strict sense of the term, and becomes a

"*Prelude*".

The moment this distinction arises,— in consequence of the separating effect of the perfect Cadence,— the necessity of preserving close thematic and organic relation with the following Period is cancelled, and complete independence of character (in everything excepting tonality, meter and tempo) may be imparted to the Prelude.

Comparatively close organic relation with the following Period exists in the Preludes to "Songs without Words" No. 19 (comp. Song No. 1); No. 6 (first seven measures); No. 21 (first eight measures); and even in Nos. 3, 28 and 41, though these are severed from the first Period by a double-bar. See also: CHOPIN, Mazurkas Nos. 3, 42, 46.

Entire independence is illustrated in the Preludes to "Songs without Words" No. 4, No. 35, No. 16 and No. 9. The opening (4) measures of No. 27 defy exact classification; in the independence of their character they suggest the Prelude-class, but they lead, like an Introduction, directly and smoothly into the first Period, from which only a Dominant *Semicadence* separates them.

46. It is of course possible to interline a brief "introduction" to the Consequent Phrase also, but examples of this kind are *very rare*, because of the attendant danger of destroying the necessary continuity between the two Phrases. Such an introduction to the Consequent will sound most plausible when corresponding in thematic character and style to an introduction to its Antecedent Phrase; and it must be so skilfully handled as not to interfere with the impression intended to be conveyed by the original (unextended) Period. For example:

52.

V Introd.—

cresc.

Consequent Phrase.

SCHUBERT.

V I

*1) The vocal melody of this example ("Winterreise", No. 2) fixes the design of the "Period", beyond the possibility of misconception.

5. The extensions at the End of either Phrase, or of both Phrases.

47. The extensions at the end are much more likely to be applied to the Cadence of the *Consequent* Phrase than to that of the Antecedent. They conform exactly to those explained in paragraphs 25, 26, which review. One peculiarly instructive illustration will suffice:

*1) Correct perfect Cadence, omitted (or, more properly, suppressed) on account of the extension to follow.

*2) "Intercepted" form of the perfect Cadence (comp. Ex. 32, note *4)). It is expanded to two measures.

*3) This, and the seven measures which follow, constitute a "new Cadence-member" (see par. 29*d*; Ex. 42).

See also: MENDELSSOHN, "Songs without Words", No. 23, meas. 1–9 from the first double-bar; compare carefully with meas. 25–10 from the end. Also No. 27, meas. 16–4 from the end (cited in Ex. 32–2); No. 31, meas. 1–11 (4-measure Period, *repeated*, and extended at its end); No. 38, meas. 1–10.

CHOPIN, Pfte. Concerto, *e* minor (op. 11), *Romance*, meas. 13–22 (quaint repetition of 2nd half of Consequent Phrase).

48. An extension at the end of the Antecedent Phrase will be, as intimated, a comparatively rare occurrence, owing to the danger it involves of severing the continuity of the two Phrases.

It can scarcely be any more than a brief repetition, or expansion, of the chords which constitute the Semicadence (which it must confirm, and not destroy), or of the entire semicadence-member; and it will generally be balanced by a similar manipulation of the final cadence (of the Consequent) also. For example:

*1) Or, more accurately (in both cases), an "expansion" of the Cadence-tone in the melody.

*2) This Cadence is incomplete, because the new section which follows is to be entered without interruption. (See the Note following par. 93*a*.) This example, from the third movement of the first Symphony of BRAHMS, is a unique illustration of "opposite construction" (39*b*).

See also: BRAHMS, op. 117, No. 3, meas. 1–10, 11–20; same work, second tempo (*più moto ed espress.*), meas. 1–10, 11–20, 21–30. These Periods are all of parallel construction, and all extended in the same way,— at the Cadences. Also op. 118, No. 1, meas. 1–10.

See also: MENDELSSOHN, "Songs without Words" No. 37, meas. 30–39 (extension at end of *Antecedent only*).

SCHUBERT, "Winterreise", No. 14, last fifteen measures (extension at end of each Phrase); "Winterreise", No. 19, meas. 6–13 (two 3-measure Phrases; followed by modified repetition, meas. 14–21); "Winterreise", No. 22, meas. 5–18 (5-measure Phrases), and meas. 16–5 from the end.

CHOPIN, Mazurka No. 20, meas. 9–24 (repeated Consequent).

6. EXTENSIONS IN THE COURSE.

49. This mode of enlargement is applied most frequently, and, at all events, most extensively, to the *Consequent* Phrase (see par. 30). The details are enumerated in paragraph 29, which review. For illustration:

*1) The Semicadence is not bridged over, in this case, for the obvious purpose of rendering the following extension perfectly distinct.

*2) Modified repetition of second half of the Antecedent Phrase.

*3) A somewhat disguised sequence of the first half of the Consequent Phrase.

See also: MENDELSSOHN, "Songs without Words", No. 11, meas. 22½–9 from the end; a 4-measure Antecedent, and a Consequent containing course-extensions (in its first and third measures); the perfect Cadence is twice evaded (in measures six and eight of Consequent Phrase), and, finally, a "new cadence-member" of two measures closes the Period.

50. Such extensions in the course of either Phrase are not unlikely, here again, to result in "chain-phrase" formation, as explained in paragraph 31. As usual, this is far most likely to be the case with the *Consequent* Phrase.

See MENDELSSOHN, "Songs without Words", No. 10, meas. 11–24 (a 4-measure Antecedent); and No. 38, meas. 22½–41 (ending with an imperfect Cadence, before final Phrase of the Song).

CHOPIN, Prelude, op. 28, No. 1, meas. 1–25.

But this may even occur in the Antecedent, as the following (rare) example shows:

*1) The Antecedent, ending with this emphatic semicadence, is thirteen measures long. Its thematic evolution is indicated by the lettered brackets. The Consequent which follows is an example of the 5-measure Phrase.

*2) Pfte. Sonata, op. 49, No. 1, *Finale*, meas. 29½–12 from the end.

7. The Codetta.

51. To the class of extensions at the end belongs, furthermore, the Codetta (i. e., little Coda); but it differs from the extensions explained in paragraphs 24, 25, 26, and 47, in being more *independent* of the Phrase or Period to which it is added. For in the majority of cases it follows *after the complete perfect Cadence has been made*, and becomes by that means *detached* from its Phrase or Period. (It is most nearly, though not strictly, analogous to paragraphs 26*b*, *c*, *d*).

For this reason it need not be thematically related to the Melody of the Cadence-member, but may derive its Melody from *any* member of its Phrase or Period; or it may even consist of an entirely new, though strictly kindred (organically related), melodic motive. Review also paragraph 32.

Its harmonic basis may be a reiteration, in almost any metric form, of the Dominant and Tonic chords of the Cadence;

Or it may be an optional line of chords, upon the Tonic organ-point;

Or it may incline towards the Subdominant chords and keys, as broader exposition of the Plagal ending (26*d*). The latter is probably the most common.

The length of the Codetta, as applied to any of the foregoing forms, while optional, should not as a rule exceed two measures; but it may be, and usually is, *repeated*, and even extended.

It is very rarely added to anything smaller than the *Period-form*.

For illustration, to the Period given in Example 50, the following Codetta is added:

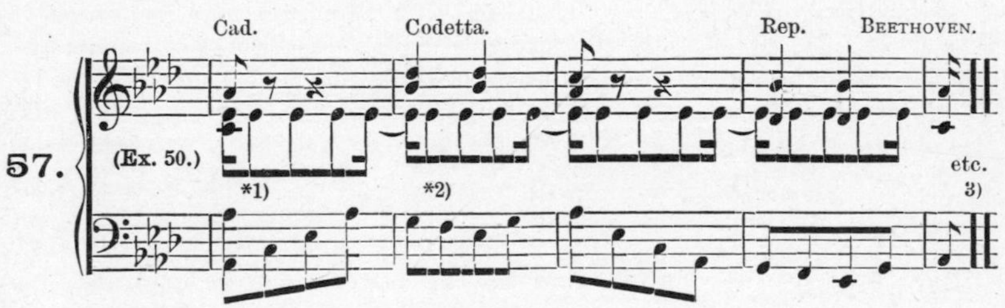

*1) This is the Cadence-measure, bridged over as shown in paragraph 18.

*2) The following two measures cannot be called an "extension of the foregoing Phrase, or Cadence-member", for they are melodically independent of the latter. Hence the independent term Codetta (appendix), to indicate the independent addition.

*3) In the original, (BEETHOVEN, Pfte. Sonata, op. 10, No. 1, end of *Adagio*,) six more measures follow, as additional repetition and extension of this Codetta; but they are necessitated simply by the proportions of the *entire Movement*, and are therefore omitted here.

Furthermore, to Ex. 41, No. 3, is added the following:

58.

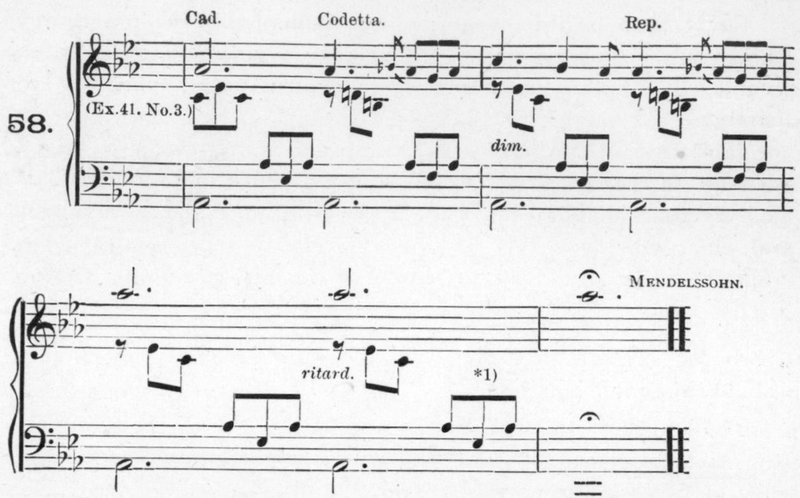

*1) The form "tapers" to the end, from the large 2-measure Phrase which precedes,—through the 1-measure Codetta, its repetition, and the half-measure extension, down to the single Tonic chord, which fades away as its resonance diminishes, without regard to measure. And the "*ritard.*" adds emphasis to the purpose of gradual relaxation.

See also: Mendelssohn, "Songs without Words", No. 1, last six measures (Codetta to preceding seven measures, with which it is to be compared); No. 13, last four measures (with preceding eight measures); No. 20, last five measures (with preceding twelve measures: Phrase repeated and extended); No. 27, last four measures; No. 40, last six measures.

Chopin, Prélude, op. 28, No. 21, last fourteen measures (two Codettas). And Ex. 70, note *4).

52. The Codetta is the counterpart of the Introduction or Introductory Phrase; and, just as the latter may deteriorate, by separation from its Period, into a "Prelude", so the Codetta may become a

"*Postlude*"

by still more complete separation from the sentence which precedes it, and by greater difference of style. Compare paragraph 45.

The Postlude is more common in larger forms, than in the Period. It is most likely to occur when the form began with a Prelude, and will, in that case, usually correspond exactly to the latter.

See Mendelssohn, "Songs without Words", Nos. 4, 9, 16, 23, 28, 35, 41, beginning and ending of each.

53. From all the foregoing it is evident that the processes of Phrase- or Period-extension are employed preponderantly in the second half, i. e., *in the later course*, towards, or at, the end of the sentence.

The first obligation of the composer is *to state the leading musical thought clearly*, *simply*, without confusing modifications. The variation, elaboration, and, most especially, the development and enlargement of this leading thought will follow, earlier or later, in fulfilment of the conditions of variety in unity. Review, briefly, paragraphs 30, 42, 47.

A peculiarly significant reason for extensions at the *very* end is touched upon in paragraph 27, and Example 58, note *1).

MISCELLANEOUS EXAMPLES OF PERIOD-EXTENSION.

CHOPIN. Prélude, op. 28, No. 1 (Antecedent Phrase, eight measures; Consequent Phrase, chain-form, sixteen measures; Codetta I, two measures and repeated; Codetta II, one measure, repeated three times; expanded Tonic at end).

SCHUBERT. "Die schöne Müllerin", No. 8, entire (4-measure Prelude; two 6-measure Phrases, Consequent extended; 2-measure Codetta).

BEETHOVEN. Pfte. Sonata, op. 10, No. 1, *Finale*, meas. 17–28.

BEETHOVEN. Pfte. Sonata, op. 81, *Finale*, meas. 37–52 (repetition of whole Period); also the following measures, 53–81, up to the double-bar (repetition, extension, and Codetta).

BEETHOVEN. Pfte. Sonata, op. 31, No. 3, first movement, meas. 46–68 (repetition with intermediate Interlude; Codetta).

BRAHMS. Op. 116, No. 1 (Capriccio), meas. 1–19 (repeated and extended).

BRAHMS. Op. 116, No. 2 (Intermezzo), meas. 1–18 (extended and repeated, with instructive modifications; *see also the last twenty-one measures*).

BRAHMS. Op. 116, No. 5, First Part (extension at end).

CHOPIN. Mazurka No. 3, meas. 49–64 (quaint repetition).

CHOPIN. Mazurka No. 17, meas. 1–20 (Introduction and repetition).

CHOPIN. Mazurka No. 20, meas. 1–24 (Introduction and extensions); also meas. 41–56 (repetition).

EXERCISE 12.

Former Periods, or new ones, with Introduction or Introductory Phrase (par. 44, 45, 46).

The same, with extensions at end of either Phrase, or of both Phrases (par. 47, 48).

Here, again, it will be wise to write out the Period first in its primary (unextended) form, and to elaborate it during its *repetition*.

EXERCISE 13.

The same, with extensions in the course of either Phrase or both Phrases (par. 49, 50).

The same, with Codetta (par. 51, 52).

These extensions may, finally, *all* be introduced into one and the same elaborate Period (illustrating the entire material of paragraphs 44, 47, 49, 51, in one example).

Write out each Period first in its unextended form.

CHAPTER VII.

GROUP-FORMATIONS.

The Period with Consequent-Group.

54. The term "Consequent-group" has been adopted by the author as a substitute for "Consequent-repetition", in application to those forms in which the reproduction of the Consequent phrase is modified to such an extent, or in such a manner, that the epithet "Repetition" is not strictly permissible. It is to all intents and purposes a *reproduction* of the second Phrase of the Period, but it is not a simple (or even unessentially modified) *repetition*. The term indicates that the two phrases thus obtained constitute a *double version* of such unquestionably uniform contents as to be virtually one and the same Consequent (a "Double-Consequent").

55. The details of the apparently subtle distinction between such a "reproduction" and a genuine "repetition", are as follows:

1st, any *essential* difference in the harmonic formation of the two Cadences (of the two versions of the Consequent Phrase) would antagonize the principle of "repetition", as defined in par. 21 (which carefully review). For illustration:

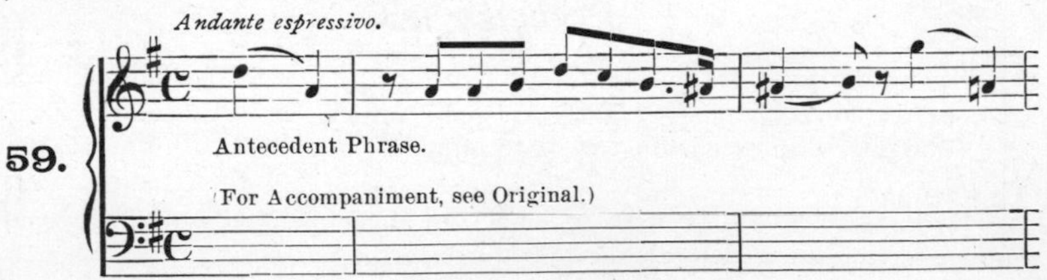

Semi-cad.
1st version of
Consequent Phrase.
*1)
2nd version of Conse-
quent Phrase.
MENDELSSOHN. No. 25.
etc.
*2)
I2 expanded
(Cad.-expansion.)

*1) This first Cadence of the Consequent Phrase is made upon the Relative Tonic, (e minor, instead of G major,) and thus the idea of "repetition" is already frustrated, because the *final* Cadence is to be made upon the original Tonic, G major.

*2) The similarity between the two versions of the Consequent Phrase is so great that it appears at first glance to be simply Phrase-repetition. But closer scrutiny of the two *essentially* different Cadences reveals the necessity for the above distinction. It is not a repeated Consequent, but a "Group of Consequents." The importance of this distinction, as defined by the formation of two successive cadences, is also shown in paragraph 39*a*, where it is the obligatory condition which distinguishes the "parallel Period" from the "repeated Phrase", or, in a word, the "repetition" from the "reproduction". See also Ex. 70, note *2).

See also: MENDELSSOHN, "Songs without Words", No. 14, meas. 11–23 from the end (final Cadence modified by chord-Fifth in Bass, on account of thematic connection with following Phrase).

MOZART, Pfte. Sonata, No. 8 (Cotta ed.), *Andante*, meas. 28–43 (second version of Consequent extended at end).

Compare these examples carefully with the illustrations given in Ex. 50; Ex. 51; Ex. 62, note *2); with especial reference to the condition of the Cadences. The latter are examples of Consequent and Antecedent *repetition*, because the cadences are essentially, if not exactly, the same; and are not to be confounded with the above (Ex. 59), which is a Consequent-*group*, because of the *essential* difference of cadences.

2ndly, a reproduction of the Consequent Phrase *upon other scale-steps*, as sequence, should not be called a repetition, even if the melodic design remain exactly, or nearly, the same. A "sequence" is a "reproduction", but never a "repetition" in the strict sense here necessarily maintained. For example:

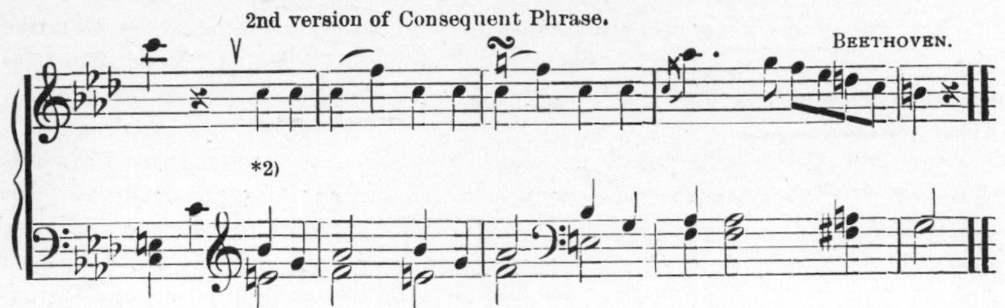

*1) Pfte. Sonata, op. 2, No. 1, *Finale*, first twelve measures.

*2) The third of these three Phrases is mainly a *sequence* of the second one, and with a "reversed" Cadence-member; consequently, the form is "Period with Consequent-group".

See CHOPIN, Prélude, op. 28, No. 24, first nineteen measures (Introduction two measures; Antecedent-Phrase four measures, with modified repetition; Consequent-Phrase first version, five measures; second version, *partial* sequence, four measures).

3rdly, the term Consequent-group should be substituted for Consequent-repetition in those cases where the reproduction embraces *more elaborate modifications* (of what is, nevertheless, unmistakably the same Phrase-contents) than would be supposable or permissible in an ordinary "repetition"; compare, carefully, all of paragraph 19. For illustration:

*1) There can be no doubt of the identity of this Phrase as *second version of the preceding Consequent Phrase*, although it diverges from the latter more and more, in its course, and ends with a totally different Cadence.

*2) See also the twelve measures which follow, in the Original (CHOPIN, Mazurka No. 11, op. 17, No. 2).

And MENDELSSOHN, "Songs without Words", No. 1, last twenty-one measures (Antecedent Phrase four measures; first Consequent four measures; second Consequent, eight measures; Codetta, five measures).—No. 31, meas. 14½–5 from the end (Antecedent, two measures; first Consequent, two measures; second Consequent, partly sequential, largely expanded, six measures).—No. 33, last twenty-three-and-one-half measures (Antecedent, four measures; first Consequent, four measures; second Consequent, ten measures, analyzed in Ex. 42, No. 2; Codetta, five measures).

SCHUBERT, "Winterreise", No. 15, meas. 19–6 from the end.

56. By exactly the same processes, the *Antecedent* Phrase of a Period may also be reproduced in this group-form. But the "Antecedent-group" is far less common than the Consequent-group. See, again, paragraphs 53, 43. One illustration will suffice:

*1) The second version is a "sequence" of the first, and, consequently, *not* a "repetition". It is an Antecedent-*group*. Compare 55, 2ndly.

*2) Here, on the contrary, a genuine *repetition* of the Consequent takes place, because (besides entire coincidence of melody) the Cadence in measure thirteen is only a concealed form of that in the final measure, without *essential* change.

*3) This measure is a quaint and characteristic expansion of the (strictly speaking, *unaccented*) first beat,—a poising of the voice upon the "up-beat" before the rhythmic movement starts into life. This accounts for the irregular (5-measure) formation.

See also: BEETHOVEN, Pfte. Sonata, op. 2, No. 1, *Menuetto*, first fourteen measures (first Antecedent-Phrase, four measures; second Antecedent, sequence, four measures extended to six; Consequent, *only two measures*, but repeated).

HAYDN, Pfte. Sonata, No. 14 (Cotta ed.), first twelve measures.

HAYDN, Symphony in B♭ (Peters ed., No. 12) *Finale*, first twelve measures.

CHOPIN, Mazurka, No. 36, first twelve measures.

CHOPIN, Prélude, op. 28, No. 5, first sixteen measures (Introduction, four measures; first Antecedent, four measures; second Antecedent, sequence, four measures; Consequent, four measures)—; the remaining twenty-three measures of the same Prélude are similarly constructed (the last seven measures are Codetta).

BRAHMS, op. 119, No. 3, last thirty measures (first Antecedent, four measures; second Antecedent, four measures; Consequent, a long Chain-Phrase to end).

THE PHRASE-GROUP.

57. The Phrase-group is a series of Phrases (at least three in number), in coherent succession, and of similar or kindred character and style; but either *too similar* to, or else *too independent* of, each other, to exhibit the distinctive condition of the Period-form, viz., the opposition of a mutually dependent thesis and antithesis (see par. 37, last clause).

The Group will never contain less than *three* Phrases, because two such, *if coherent* (not separated, as in Ex. 74), will invariably represent the *Period*-relation, in one or another of its many possible phases. On the other hand, the Group may embrace as many more than three Phrases as can be added without sacrificing coherency, or extending to an absurd extreme of "formlessness".

Each of the Phrases should close with a light *semicadence* (compare pars. 36, and 63*a*). A perfect Tonic cadence (in any key) of sufficient cadential force to complete its Phrase, can occur only at the end of the Group. There are some rare exceptions to this strict rule, but they do not concern the beginner. (This is in accurate keeping with the rules given in paragraph 31 for the Chain-Phrase, which review. The "Group of *Phrases*" is simply a larger growth of that "Group of *Members*" which constitutes the Chain-Phrase).

The following example illustrates the Group of *similar* Phrases:

*1) The similarity between these three Phrases is strikingly exhibited in the first half of each,—the melodic members being almost identical.

*2) The Bass makes this irregular leap upward from the Leading-tone (a), simply in order to evade the complete Tonic cadence.

*3) This final Cadence is unusually brief, it is true; but it, nevertheless, conforms to the conditions of the perfect Cadence fully enough to check the harmonic and melodic current, and bring the "Group" to an end. (Par. 93*a*.)

*4) Comparison of this example with the foregoing, reveals the characteristic difference between the "*Period* with Consequent- or Antecedent-Group", and the single "Phrase-Group". Ex. 59, for instance, also consists of three Phrases (like the above); but the number is *reducible to the original two of the Period-relation*, because the second and third are no more, in substance, than one (Consequent) Phrase, together. In Exs. 60 and 61 the same reasoning applies; and in Ex. 62 all four Phrases are similarly reducible to the original two. But in the above example (63), on the contrary, such a reduction to two Phrases is not tenable, because the entire sentence is simply three different versions of *one* primary phrase.

58. The Group of *independent* (or dissimilar) Phrases, on the other hand, is probably more common. The reduction of the series to two primary Phrases will not be possible, on account of the thematic individuality of the several members of the Group; but at least *general resemblance*, and close organic relation, must be preserved; and, as before, no complete perfect cadence should occur until the end is reached. For example:

64.

*1) It is evident that this series, again, cannot be reduced to *two* Phrases and be thus demonstrated as an extended "Period" of some kind, for each of the three Phrases is an independent melodic factor of the collective sentence, though perfect organic cohesion is maintained (chiefly through the uniform accompaniment).

See also the following general illustrations of the Phrase-group (both similar and dissimilar): Mendelssohn, "Songs without Words", No. 13, last twenty-three measures (four Phrases, Nos. 1 and 2 similar—*almost* repetition; No. 4 extended four measures at end; Codetta).—No. 16, meas. 4–9 (three 2-measure Phrases).—No. 20, meas. 28–17 from the end.—No. 26, meas. 28½–11 from the end (Phrase 1, two measures; Phrase 2, two measures; Phrase 3, four measures; Phrase 4, two measures; Phrase 5, two measures; Phrases 4 and 5 repeated and extended).—No. 41, meas. 15–5 from the end (three Phrases; No. 3, three measures).—No. 3, meas. 5–29 (six Phrases).

CHOPIN, Mazurka, No. 33, first twenty-two measures (five Phrases, *partly* similar, the last one extended).

CHOPIN, Prélude, op. 28, No. 9 (three similar and regular 4-measure Phrases). Prélude, op. 28, No. 2 (three Phrases, similar, each expanded).

SCHUBERT, Pfte. Sonata, No. 4 (op. 122, *Menuetto*, first twelve measures. Pfte. Sonata, No. 8 (C minor), First movement, meas. 40–53 (three similar Phrases, of unequal length; entire Group repeated, in the following fourteen measures).

GRIEG, Lyric Pieces, op. 12, No. 1 (three Phrases; rep., abbrev., and mod.).

BRAHMS, op. 118, No. 6, first twenty measures (five similar Phrases, No. 2 a repetition of No. 1); the *following twenty measures* are a modified repetition of this Group; the following eighteen measures are a Group of four Phrases (1 and 2 regular, 3 extended, 4 a sequence of 3); the following measures, up to the end, are a modified reproduction of the first Group.

To what length the Group of Phrases may possibly extend, may be seen by reference to paragraph 104. But the pupil must carefully shun such difficult experiments for a time. And he must look upon the idea of the Group-form with distrust, in any case, as being the type,—not of good consistent "Form",—but rather of "Formlessness".

59. This same idea is also applied (though far more rarely) to the *Period*, of which similar Groups may be formed, especially when the Periods are small (four measures). Such Period-groups will present the appearance, usually, of large *Phrases* with a slight semicadence in their center; and it is possible that this break may be present in some and absent in other of the Members.

See SCHUBERT, Pfte. Sonata, No. 7 (op. 164), *Finale*, first thirty measures (each Period expanded; the second one extended at end).

MENDELSSOHN, "Songs without Words", No. 32, meas. 16–28.

HAYDN, Symphony 5 (Peters ed.), Third movement, *Trio*, first twenty-six measures.

THE ELISION.

60. When the Cadence of a Phrase or Period corresponds harmonically so accurately to the beginning of the following Phrase or Period that end and beginning are practically identical, it is possible to *suppress the entire Cadence-measure*, and hasten on into the next Phrase without the pause or check for which Cadences are expressly made (par. 2*b*).

This suppression or "Elision" of the Cadence is almost exclusively applied to the perfect Cadence, though possible at semicadences also. It may be effected, firstly, when the *approach to the Cadence* has been so indicative or suggestive of the latter that its absence will be sufficiently compensated for;

Or, secondly, when the *beginning of the succeeding Phrase* is striking enough to remove any misconception of the form (see par. 93*a*, first and last clause).

The object of the elision is either to avoid an unnecessary and stagnating pause, or to obtain an exhilarating, urging effect, which is sometimes very effective. But it must be distinctly understood that it is a comparatively rare and dangerous artifice, the expediency of which should be carefully tested in each case. For illustration:

*1) These small notes represent the perfect Cadence which is due and expected at this point, but which is suppressed (omitted), causing the elision of the entire Cadence-measure. In other words, this is the fourth measure of the first phrase, and, *simultaneously*, the first measure of the following one. The latter immediately asserts itself so completely (through abrupt change of style and abrupt transition from *p* to *f*) that the actual cadence is "cut out" entirely, and the sum of measures in the two Phrases is only seven, instead of eight.

*2) The first chord in the fourth measure represents the "evaded" form of the (expected) cadence; but, at the same time, it corresponds exactly to the beginning of the first melodic member of the Phrase, which it is the author's intention to repeat, and which he proceeds to repeat *immediately*, without the—in this instance undesirable—delay which a full exposition of the cadence would cause.

*3) "Songs without Words," No. 42, near the end; the "extension" is cited in Ex. 41, No. 2. See also Ex. 70, Note *4).

BEETHOVEN, Pfte. Son. op. 2, No. 3, *Adagio*, between meas. 10 and 11.

MENDELSSOHN, "Songs without Words" No. 4, bar 5 from the end.—No. 9, bar 3 from the end.—No. 11, between meas. 4 and 5 (compare with measure 19 from the end, where the Elision does *not* appear).—No. 31, bar 5 from the end.

MOZART, Pfte. Son. No. 11 (Cotta edition), between measures 7 and 8; also last movement (*Rondo*), measures 13–19 (repeated Phrase with Elision).

On the other hand, care must be taken not to confound the Elision with those forms of concealed or evaded cadence, where the same abrupt leap into the new style of the following Phrase takes place *within the Cadence-measure*, but, contrary to appearances, does *not* suppress the latter. For example:

*1) Notwithstanding the abrupt and misleading change of character at the beginning of this cadence-measure, there is no Elision, for the coming Phrase contains its four measures without this one. The "change" must be regarded as occurring upon the *second* 16th-note, not upon the first one; consequently, according to par. 2*a* (third clause, which review), this is only the preliminary measure of the 2nd Phrase; and, though thematically consistent with what follows, it is no more than one of the innumerable modes of "bridging over" the Cadence-space (par. 18).

BEETHOVEN, Pfte. Son. op. 2, No. 3, meas. 12–21, is a still more delusive illustration of the absence of an Elision where one is apt to be suspected (between measures 12 and 13). But, here again, the new Phrase (and its subsequent reproduction, also) begins upon the *second* 16th-note of the cadence-measure, and has its quota of 4 measures without the "bridging", though the latter is directly characteristic of the coming Phrase. Of all the possible ways of bridging over the space between one Phrase and the next, *this must be conceded to be the most consistent and admirable;* i. e., with material which anticipates the coming Phrase.

See also MENDELSSOHN, "Songs without Words", No. 28, meas. 5 from the end; here, also, "end" and "beginning" are interlocked, but there is no Elision.—No. 26, meas. 11 from the end; no Elision,—comp. 2 meas. later.

EXERCISE 14.

Former Periods, or new ones, with Consequent-group, in each of the three varieties of structure explained in par. 55.

The same, with Antecedent-group (par. 56).

Work from Cadence to Cadence; *make all Cadences sufficiently emphatic*, —rather too distinct than too vague. Still avoid, for a time, any elaborate modes of evading or concealing the Cadences, such as may too completely disguise their purpose, and impair firm outlines of form.—*Review the directions given in Exercise 9.*

EXERCISE 15.

Write a number of Phrase-groups, of both similar and dissimilar thematic contents, according to par. 57 and 58. Each group must be limited to *three* fundamental Phrases, at present, though this number may be optionally increased *by the repetition* (exact or modified) of any of the Phrases.

And make a few experiments with the Elision; best in connection with *repetition* of Phrase or Period.

CHAPTER VIII.

THE DOUBLE PERIOD.

61. The Double period consists in the union of TWO PERIODS, and embraces, consequently (when regular), *four Phrases*, so conceived and distributed that the Period-relation is apparent between Phrases 1 and 2, between Phrases 3 and 4, and also, on a broader scale, between these two pairs.

62. The two Periods of a legitimate *Double*-period form are just as coherent, and just as closely dependent one upon the other, as the Antecedent and Consequent Phrases of the *simple* Period forms are. And, for this reason, the Cadence in the center (i. e., at the end of the 2nd Phrase) must be in the nature of a *Semicadence*, though almost unavoidably somewhat heavier than an ordinary light semicadence.

The Double period must be conceived simply as an expanded growth of the single Period, the Phrases of which assume such a breadth (length) that they almost necessarily separate slightly in their respective centers. These intermediate points of repose will, naturally, be lighter than the one in the center of the whole. The latter, though still only a *Semicadence* (inasmuch as it corresponds to the semicadence of the simple Period), will be rhythmically, and perhaps even harmonically, stronger or heavier than those at the termination of the 1st and 3rd Phrases.

The various degrees of rhythmic and harmonic weight which it is possible to impart to a semicadence-chord, are distinctions which increase in importance as the forms enlarge. Therefore, the following general rules must be observed: A semicadence is harmonically "heaviest" when made upon some Dominant *Triad*, or upon the Tonic Triad of a related key, as these are strong chords, but chords which, while they invite repose, still suggest inevitable onward movement. A semicadence upon any form of any other chord, or upon the *dissonant* forms of Dominant (or other) harmony, is "lighter", either because it presses forward too vigorously of itself, or because, if itself a heavy, stagnating chord, it gives immediate birth to an active counteracting agency. Further: a semicadence is rhythmically heavy or light in exact proportion to the *duration of the chord*,—the length of time spent in pausing,—and the consequent length or brevity of the "bridging" which follows. Finally: the *rhythmic* distinction is far the more important of the two.

63. The Cadence-conditions of the regular Double period are, then, as follows:

(a) At the end of the first Phrase a *light* semicadence, consisting perhaps most frequently of the *Tonic* chord, with Third or Fifth (instead of Root) in one of the outer parts; or the Dominant chord, consonant or dissonant,—the latter being lighter than the former; or possibly some other chord in one of its lighter forms. And, in any case, rhythmically more or less brief, exactly according to the *degree of interruption* desired (see par. 2*b*, final clause).

(b) At the end of the 2nd Phrase a *heavier* semicadence, corresponding generally, in choice of chord, to the table given in par. 36 (to which strict attention must be given), but probably with more rhythmic stress, i. e., longer duration, than in the single Period. It is most apt to be a Tonic chord of the *Dominant Key;* or, more rarely, a Tonic chord of the Relative, or some other next-related key, approached with a more elaborate and emphatic modulation. *But it must never be so heavy as to lose its semicadence effect*, and thus destroy the continuity of the whole.

(c) At the end of the 3rd Phrase a *light* semicadence again, perhaps corresponding to the first one, though a little more likely to incline toward the *Subdominant* harmonies; and again, with a more emphatic modulatory manifestation.

(d) At the end of the 4th Phrase (in the regular, complete Double period) the Tonic perfect Cadence.

64. The necessary cohesion between the two Periods is most effectively preserved by constructing the 2nd Period melodically PARALLEL with the 1st. See par. 39*a*.

The parallelism need not, however, be maintained any farther than during the first melodic member of the 2nd Period; although, generally, the entire 3rd Phrase corresponds exactly or nearly to the

1st Phrase; and, in cases of extreme parallelism, even the 4th Phrase follows the thematic design of the 2nd Phrase, nearly to the end. Phrase 2 should *contrast* with phrase 1.

The following example illustrates the Double period as an "expansion of the single Period", in parallel construction:

*1) This cadence, like that which precedes it in the 4th measure, is made upon the Dominant harmony with the chord-fifth in the Soprano. But it is *rhythmically* stronger here than in the 4th measure.

*2) The parallelism of construction extends up to this point, with no other than the purely unessential modification in the 9th measure.

*3) There is no reasonable doubt of this being the *Double*-period form; but, the measures being small and the tempo somewhat active, it creates the impression of a Large *single* Period (of 8-measure Phrases and parallel construction) with a semicadence in the middle of each half, coinciding, on a larger scale, with the syntax of Ex. 13, No. 3—which see. This latter analysis (i. e., Large *single* Period) would certainly be correct if the tempo were *allegro* or *presto*.

65. The transitional grades and progressive shades of distinction from the perfectly unmistakable Single-period form with no intermediate interruptions, into the perfectly unmistakable Double period with its four legitimate cadences, are so innumerable, that it will often be impossible to define accurately the denomination of certain examples of this kind found in musical literature; and even so slight a thing as a deviation in the tempo or "phrasing" of the performer may influence, perhaps positively alter, the structural impression and analysis. Of one thing the student may rest assured, namely: in proportion as the distinction becomes thus more minute and questionable, *it becomes of less and less moment to define it, and less wise to insist upon an absolute definition*. See par. 10; and par. 77.

For examples of doubtful form, between Single and Double period, see:

Mendelssohn, "Song without Words" No. 12, meas. 7-22 (a noticeable semicadence in the center of the first half, *but none whatever in the second half;* like Ex. 13, No. 1). No. 22, first 9 measures (exactly the same). No. 8, first 17 measures (probably Double, despite the rapid tempo). No. 19, measures 3-11 (probably Double). No. 25, first 10 measures (probably Single; extended at end). No. 32, measures 4-14 (probably Single; extended at end). No. 48, first 8 measures (probably Single).

Beethoven, Pfte. Son. op. 10, No. 1, *Adagio*, first 16 measures (probably Double); op. 10, No. 3, *Menuetto*, first 16 measures (probably Single); op. 14, No. 1, *Allegretto*, first 16 measures (probably Single); *Rondo*, op. 51, No. 1, first 8 measures (probably Single).

Chopin, Préludes, op. 28, No. 8, first 8 measures (probably Single).

The following examples, on the contrary, are beyond a doubt genuine Double periods, of parallel construction:

*1) This cadence, it is true, cannot be called heavier than the one in the 4th measure; nevertheless, it serves its purpose sufficiently well. The construction of the 2nd Period is here again extremely parallel, almost to the cadence; but compare with Ex. 49; and observe that the *parallel Double period* differs from the *repeated Period* in the differentiation of its 2nd and 4th cadences.

See also: Beethoven, Pfte. Son. op. 22, *Finale*, first 18 measures.

Chopin, Préludes, op. 28, No. 7; No. 10 (Phrase 3 *sequence* of Phrase 1; Phrase 4 like 2, *excepting Cadence;* slight cadence-extension); No. 14 (Phrase 2 extended to 6 measures; Phrase 4 only 3 measures; Codetta 3 measures); No. 23 (Phrase 4 extended to 5 measures; Codetta, 6 measures, beginning after —or with—an Elision); No. 17, first 18 measures; No. 19, first 16 measures.

Chopin, Nocturne No. 1 (op. 9, No. 1), first 18 measures (cadence-extension); Nocturne 5 (op. 15, No. 2), first 16 measures (regular, and extremely parallel,—*almost* Single period repeated).

Mozart, Pfte. Son. No. 7 (Cotta ed.), *Adagio*, first eight measures; Pfte. Son. No. 13 (Cotta ed.), *Finale*, first 16 measures; Pfte. Son. 14 (Cotta), *Finale*, first 16 measures; Pfte. Son. No. 15 (Cotta), 2nd movement, first 16 measures.

Schubert, Pfte. Son. No. 10 (B♭ major), first 18 measures (the 2nd cadence expanded); Pfte. Son. No. 2 (op. 53), *Scherzo*, first 40 measures (very large; 8-meas. Phrases, Nos. 2 and 4 extended at end to 12 measures).

Mendelssohn, "Songs without Words", No. 15, first 22 measures (Introd. 6 meas.); No. 18, first 17 measures; No. 24, first 18 measures; No. 30, first 15 measures (4th Phrase short); No. 37, first 17 measures.

Brahms, op. 116, No. 6, "Trio" (5-sharp signature).—Op. 116, No. 7, first 20 measures (each Consequent extended); compare last 31 measures of same work.—Op. 117, No. 1, "*più Adagio*".—Op. 117, No. 2, measures 22 (second half) to 38.—Op. 118, No. 5, first 16 measures.—Op. 119, No. 1, measures

1–16.—Op. 119, No. 2, second tempo (4-sharp signature) first 16 measures.—Op. 119, No. 4, measures 1–20; measures 21–40; measures 41–60 (each a regular parallel Double period, of 5-measure Phrases).

66. The CONTRASTING construction (39*c*) of the 2nd Period, in the Double-period form, is far more unusual and confusing than the parallel construction; because, when the 3rd Phrase does not melodically confirm the 1st one, it is much more difficult to preserve the cohesion of the two Periods (demanded in par. 62), *and to prevent the impression of two separate, independent Periods* (as in the Two-Part Song-form: see par. 74).

Still, "four Phrases" in *coherent* succession, if such be carefully sustained, are likely to be a Double period from sheer symmetry of design, whether Phrase 3 is like Phrase 1 or not; only excepting, of course, possible cases where the 4 Phrases are *reducible*, by clear evidence of repetition, to a "repeated Period", or to a "Group of 3 Phrases." But the continuity of the Double-period form must be assured, by avoiding too complete a Cadence at the end of the 2nd Phrase.

See again MENDELSSOHN, "Songs without Words", No. 13, last 23 measures, already cited as example of the Group of 4 Phrases.

And CHOPIN, Prélude op. 28, No. 18 (Phrase 1, 4 measures; Phrase 2, similar, 5 measures; Phrase 3, four measures; Phrase 4, extended to 8 measures). This *might* be called a Contrasting Double period, but the title "Phrase-group" is more consistent with its *character*.

Furthermore, the Contrasting Double period may represent a Large contrasting Single period, with interruption in the center of each half (see par. 62, second clause). For illustration:

*1) Thematically (i. e., melodically), Phrase 3 is totally unlike Phrase 1; and there is likewise no resemblance between Phrases 4 and 2. It is "contrasting" construction. But close *formative* relation is preserved, throughout, by uniformity of style and character; and the continuity of structure is absolute.

*2) The "perfect-cadence Tonic" is wanting in Bass, here, because an extension follows, to which reference will be duly made.

*3) "Song without Words" No. 2, near the end. *Compare these measures with the first 16 measures* of the same Song, where the construction is parallel.

See also: MENDELSSOHN, "Songs without Words", No. 6, measures 18–34; No. 3, first 16 measures after the 2nd double-bar.

MENDELSSOHN, op. 16, No. 1, first 21 measures (4th Phrase short; Codetta, 2 measures, repeated and extended).

HAYDN, Symphony No. 6 (Peters ed.), *Menuetto*, first 18 measures (Phrase 4 extended, as shown in Ex. 39, No. 1).

CHOPIN, Mazurka No. 32 (op. 50, No. 3), first 16 measures.

BEETHOVEN, Pfte. Son. op. 22, *Adagio*, first 9 measures (a little doubtful whether Single or Double period,—probably the latter).

THE EXTENSIONS OF THE DOUBLE PERIOD.

67. Nothing further need be said, here, concerning the details of ordinary Phrase-extension (par. 24 to 30), than that they may, as a matter of course, be applied to *any* of the Phrases which collectively constitute the Double period. But see par. 53. The only devices of enlargement to be specially considered in this place, are those of modified *repetition*, and *Group-formation*, which may be utilized as follows:

(a) The modified repetition of the *entire* Double period, of which an example will be found in MOZART, Pfte. Son. No. 11 (Cotta ed.), *Andante*, first 32 measures (rep. variated).

See also: SCHUBERT, Pfte. Son. No. 6 (op. 147), *Finale*, measures 51 to 80 (quaintly modified repetition, *contracted* two measures at end; but otherwise preserving all salient traits).

CHOPIN, Mazurka No. 13, first 36 measures (Introd. 4 measures); Mazurka No. 37, first 44 measures (Phrase 4 each time extended to 10 measures; repetition modified); CHOPIN, Nocturne No. 3 (op. 9, No. 3) first 40 measures (Phrase 4 extended to 8 measures; repetition elaborate).

(b) The modified repetition of either, or each, of the two Periods.

This is a somewhat misleading device, especially when applied to the *first* Period (comp. par. 42). A Double period, if interrupted in the center for the sake of repeating its first Period, will almost certainly present the appearance of two *separate* Periods, and become a Two-Part Song-form. But see CHOPIN, Mazurka No. 29, first 32 measures (contrasting construction; each Period *exactly* repeated, and evidently without completely disturbing the continuity of the whole).

See also: BEETHOVEN, Pfte. Son. op. 31, No. 2, *Finale*, measures 1–31 (2nd Period repeated and extended); Pfte. Son. op. 106, *Adagio*, measures 1–26 (ditto; Introd. one measure).

(c) The enlargement of the Double period to 5 or more Phrases by repetition of the last Phrase, or Group-formation of the final Consequent.

This process of extension can scarcely be applied to any other than the Double period of *parallel* construction, *in which identity of design is so fully assured by the correspondence of Phrase 3 to Phrase 1*, that it cannot be destroyed by anything that follows (in the same section).

The *repetition* of the last Phrase is, of course, imaginable even in a Double period of *contrasting* construction. But *Group*-formation would be so difficult to prove at the end of a contrasting Double period, that the entire sentence would almost certainly be called a "Phrase-group", from sheer expediency.

For illustration:

Andante cantabile.
70.
PERIOD 1.
Phrase 1
3
3
3
(etc. See Original.)
Phrase 2.
3
3
PERIOD 2
Phrase 3 (like 1.) *1)
3
Phrase 4.
(first version).
*2)
Phrase 4.
(second version).
*3)

*1) At this point, already, the identity of the "Double-period" form is so fully established, that no reasonable amount of enlargement by the addition of Phrases (whether similar or not) could change the denomination.

*2) The perfect cadence, due and expected at this place, is completely evaded. The following Phrase is therefore *not a repetition, but a reproduction*, of the preceding. It is a "Consequent-group", as shown in par. 54.

*3) Although this is the genuine form of the perfect cadence (Root in both outer parts), it is made so brief, and followed so abruptly by the new harmony, that it assumes the nature of the "concealed cadence"; the following 2 measures are a modified repetition of the second half of the Phrase.

*4) At this place there is an unusually distinct "Elision" of the cadence-measure. This chord certainly stands for the end of the foregoing Phrase; but it is just as certainly, at the same time, the beginning of the Codetta, as comparison with the first thematic member of the Double period proves.

68a. The enlargement of the Double period, finally, by the addition of an Introduction (par. 28), an Introductory Phrase (par. 44), a Prelude (45)—or by the addition of a Codetta or Postlude (par. 51-52),—is not only possible, but *more appropriate and necessary than in smaller forms.* Illustrations are contained in some of the above references, and will also be found in the following

MISCELLANEOUS EXAMPLES OF DOUBLE-PERIOD EXTENSIONS.

MENDELSSOHN, "Song without Words" No. 20, first 21 measures (five 4-measure Phrases, No. 5 *new*, obtained by Group-formation of second Period); No. 21, first 32 measures (Prelude 8 measures; Double period extended by Group-formation; Phrase 4 three measures, Phrase 5 nine measures); No. 26, first 15 measures (two-measure Phrases, Group-formation of 2nd Period); No.

32. first 14 measures (Introd. 4 measures; 2-measure Phrases, Group-formation); No. 36, first 27 measures; No. 39, first 15 measures (2-measure Phrases, a little doubtful whether Single or Double-period form; Group-formation; Codetta of 1 measure, repeated); No. 2, first 29 measures (*seven* Phrases, but unmistakably Double-period form, parallel construction, enlarged by Group-formation of 2nd Period).

CHOPIN, Préludes, op. 28, No. 3 (Introd. 2 measures; Phrase 2, five measures; Phrase 5, eight measures; Codetta); No. 4 (Phrase 2, eight measures; Phrase 4, five measures extended to nine); No. 5 (Introd. four measures; construction parallel; *Antecedent-group* in each Period); No. 6 (Phrase 3, six measures; Phrase 4 reproduced ,—Group-formation, as in Ex. 70; Codetta); No. 13, first 20 measures.—CHOPIN, Mazurka 31 (op. 50, No. 2), first 28 measures (Introd. 8 measures).

BACH, Ouverture à la manière française, "Echo", measures 1–22 (Phrase 2 eight measures; Phrase 4 also extended).

SCHUBERT, Pfte. Son. No. 8 (C minor), *Adagio*, measures 1–18 (4th Phrase short); Pfte. Son. No. 10 (B♭ major), 1st movement, measures 1–18 (2nd cadence expanded).

BRAHMS, op. 116, No. 3 (Phrase 1 of each Period repeated).—Op. 117, No. 2, first 22 measures (Consequent-group at end).—Op. 119, No. 1, measures 17-42 (parallel; cadence imperfect; each Consequent extended).—Op. 119, No. 3, measures 1–24 (parallel; each Consequent extended).

(b) The device of transforming the (Large) Single period into a Double period, by occasioning a semicadence in the center of each half (par. 62, last clause), may also be applied to the Double period, —which, if large enough, may thus assume the design of a

"QUADRUPLE PERIOD".

See MENDELSSOHN, "Song without Words" No. 13, first 20 measures (extended; it is not only possible, but perhaps necessary, to regard this as a form of 4—or 5—four-measure *Periods*, consisting of 2-measure Phrases).

CHOPIN, Mazurka 28 (op. 41, No. 3), first 38 measures; CHOPIN, Polonaise No. 6 (op. 53), measures 17-48 (quasi *repeated* Double period); CHOPIN, Prélude, op. 28, No. 16 (extended 13 measures at end).

SCHUBERT, Pfte. Son. No. 5 (op. 143), first 46 measures.

EXERCISE 16.

Write a number of regular (i. e., unextended) Double periods, of Parallel construction (par. 61–64).

Use both the major and the minor modes, best in alternate examples. Employ different varieties of duple and triple time, and the different grades of tempo from *Adagio* to *Presto*. And adopt different styles, imitating (even closely or literally, if necessary) the style of certain given illustrations, or of any other familiar or favorite composition.

See the N. B. on page 52.

Work towards the Cadence during each Phrase, *and from Cadence to Cadence.* Avoid vague forms of Cadence, as a rule, but employ freely the varieties of concealed and evaded Cadence already learned and mastered.

A few illustrations of the Contrasting Double period may be attempted; best, as Large Single period with intermediate interruptions (par. 66).

EXERCISE 17.

The examples of Exercise 16, or new ones, extended in the manner indicated in par. 67*a*, *b*, *c;* and par. 68*a*.

DIVISION TWO.

THE SONG-FORMS,* OR PART-FORMS.

INTRODUCTORY.

69. The comparative definition of the various members and distinctive elements of form which enter into the composition of this second, larger, Division of structural evolution, is as follows:

(a) The PHRASE: is an *uninterrupted* series of "Chords", and coherent melodic "Members", of such a length as can be reasonably sustained without palpable interruption,—generally from 2 to 8 measures; closing with a Cadence (perfect Cadence or Semicadence).

(b) The PART: is a *coherent* series of such "Phrases", to the number of two, three, four or more; (possibly only *one;* and, on the other hand, never more than can be held without effort in close relation and connection with each other); terminating, as a rule, with a strong Tonic Cadence.

(c) The SONG-FORM: is a coherent series of such "Parts", to the number of 2, 3 or more; ending, as a rule, with the complete Tonic perfect Cadence.

The cohesion of the members is observed to relax, in proportion to the growth, or increase in length, of the form; simply because, the greater the dimension, i. e., length, of the several sections of the design, the greater the necessity of more emphatic points of repose, and of more variety and contrast between the individual members. Hence:

Between the "Members" of the Phrase (i. e., the Chords and melodic Motives) there is little or no separation (at most, a Quarter-cadence);

But between the "Phrases" of a Part there stands a Semicadence;

---

* So called in analogy to the *vocal* forms from which they are derived; but just as common in instrumental as in vocal composition.

And between the "Parts" of a Song-form there stands, as a rule, a complete Tonic Cadence.

Furthermore:

The melodic and rhythmic elements of a *Phrase* must be very closely related;

The Phrases of a *Part* are organically related, but somewhat independent;

The Parts of a *Song-form* are still kindred, but sundered, and often quite independent of each other, in certain outward respects.

70. According to par. 69*b*, the name "Part" is given to any series of Phrases, in comparatively unbroken succession, extending up to a cadence of sufficient force to check both the harmonic and melodic currents, and so to complete the musical purpose of that section as to set it temporarily apart; but not of sufficient culminating force to dispel the natural expectation of a following, kindred, section, which may more fully consummate and confirm this musical purpose.

(a) It is possible, as already hinted, that one single Phrase, when of sufficiently opulent character, and especially *when repeated*, might constitute an entire Part. But it is not probable; and examples of so small a Part, excepting when occupying an intermediate position, between larger Parts, are rare. See Ex. 74; and Ex. 78.

(b) As a rule, therefore, the "Part" will contain at least two Phrases; and may contain as many more as the limitation dictated in par. 69*b* will admit. In a word, *each of the designs explained in the first Division of this book*,—from the repeated Phrase up to the enlarged Double period,—represents the elements, and is an example, of the *Single Part*. And it is perfectly proper to speak of them as the "One-Part" forms.

CHAPTER IX.

THE TWO-PART SONG-FORM.

71. In the Two-part Song-form, or, as it is also called, the *bipartite* form, there are two such Parts; usually, though not necessarily, of corresponding general character and design, but effectually disconnected from each other by a cadential interruption.

72a. Of these, the First Part, as already stated, may consist of a Repeated Phrase (rare); a Period, regular or extended; a Double period, regular or extended; or a Group of Phrases. It is, perhaps, most commonly a Period, and regular in structure, in keeping with the principle enunciated in par. 53 (which review).

The First Part of a Song-form is the "statement" of the leading musical thought,—the motive, text, or subject; which, while it must be sufficiently impressive, interesting, and pregnant to excite attention and give gratification by itself, should depend chiefly upon the following Part (or Parts, if there be more than two) for its development, elaboration and corroboration.

The First Part may be, and very commonly is, repeated.

(b) The Cadence of the First Part, as stated in par. 69*b*, will be made, as a very general rule, upon some Tonic harmony, in its strongest form, and in strongest rhythmic location. It may be (in the order of preference):

(1) The Tonic of the *Dominant* key, in a Song-form beginning in major;

(2) The Tonic of the *Relative* key, in a Song-form beginning in minor;

(3) The Tonic of the *Original* key itself.

(4) Or it may be the Tonic of some other Next-related key; i. e., the Dominant from *minor*, or the Relative from *major*,—instead of the opposite, as given above; further, the Relative of the Dominant; more rarely, the Relative of the Subdominant key; and, most rarely, the Subdominant key itself; possibly some Remotely-related key, as the "Modulatory Stride",* or one of the "Mediant"* keys.

(5) Other Cadence-conditions, to be avoided here, are explained in par. 93, to which brief reference may be made.

(c) The general modulatory current of the First Part will be determined by the choice of Cadence. Review, in this connection, par. 37, recollecting that in a 2-Part form the First Part is an "Antecedent", simply magnified in dimension.

But, within this general modulatory design, there exists the opportunity for *transient* modulations, more necessary here than in smaller forms, because the increase in dimension magnifies the simpler *Chord*-relations into *Key*-associations. But see par. 72*a*,

---

* See the Author's "Material used in Mus. Composition", p. 149, and p. 155.

second clause; and avoid overloading the *First* Part with harmonic and modulatory color. See also par. 94.

73a. The SECOND PART, in the 2-Part Song-form, is probably most prone to assume the same form, or length, as its First Part, though many digressions from this condition of symmetry are possible and common. In case of differentiation, the Second Part will almost certainly be the longer of the two.

Like Part I, the Second Part may be repeated.

(b) In character, the Second Part must maintain fairly close agreement with its First Part; not, by any means, servile *thematic* relations (i. e., in respect of melodic design), but close *formative* connection (in respect of general harmonic character, rhythmic character and technical style). As Part I is an "Antecedent", Part II is its "Consequent"; therefore, a certain impression of *consistent opposition* between the two Parts should be created, such as distinguishes, on a smaller scale, the Period-relation. This is very frequently effected by basing the first member of Part II upon the Dominant harmony, in opposition to the Tonic basis upon which Part I starts out.

In other words, while CADENTIAL SEPARATION is necessary, no radical change of CHARACTER should be perceptible in passing out of the First Part into the Second. See par. 69, the very last clause. It is precisely such a *distinct alteration of style*, that ushers in a new "Subject" or new "Song-form" (like the "Trio" in the Minuet,—pars. 117, 119,—or the "Subordinate Theme" in the Rondo and Sonata-*Allegro* forms). The end of the First "Part" is sufficiently marked by the complete cadential break, demanded in par. 72*b*; but the condition of coherency and consistency, *uniformity of style and general character*, should prevail throughout all the component Parts of a Song-form. On the other hand, as already stated, the *thematic* (melodic) conduct may be as independent as is desired, and a certain amount of individuality is quite essential.

(c) The Second Part ends with the complete Tonic perfect Cadence, in the original key; probably emphasized by a Codetta, or, at least, by an extension at the end of the final Phrase. (See par. 79*b* and *c*.)

In its modulatory design, the Second Part will be found, in the most perfect models of the 2-Part form, to incline toward the lower (i. e., Subdominant) keys,—just as the First Part favors the higher (i. e., Dominant) direction.

Two-Part Song-form, Primary Design.

74. The type of the primary 2-Part Song-form (the design out of which it is evolved) is the Double period, especially that of contrasting construction, in which the continuity insisted upon in par. 62 is disturbed by a cadential break in the center, so complete that it resolves the "*One*-Part" Double-period form into a "*Two*-Part" Song-form. (See pars. 66, and 62.)

Hence, the Primary design of the 2-Part Song-form is that in which each Part is in the ordinary Period-form, with or without repetition.

Examine the following illustrations of this Primary design scrupulously, testing the minutest traits as they may be borne upon by the conditions enumerated in paragraphs 71, 72 and 73:

71.

*1) An unusually brief (light) Semicadence.

*2) This is a complete Tonic Cadence in the Dominant key, of such weight and emphasis as totally to sever all purely external connection between the two Periods, which, consequently, represent here two *Parts*. (Compare par. 63*b*, last clause.)

*3) The Second Part starts out from the Dominant, while Part I began upon a Tonic basis.

*4) The "consistent opposition" of the Parts, mentioned in par. 73*b*, is clearly illustrated here by the rhythmic form of this first measure, which corresponds to that of the *second* measure in Part I. Thus, while the rhythmic figure of the very first measure of the Song-form becomes the rhythmic type of Part I, that of the second measure characterizes the greater portion of Part II; *and the first two "measures" constitute the rhythmic germ of the two "Parts"*. This is consistent Musical Form.

*5) Here the Subdominant inclination of the Second Part (par. 73*c*) manifests itself.

*1) A complete Tonic Cadence in the Relative key; see par. 72*b* (2).

*2) In its thematic (melodic) aspect and style, this Second Part closely resembles its First Part. But "consistent opposition" is nevertheless obtained by enlarging the *one*-measure Sequence of Part I, to a *two*-measure Sequence in Part II.

*3) Theme of the "Variations sérieuses", op. 54. *See also the individual Variations*, which, while they nearly all preserve the 2-Part design, present many instructive modifications in the treatment of the Cadences; viz., the Cadence at the end of Part I is always bridged over, sometimes reduced to a Semicadence, and is therefore more vague than in the Theme,—especially so in Var. 1, 2, 6 and 13;—Var. 3, 4, 7, 9, 11, 12 and 14 all approach the Double-period form, because the middle Cadence is not strong enough to divide the design into two *Parts;*—Var. 10, 15, 16 and 17 approach the form of a Group of Phrases;—In Var. 5, 8 and 16, the middle Cadence is altered to a different key;—In Var. 14, being Major, the *Dominant* (Semi-) Cadence is used.

See also: CHOPIN, Mazurka No. 50 (Peters ed.) first 32 measures (each Part repeated).

BEETHOVEN, 9 Variations in A major, Theme (by PAISIELLO),—Second Part repeated. BEETHOVEN, Symphony No. 2, *Larghetto*, first 32 measures (each Part repeated).

HAYDN, Pfte. Son. No. 4 (Cotta ed.), *Largo* (final Cadence on Dominant, for an obvious reason); Pfte. Son. No. 5 (Cotta ed.), *Presto*, first 16 measures (two *complete* repetitions, the second one very much altered); Pfte. Son. No. 7 (Cotta ed.), *Finale*, first 18 measures; Pfte. Son. No. 11 (Cotta ed.), first 16 measures; Symphony No. 9 (Peters ed.), *Andante*, first 10 measures; Symphony No. 6 (Peters ed.), *Andante*, first 32 measures (each Part repeated).

SCHUMANN, "Bunte Blätter", op. 99, No. 1 (Cadence of Part I somewhat vague,—see par. 93); "Waldscenen", op. 82, No. 7 ("Vogel als Prophet") first 18 measures (Codetta of 2 measures).

BEETHOVEN, Pfte. Son. op. 28, "Trio" of 3rd Movement (Part I repeated literally; Part II repeated with modification; melodic relation between the Parts unusually close); Pfte. Son. op. 57 (Appassionata), *Andante*, the Theme, and its Variations also.

75. A very common,—almost characteristic,—trait of the 2-Part Song-form, exhibited in many examples in musical literature, consists in the *similarity between the respective endings* of the two Parts.

Sometimes the resemblance is *literal* (as in Ex. 73); sometimes the endings differ only in key (in case Part I does not close in the original key,—as Part II *must*); in some cases there is only a general resemblance; occasionally the coincidence embraces the entire last Phrase of each Part; and again, on the contrary, it is very brief.

This point of resemblance between the *endings* of the Parts must not be confounded with that essential condition of parallelism which prevails at the *beginning of each Period* in the Double-period form (par. 64), for their respective influences upon the formal conception are precisely opposite. The agreement at the beginning confirms and supports the *coherency* of the members; while the agreement of the endings, on the contrary, serves to emphasize their *separation*, inasmuch as the central cadence thus assumes a form and weight similar to that of the final cadence, and closes its Part as completely as the latter does the entire sentence.

N. B. Very particular care must be taken to limit any such resemblance as this strictly to the *ending* of the Parts, and to repress the tempting inclination to introduce, in the course of the Second Part, any member which exactly corroborates *the beginning of the First Part!* Such a feature would transform the imagined 2-Part form into some variety of the *Three*-Part design. See par. 81*a*.

For example:

*1) This is the comparatively rare termination of Part I with a perfect Cadence in the original key; see par. 72*b* (3).

*2) The Theme of 8 Variations in B♭ by BEETHOVEN (a popular German song). The parallel endings are indicated by the brackets. *See also the individual Variations*, and observe to what extent this structural feature is preserved in some of them.

See also: BEETHOVEN, 9 Variations in C minor (March by DRESSLER), Theme, and *all the Variations* (resemblance covers the entire last Phrase, but involves transposition).

MOZART, G minor Symphony, *Finale*, first 16 measures.

EXERCISE 18.

A. Write two examples of the 2-Part Song-form, *Primary design*, *in Major;* with scrupulous regard to the details of structure and cadence given in par. 72 and 73.

Use some variety of duple time for one, and triple time for the other; and choose radically different style and tempo for each.

REVIEW THE DIRECTIONS GIVEN IN EXERCISE 9.

B. Write two examples of the same form and design in *Minor*, observing all the above directions; in one instance introducing the similarity of ending, explained in par. 75, and carefully guarding against the error pointed out in the final clause.

THE DIMINUTIVE TWO-PART SONG-FORM.

76. As already declared in par. 70*a*, it is possible that a Part may consist of no more than one single Phrase, and, though naturally rare, such examples may be found.

This may be true of either Part, or even, though still more rarely, of both. As usual, it is least likely to occur in the Second Part (par. 73*a*, last clause).

How difficult it is to impart sufficient contents to a *single Phrase*, and to separate it so positively from its companion as to establish its dignity and independence as an adequate "Part", the student will soon discover. Review par. 57, second clause, and par. 70*b*; and reflect to what extent, on the other hand, the *continuity* of Phrase-succession is maintained as One-Part form in some of the given illustrations of the extended Double period, the Phrase-Group, and the Quadruple period.

The conditions are most favorable when the Phrase, thus made to represent an entire Part, is either of the large (8-measure) species, or broad in tempo and character; when it has a very firm Cadence; and *when it is repeated*. For illustration:

*1) This is an unusual example of the 2-Part form, each Part of which is only a 4-measure Phrase. But the breadth of character and contents, the comparatively moderate tempo, and the *repetition* of each Part, establish the form beyond question. (There is even a remote possibility of assuming the Period-form, instead of Phrase, in each Part; compare par. 10.) It is to be found in BEETHOVEN's Pfte. Son. op. 27, No. 1, first movement, and *must be referred to.* The illustration here given covers the first 8 measures (or 9, with the second ending); the following 12 (13) measures illustrate exactly the same variety of the Diminutive 2-Part Song-form, the repetition of Part II being written out, on account of unessential modifications; the 16 measures which follow are a recurrence of the above illustration, *but with the repetitions written out and modified;* these are succeeded by an Allegro-Theme (also 2-Part form, but "irregular," because the repetition of its Second Part is "dissolved"—i. e. conducted, as Re-transition, away from its own key into that of the next Theme); then follows another recurrence of the first Theme, with still other varieties of modified repetition; a Codetta of 8 measures concludes the movement.

See also: BEETHOVEN, Pfte. Son. op. 26, second movement, "Trio" (Part I an 8-measure Phrase; Part II a Period).—Pfte. Son. op. 79, *Andante*, first 8 measures (Part I a Period, Part II a repeated Phrase); same Sonata, *Finale*, first 16 measures (Part II a repeated Phrase).

BEETHOVEN, 10 Variations in B♭ (SALIERI), Theme (Part I a repeated Period, with peculiar transformation of the Dominant Semicadence into a complete Cadence effect, by one measure of extension in the 2d ending; Part II only a Phrase, but extended); *see also each Variation* (—of Variation 10, only the first 45 measures).—BEETHOVEN, Pfte. Son. op. 31, No. 1, *Rondo*, first 32 measures (Part II a repeated Phrase; the entire Song-form repeated and variated).

SCHUMANN, Jugend-Album, op. 68, No. 23 (Reiterstück); each Part repeated literally, and then the entire Song-form repeated, with modifications; a long Coda follows.

SCHUBERT Songs, "Winterreise", No. 5 ("Der Lindenbaum"), measures 9–24 (Part I is a repeated Phrase).

CAREY, "God save the King"—(Part I a 6-measure Phrase).

77. Reverting to par. 65, which review, attention must here again be drawn to the perplexing, but altogether natural and essential, points of external resemblance between different denominations of formal design. The transitional stages from each one into the next higher, or larger, species are so imperceptibly graded, that positive definition becomes, at a certain stage, difficult and even impossible,—but also unnecessary.

Thus, it has already been seen (and in the student's subsequent personal analysis of compositions, many further proofs will be encountered), that both the Period-form and the 2-Part Song-form may consist of two Phrases; that, by inference, the extended Period, the Double period, the Phrase-Group (not to mention the unusual designs of the Period-Group and Quadruple period) might be *greater*, in temporal dimension, than some specimens of the structurally higher graded 2-Part Song-form; that the external resemblance between a Period in which each Phrase is repeated (Ex. 51), and a 2-Part Song-form in which each Part is a repeated Phrase (Ex. 74), is complete, save in respect of those few *essential* conditions upon which the distinction depends; that a contrasting Double period can often scarcely be distinguished from a 2-Part Song-form (see BEETHOVEN, 24 Variations in A, Theme); and so forth.

The essential distinction between the "One-Part" forms and the "Two- (or Three-) Part" forms is clearly stated in par. 73*b*, second clause, and hinges mainly upon the idea of *Separation* (which is as possible among kindred, as among foreign members). Hence it is, that the *repetition* of either Part serves to individualize it and separate it from its fellow; that a sufficiently pronounced difference in character, assumed perhaps abruptly, will have the same effect; and that, finally, simple emphasis of Cadence may suffice, even in case of very close similarity of melody and style, to sever the Parts unmistakably. See also par. 93.

EXERCISE 19.

A. Analyze the following (doubtful) examples, and endeavor to determine whether the form is Two-Part or One-Part, and, if the latter, exactly what species; pars. 93 and 104 may be referred to for additional clues:

BEETHOVEN, Pfte. Son. op. 10, No. 1, first 30 measures.—Pfte. Son. op. 10, No. 3, "Trio" of *Menuetto*.—Pfte. Son. op. 13, *Finale*, first 17 measures.—Pfte. Son. op. 31, No. 1, first 30 measures.—Pfte. Son. op. 79, first 24 measures.

MENDELSSOHN, Caprice, op. 16, No. 1, Andante section.

SCHUMANN, Songs, op. 24 ("Liederkreis"), No. 8.

GRIEG, Lyric Pieces, op. 12, No. 2, measures 1–18.

B. Write two examples of the Diminutive 2-Part Song-form (par. 76), one in major and one in minor; one in Adagio, the other in Allegretto tempo; one in duple, the other in triple time.

CHAPTER X.

THE FULLY DEVELOPED TWO-PART SONG-FORM.

78. Here, all likelihood of a misconception of the form (touched upon in par. 77) is precluded, because of the dimensions generally reached, and the consequent opportunity, and even necessity, of more distinctly individualizing and separating the two Parts.

The conception of Part I will not differ in any other respect from par. 72*a*, *b*, *c* (which review) than in that it will surely never be less than Period-design, and may be larger.

But the structure of Part II, while naturally adhering to the conditions defined in par. 73*a*, *b*, *c* (which review), will, in the fully developed form, usually be more elaborate (longer, and with more extensions) than in the smaller varieties explained in the preceding chapter.

The designation "Fully developed" may be construed as applying to all examples of the 2-Part Song-form in which *each Part is at least a Period*, and to some degree *extended*. Commonly, it is true, wider differentiation of the Parts, in favor of greater length and independence of the Second Part, will be observed.

79a. The EXTENSION of the Two-Part Song-form by repetition of either Part, or of each Part, or of the *entire* Song, has already been indicated in the text, and encountered in some of the quotations.

The "Variations" upon a 2-Part Theme, cited above, may be regarded as "modified repetitions" of the entire Song-form; in a broader sense, however, than the pupil should undertake to exemplify for the present.

(b) Besides this means of enlargement and development (to which may be added all the other ordinary varieties of extension *in the course* of a Phrase, or of a section of any kind), there are also those adjuncts of a more external nature, represented by

the Introductory Phrase,
the Prelude,
the Codetta or Coda, and
the Postlude.

(c) It is only necessary to remember that these auxiliary members become more and more desirable, and are apt to assume greater length, the larger the form to which they are attached. Thus, the Introductory member of a 2- or 3-Part Song-form, will probably, though by no means certainly, be longer, and perhaps more independent, than that of a One-Part form.

Review pars. 44, 45; and see MENDELSSOHN, "Songs without Words", No. 6, first 7 measures; No. 23, first 6 measures. In both of these cases the Introduction or Prelude takes a more active part in the plan of the whole, than in some of the other "Songs without Words" to which reference has been made; and it will be observed that they recur at the end, as Codetta or Postlude.

And, furthermore, the comparatively brief "Codetta" or Postlude added to a Period, or Double period (pars. 51, 52, 68*a*), becomes sometimes a complete "Coda" even in the *Two*-Part Song-form; while in any still larger form this enlargement is all the more probable.

The details of the distinction between Codetta and Coda are given at length in par. 98, to which reference may be made, although the formation and employment of the Codetta or Postlude must yet be restricted to the directions hitherto given.

Illustration of the fully developed 2-Part Song-form:

75.

*1) *Gavotte* from the 6th French Suite. (The present author is responsible for the phrasing and marks of expression.) Part I is a regular parallel Period, with perfect Cadence in the Dominant key, according to the rule. Part II is a Group of 3 Phrases, exhibiting the usual traits of established form: the outset upon the Dominant harmony; the inclination toward the Subdominant key in the center, and again near the end; and the general similarity between the respective endings of the two Parts (more common, by the way, in older than in modern music).

See also: BEETHOVEN, Bagatelle, op. 119, No. 8.—BEETHOVEN, 8 Variations in F major (SÜSSMAYR), Theme; 33 Variations in C major, op. 120 (DIABELLI), Theme, and also the Variations (each Part a Double period; very similar endings).

MOZART, Pfte. Son. No. 3 (Cotta ed.), *Andante*, first 20 measures (design exactly like that of Ex. 75; the 16 measures which follow are a 2-Part Song-form of Primary design).

HAYDN, Pfte. Son. No. 8 (Cotta ed.), last Movement, "Trio" (here Part I is the larger design of the two, being a Group of 3 Phrases, while Part II is Period-form; but the number of measures is equal).

SCHUBERT, Pfte. Son. No. 9, *Andantino*, first 32 measures (an extraordinary example; Part I a Double period; Part II *almost identical with Part I in its melody*, but harmonized chiefly in the relative key, and contracted,—by which means it sufficiently establishes its identity as a separate Part; a *complete repetition*, with 4 measures of Plagal extension, follows).

CHOPIN, Mazurka No. 45 (op. 67, No. 4), first 32 measures (each Part repeated, Part II literally; Second Part a Double period).

CHOPIN, Nocturne No. 10 (op. 32, No. 2), "*Più agitato*" ($\frac{12}{8}$ time; Cadence of Part I very vague, but sufficient, under the circumstances; the entire Song-form is *sequentially reproduced*, a half-step higher, and led without cadence into the following section).

More elaborate and extended illustrations will be found in MENDELSSOHN, *Scherzo a capriccio* in F♯ minor, first 36 measures (Part I a little longer than II); the ensuing 10 measures are a Codetta, repeated and extended; and the next 32 measures are again in the 2-Part Song-form.—MENDELSSOHN, "Songs without Words", No. 6, entire.—MENDELSSOHN, op. 72, No. 2, entire (4-measure Prelude and Postlude).—MENDELSSOHN, Étude in *a* minor, op. 104, No. 3, entire (Part I an extended Double period—possibly Single period; Part II Double period, or, more probably, a Group of 4 Phrases, No. 4 reproduced, Cadence somewhat vague; Coda 13½ measures, to end).

CHOPIN, Mazurka No. 25 (op. 33, No. 4), entire section up to signature of 5 sharps (Part I, extended Double period, repeated; Part II, Period with repeated Antecedent and extended Consequent; entire Song-form repeated literally).

BRAHMS, op. 117, No. 3, first tempo (each Part a slightly expanded Period; entire Song-form repeated, with modifications).

SCHUBERT, Impromptu, op. 90, No. 3, first 48 measures (Part II repeated); also the following 53 measures (Part I has a 4-measure Codetta, repeated).

BACH, Well-tempered Clavichord, Vol. I, Preludio No. 8 (E♭ minor),—Part I, a group of 4 regular Phrases, resembling Double period; Part II, a Group of 3 Phrases, to which 2 others are added, after a striking evasion of the expected perfect Cadence (in measure 29); Codetta, 3½ measures.

THE LARGE TWO-PART FORM, AS TYPE OF THE SONATINA-FORM.

80. From the fully-developed 2-Part Song-form, of the extent exhibited in the illustrations last cited, it is only one further step into that LARGE 2-PART FORM out of which the Sonatina-form emerges, and to which the latter probably owes its origin. The demonstration of this Higher form must be reserved for a later volume, as the student is not yet sufficiently equipped for its successful manipulation. He is to make no other use of the Large 2-Part Song-form at present than to analyze the following examples. It will be observed that each Part is allied to the Phrase-group form, usually with a Codetta; and that the parallel structure of the endings (cited in par. 75,—Ex. 73) generally extends over the entire second half of each part,—often more.

See HAYDN, Pfte. Son. No. 3 (Cotta ed.), *Larghetto;* Pfte. Son. No. 2 (Cotta ed.), *Adagio;* Pfte. Son. No. 11 (Cotta ed.), *Adagio* (a Coda of 15 or 16 measures is added).—DOMENICO SCARLATTI (BÜLOW'S revision, Peters ed.), Suite I, "Sarabande" (Part I, extended Double period; Part II, group of Phrases); same Suite, "Burlesca", "Menuetto", "Gigue" (with brief Coda), and "Toccata".—HUMMEL, Pfte. Son. No. 1 (op. 2), *Adagio* (brief Coda).—J. S. BACH, Well-tempered Clavichord, Vol. II, Preludio No. 15 (G major).—BRAHMS, Intermezzo, op. 76, No. 3; this example is very diminutive, it is true, but can scarcely be assigned to any other class of forms than that of the "embryo Sonatina"; (Part I, 10 measures, Codetta and Retransition 5 measures, Part II similar); it approaches the "Large Double period" with Codetta to each Period.

EXERCISE 20.

A. Write two examples of the fully-developed 2-Part Song-form; one of them in major and the other one in minor; one in *Andante*, the other in *Allegro* tempo; one in duple, and the other in triple time; the second one considerably larger than the first one. Add a Codetta to each. Observe the directions given in par. 78.

For this work, one of the Periods invented in Exercise 9 might be utilized.

B. Write a third example, with free choice of all conditions; but with either an Introductory Phrase or a Prelude, and either a Codetta or a Postlude.—Again, some former Period-form may be used.

CHAPTER XI.

THE THREE-PART SONG-FORM.

81a. The ruling principle of all 3-Part (or, as they are often called, *tripartite*) Forms is, *the Return to the Beginning*, or to the first (or principal) thematic section.

In order to be an unmistakable and perfectly genuine RETURN, it can only succeed an equally genuine and positive DEPARTURE; and this Departure is embodied in the correspondingly distinct Second Part, which intervenes between Part I (the definite STATEMENT) and Part III (the RECURRENCE of the Statement).

(b) This specific return to the beginning, or, more properly, this *recurrence of the first thematic member* as a distinctive trait of the 3-Part forms, must not be confounded with those examples of apparently similar recurrence that have been seen in repetitions, and in the Period and Double period of parallel construction. For instance, in Ex. 25 the initial melodic member is observed to recur in the 5th measure; but this initial member is connected with all that follows during 4 measures, exactly as in the preceding 4 measures, so that the contents of measures 5, etc., are an *immediate* repetition without any intervening digression or definite Departure. And even in Ex. 31, where there *is* an intermediate passage between the first Phrase and its recurrence as repetition, it is merely an "Interlude," with none of the elements of a "Departure." See the last clause of par. 20.

In Ex. 46 the recurrence, in measures 5, etc., of the first members (contained in measures 1 to 4) is again an *immediate* reproduction, not separated by an intermediate Departure. The same is the case in Ex. 67, though there is much more reason for misconception here than in the smaller examples, because something really appears to intervene between the first melodic member and its recurrence in measures 8, etc.; but this intervening section, while it is an *entire Phrase* (Phrase 2 of the parallel Double period), is uninterruptedly connected with the first Phrase, and does not constitute that degree of "genuine and positive Departure" upon which the "Return" depends, as distinctive condition of the 3-Part forms. Here, again, it is simply a question whether the form is only "One-Part," or more; and the decision, as shown in par. 77, depends upon the degree of *separation*, which either is, or is not, sufficient to define a genuine Departure. Comparison of the above example (67) with Ex. 76, where the interruption is complete, will make this plain.

(c) The influence which this leading principle exerts upon the conception of the *Second* Part, is obvious. In the 2-Part forms, Part II was found to be a coördinate companion to Part I, carrying on the development of the melodic purpose with preponderant parallelism of design, as "continuation" of the musical sentence; and keeping the perfect cadence of the original key in view, as final aim.

But in the 3-Part forms, on the contrary, Part II is not so much a continuation as it is a "digression"; it is not coördinate with Part I, and the idea of opposition will be more likely to predominate than that of parallelism; it is not a *final*, but an *inter-*

mediate section of the form, and does not tend to a point of rest, but strives (from the moment when its identity as "Departure" has been assured) to regain, or lead back into, the original melodic current, i. e., to prepare for the recurrence of Part I. See pars. 87 and 88.

THE THREE-PART PERIOD.

82. The embryo of the 3-Part Song-form is a diminutive design, which embodies all the essential conditions of the fully developed form, and for which the term THREE-PART PERIOD seems most appropriate.*

It bears the same proportion to the full 3-Part Song-form, that Ex. 74 does to the full 2-Part Song-form, inasmuch as each of its three sections is only a Phrase. The feasibility of this diminutive design is indirectly demonstrated in par. 76, which review.

The designation "Period" instead of "Song-form", though somewhat inconsistent, is justified by the resemblance of this form to the different varieties of Periods extended to the sum of three Phrases (i. e., Period with Consequent repeated, or Consequent-group; Period with Antecedent repeated, or Antecedent-group), in each of which a *reduction of the three Phrases to two* is possible. The impossibility of such a reduction in the "Phrase-group" is the very reason why the latter could not be spoken of as a "Period" (Ex. 63, note *4)).

83a. In the genuine 3-Part Period (as type of the corresponding Song-form) the First Phrase ends with a *perfect cadence*, either in the original key, or in some next-related key; and it is generally repeated.

The Second Phrase ends, as a rule, upon the *Dominant* harmony, because that is the most favorable point from which to regain the Tonic harmony with which the first Phrase (presumably) began. Phrase II is not repeated alone, as a rule.

The Third Phrase is a more or less exact reproduction or recurrence of Phrase I. At least the *first member* should thematically corroborate that of the first Phrase. Phrase III is not repeated alone, *but Phrases II and III are frequently repeated together.*

For example:

---

*The designation "Diminutive 3-Part Song-form" might seem more appropriate than "3-Part Period", from analogy with par. 76. But the latter is, for valid reasons, nevertheless the preferable term. See Ex. 76, Note *1).

*1) The weight of this perfect cadence is sufficient to detach the Phrase positively from those which follow, and to make it as completely a Part as is the case with the first Phrase in Ex. 74. This betrays the sole comparative inconsistency of the term 3-Part *Period*, to which reference has been made.

*2) The cadence of Phrase II is made at this point, upon the Dominant harmony, and is so bridged over as to lead without the slightest check (almost like an Introduction) into the initial motive of Phrase I,— now Phrase III.

*3) The first ending of Phrase III (which is a *literal* recurrence of Phrase I) is as conclusive as at first;

*4) but in the second ending the perfect cadence is evaded, and spun out, in Chain-phrase formation, into what, for convenience, may be called a Codetta.

See also: SCHUMANN, "Album-Blätter", op. 124, No. 2 and No. 9 (containing all the repetitions).

SCHUMANN, "Jugend-Album" op. 68, No. 1 (all the repetitions); No. 10, F major (Phrase II only 2 measures; all repetitions); No. 17, A major (Phrase III modified and extended; Codetta, 9 measures).

BEETHOVEN, Bagatelle, op. 33, No. 4, first 16 measures (all legitimate repetitions); Bagatelle, op. 33, No. 6, first 20 measures (Phrase III is repeated alone, like Phrase I, before the repetition of Phrases II and III together begins).

BEETHOVEN, Pfte. Son. op. 2, No. 2, the "Trio" of the 3rd movement (8-measure Phrases).

HAYDN, Pfte. Son. No. 12 (Cotta ed.), *Presto*, measures 25—44 (Phrase I repeated; Phrase III modified, and extended to 8 measures).

CHOPIN, Nocturne No. 16 (op. 55, No. 2) first 12 measures (a superb illustration; Phrase II closes with decided cadence upon the Dominant of the relative key, and the remainder of the measure,—the 8th,—is retransitional "bridging" of the cadence-measure; the first measure of Phrase III is a somewhat disguised recurrence of the beginning, but unmistakably the same member; and the rest of the Phrase is a correspondingly ingenious ornamentation of Phrase I).

CHOPIN, Mazurka No. 4 (op. 6, No. 4), each Phrase repeated—*even the Second one;* CHOPIN, Mazurka No. 9 (op. 7, No. 5), each Phrase repeated; Phrase II a simple transposition of Phrase I into the Dominant key; Phrase III a literal "da capo," and, as expressly stated, running on "without end."

(b) Other, more irregular, varieties of the 3-Part Period afford perhaps greater justification of the denomination "Period," but resemble the genuine 3-Part forms all the less. In all of these cases, it is true, the Third Phrase is substantially the same as the First one, but the condition of the cadences does not conform to the rules given in par. 83*a*. For illustration:

*1) The First Phrase closes, irregularly, with an imperfect cadence (the chord-third in Soprano); but it is of ample weight to define the termination of its Phrase, and it will be observed that the same imperfect cadence recurs at the very end,—a peculiarity of certain Folk-melodies.

*2) This cadence is exactly the same as that of Phrase I; therefore it furnishes no sufficient proof of the qualities which identify the "Second Phrase" of a tripartite form, and even seriously disturbs the coherent connection with, and *impulse into*, the Third Phrase (par. 83*a*). But, notwithstanding this default in its preparation, Phrase III is clearly recognizable as a Recurrence of Phrase I, chiefly because of its distinct rhythmic character.

See also: SCHUMANN, "Jugend-Album" op. 68, No. 19, *a* minor (Phrase I closes with a Dominant *semicadence;* Phrase II is only 2 measures long; the beginning of Phr. III is disguised; all the legitimate repetitions occur); No. 38—"Winterzeit, I."—(Phrase I ends with a *semicadence;* Phr. III considerably altered in its second half; all repetitions).—SCHUMANN, "Album-Blätter" op. 124, No. 13 (instead of repetition, Phrase I is reproduced as *sequence;* Phr. II closes with the same imperfect Tonic cadence seen in Example 77; Phr. III is an extended Recurrence of Phrase I). In this case the designation *Phrase-Group* would be admissible, and doubtless even more accurate.

CHOPIN, Nocturne No. 7 (op. 27, No. 1), first 26 (28) measures. Each Phrase is repeated, even the Second one, alone. The repetition of Phr. I closes with an expansion of the penultimate cad.-chord, and is interlocked with the beginning of Phr. II by an Elision; Phr. II, and its repetition, end with a full cad. *upon the Tonic of the original key!* This almost totally severs its connection with Phrase III, which consequently, though an almost exact reproduction of Phr. I, assumes rather the character of a Coda. To this example, also, the conditions of the *Group of Phrases*, given in par. 58, appear to apply more exactly than do those of the 3-Part Period.

BRAHMS, op. 118, No. 4, first 16 measures (closes with semicadence; Phr. 2 extended).

These more irregular examples all point to the fact that the similarity between Phrase III and Phrase I, while corroborating the ruling principle of the 3-Part designs, is not enough, *in itself*, to establish the legitimate "3-Part form." For instance, this very likeness appears plainly in the parallel "Double period," as emphasized in par. 81*b*. It is only when associated with *other characteristic conditions*, that this structural trait becomes a perfectly valid factor of the tripartite design. And it must be remembered, that it is only because the absence of these other conditions is more easily accounted for and excused in *smaller* designs, where quick comparison is possible, that such irregular and almost indefinable forms as those last cited can exist. In the fully developed 3-Part forms there is far less likelihood of such confusing irregularities, and therefore the "Return to the beginning" may be accepted as an unfailing proof of the identity of the forms under present consideration.

EXERCISE 21.

A. Write two examples of the *regular* 3-Part Period, one in major and one in minor; choosing a different time, tempo and character for each; and adhering strictly to the directions given in par. 83*a*.

For this exercise, choice may be made among the Phrases invented in Exercises 1 and 2.

B. Write a third example, with *modified repetitions* as prescribed in the legitimate designs; and with a partial change in the formation of Phrase III (as compared with Phrase I); also add a Codetta.

The Incipient Grade of the 3-Part Song-Form.

84a. In this design the First Part is at least a full *Period*, while Parts II and III each still adhere to the diminutive form of the Phrase. The term "Song-form" must be adopted, because, as soon as *any one of the three sections* assumes the Period-form, it becomes a full "Part," and it is no longer consistent to speak of the *whole* as a 3-Part "Period."

(b) In its details, the Incipient 3-Part Song-form corresponds to the schedule given in par. 83*a*, only excepting the enlargement of Part I, cited above; namely:

Part I is a Period, of any variety, (possibly, though rarely, anything larger,) and with a complete Tonic cadence in the original key, or in the Dominant key (if major), or Relative key (if minor), or perhaps in some other related key.

Part II is only a Phrase (possibly extended), with a very definite Dominant cadence that strongly suggests, and leads into, the first thematic member of the First Part.

Part III also is only a Phrase; therefore it is not a *complete Recurrence of Part I*, and discrimination must be exercised, that, in thus abbreviating the contents of the First Part, the ruling condition of tripartite form be not sacrificed: *Under all circumstances Part III must, at its beginning, distinctly confirm* THE BEGINNING OF PART I. If Part I be a Period of parallel construction, Part III may appear to be a recurrence of the *second* Phrase of Part I, inasmuch as the beginning of that Phrase will then correspond to the beginning of the whole. But if Part I be a period of contrasting construction, then Part III must corroborate the *first* Phrase (partly or entirely), and may not resemble the second Phrase at all. It is not necessary to specify just how much of Part III may or must be derived from the First Part; but, as a rule, at least one full measure, or one complete melodic member, should agree with the initial measure or member of Part I. The remainder of Part III will be dictated by the course of the "highway to the perfect cadence" (defined in paragraphs 6 and 7). For example:

Grazioso.
Part I. (Period).
78.
p
sf
Part II. (Phrase).
sf
sf
Part III.
(Phrase).
pp

*1) Pianof. Sonata op. 2, No. 2, *Finale.* Part I is a parallel Period, with a very striking initial member, the recurrence of which is therefore quickly recognizable. It closes with a perf. cad. in the Dominant key. The Second Part is in reality only a 2-measure Phrase, made four by repetition. Part III appears, at first glance, to be a recurrence of the *second* Phrase of Part I, but on closer examination it proves to be much more nearly identical with the first Phrase,—excepting, of course, that it terminates with the regular perfect cadence. But even if it did resemble the 2nd Phrase more than the 1st, the "Return to the initial member" would be unmistakably defined; and the two Phrases of Part I, constituting a *parallel* Period, represent in total substance but little more than one Phrase, anyway.

See BEETHOVEN, the same Sonata (op. 2, No. 2), *Largo*, the first 19 measures. Here the derivation of Part III from the *first* Phrase of Part I is indisputable, for the construction of the latter is chiefly contrasting. Part II ends with the usual Dominant cadence, and the cadence-measure is so bridged over as to lead very smoothly into the initial member. Part III is extended to 7 measures, but remains a "Phrase" in form.

In BEETHOVEN, Pfte. Son. op. 7, *Finale*, first 16 measures, the resemblance of Part III to the *second* Phrase of Part I is stronger. But there is no doubt that the impression conveyed is that of a "Return to the initial member." *With this idea established, there is no danger of confounding the Incipient 3-Part form with that variety of the 2-Part form in which the Parts have only a similar ending. See Ex. 73, and the N. B. immediately preceding it.*

See further: BEETHOVEN, Pfte. Son. op. 14, No. 2, *Andante*, first 16 measures (Part III corroborates the *first* Phrase of Part I, excepting the Cadence; a Codetta of 4 measures follows).—BEETHOVEN, Pfte. Son. op. 49, No. 1, *Finale*, first 16 measures (Part III is an almost exact copy of the *second* Phrase of Part I, but the construction of the latter is parallel).—BEETHOVEN, Pfte. Son. op. 2, No. 1, *Adagio*, first 16 measures (a misleading example, open to difference of opinion; Part III is the corroboration of the initial member, in a disguised—though by no means unrecognizable—form).—A still more questionable example is BEETHOVEN, Pfte. Son. op. 22, *minore* of the Menuetto; this is very probably 2-Part Song-form.—Further, BEETHOVEN, Bagatelle, op. 33, No. 3, first 16 measures (a very clear illustration); Bagatelle, op. 119, No. 4.

SCHUBERT, Impromptu, op. 142, No. 3, Theme.

MOZART, Pfte. Son. 15 (Cotta ed.), Theme of last Movement; see also the several variations.—MOZART, Pfte. Son. 9 (Cotta), Theme of first Movement; here Part III almost exactly resembles the *second* Phrase of Part I—with an extension of 2 measures,—and represents, therefore, what might be regarded as the more questionable class of Incipient 3-Part Song-forms. What Mozart's own conception of the "Idea" was, is however manifested in the succeeding variations, in all but one of which the resemblance of Part III to the *first* Phrase is very close, to the exclusion of all but an allusion to the style of the second Phrase, in the added Extension.—MOZART, Fantasie and Sonata in C minor (Cotta ed. No. 18), *Andantino*, entire; all the legitimate repetitions are made, but written out and variated.

HAYDN, Pfte. Son. No. 4 (Cotta ed.), *Finale*, measures 21–40 (Parts II and III each extended to 6 measures); Pfte. Son. No. 8 (Cotta), *Scherzando*, first 16 measures.

GRIEG, Lyric Pieces op. 12, No. 3, first 16 measures (followed by repetition of Parts II and III).—GRIEG, Ballade op. 24, Theme.

CHOPIN, Nocturne No. 1 (op. 9, No. 1) measures 19–50; this example, (which contains all the repetitions), is again, on account of far more striking likeness of Part III to the *second* Phrase of Part I, one of the doubtful class; the evidence of a "Return to the beginning" is, however, sufficiently striking to define the tripartite design. The same is true of Nocturne 10 (op. 32, No. 2), first 18 measures (2-measure Prelude). In par. 100 may be found another possible classification of these two, and all similar, examples.*

---

*The classification of Ex. 78 (and the illustrations in the additional references) among the 3-Part forms, differs from the analysis hitherto adopted by other writers, who rank them among the *Two*-Part forms. Though this is not the only question upon which the present author holds a different opinion from that of other theorists, it is the only one to which a few words of defence are devoted. It appears obvious, from the great diversity of dimensions that the pupil has already observed to exist within one and the same structural design, and from the confusing similarity of size often attending entirely different forms, that *dimension and proportion* alone cannot be reliable criteria, and that, therefore, the classification of the various designs must depend rather upon the *idea* embodied in them. For this reason a distinction appears to be necessary between the SECTIONS of a form (which are the more mechanical divisions), and the PARTS (which are the ideal divisions). In every 3-Part Song-form a division into *two sections* will be observed, the first of which agrees with the first Part, while the 2nd section embraces both Parts II and III, which are so inter-dependent in the "idea" of the tripartite form, that their separation would violate its chief condition. The mere accident that, in the above Example (78), this 2nd section,—Parts II and III,—is precisely the same size as the first section, is not sufficient proof of the 2-Part form; for "Section" and "Part" are not the same unless they are identical in the *idea* they embody. If it be contended that the single Phrase is not enough to represent a Second Part, proof to the contrary may be found in BEETHOVEN, Pfte. Son. op. 49, No. 2, *Finale*, first 20 measures; HAYDN, Pfte. Son. No 12 (Cotta ed.), *Finale*, first 24 measures; each of these is a full 3-Part Song-form, in which Part II is

(c) How easily the Incipient 3-Part Song-form may be evolved out of the 3-Part Period, is seen in such examples as BEETHOVEN, Bagatelle op. 33, Nos. 4 and 6 (both cited after Ex. 76 as illustrations of the 3-Part Period), in which the *modified repetition* of the Phrase that constitutes Part I, is so seductively suggestive of the parallel *Period;* especially in No. 6, where Part III reproduces this repetition; and still more so in Bagatelle op. 33, No. 1, in which, besides this same misleading trait of Parts I and III, the Second Part, while only a Phrase, is extended by repetition and other means to the length of no less than 16 measures. Thus these examples, while actually only 3-Part Periods, assume the external appearance and dimensions of the broader Song-form.

EXERCISE 22.

Write two examples of the Incipient 3-Part Song-form; one in major and the other in minor; observing the directions given in par. 84*b*.

In the first one, construct Part I as parallel Period; in the other, as contrasting Period.

CHAPTER XII.

THE ORDINARY COMPLETE 3-PART SONG-FORM.

85. In this species, Part I is at least Period-form; Part II generally also at least a Period; and Part III is a nearly or quite literal Recurrence of Part I. The details of the design are as follows:

---

only a Phrase, but nevertheless a perfectly distinct "Departure." The idea of all bipartite forms is solely that of thesis and antithesis; the simple opposition of Question and Reply, or Statement and Counter-statement, be it upon parallel or upon contrasting lines. This has been found thus far in the Period, Double period, and in the 2-Part Song-forms exhibited in Exs. 71, 72, 73, 74 and 75. In Ex. 78, though it corresponds in *external* appearance to Ex. 71, 72 and 73, there is something more than this; there is the *three*-fold idea of Statement, Departure and Recurrence; on a smaller scale, it is true, than in the examples which are to follow, but just as genuine and unmistakable as in any full-fledged 3-Part Song-form, or Rondo, or even Sonata-*allegro*, for that matter. The presence of this *idea* has led the present author to classify these examples among the 3-Part forms, with no more than the just reservation indicated by the term "Incipient Grade"; and his experience, during many years' teaching, of the readiness of the pupil to grasp and apply this distinction in the work of analysis, testifies to its convenience and to more absolute reliability than can be secured in many other, far more perplexing, phases of Form-evolution.

THE FIRST PART.

86a. The First Part of the tripartite form will not differ in any essential respect from the First Part of a bipartite design. Therefore the details given in par. 72*a*, *b*, and *c* apply here, and must be carefully reviewed.

(b) The *length* of Part I should be taken into consideration, and determined if possible beforehand, in proportion to the probable, or intended, extent of the entire Song-form. As already stated, Part I should be, as a rule, a *brief*, *simple*, *clear Statement*. A long First Part involves either the necessity of extreme length of the whole Song-form, or the defect of top-heaviness. A glance at MENDELSSOHN, "Song without Words" No. 9, and then No. 10, makes this sufficiently plain.

THE SECOND PART; THEMATIC CONDITIONS.

87. On the contrary, the Second Part of a tripartite design differs essentially from Part II of a bipartite form. See par. 81*c*. The distinction tends to lower the rank, melodic importance and structural independence of the Second Part, but by no means to the exclusion of striking individual qualities.

Close FORMATIVE RELATION to its First Part (in regard to style and general character) should be strictly maintained. Review par. 73*b*. But considerable freedom may be exercised in its *melodic* delineation, which may be suggested entirely, or in part, by the melodic design of Part I, or may be entirely independent of the latter, especially when similarity of style and character is preserved.

Illustrations of various phases of thematic relation follow:—

(a) First, almost total agreement between Parts II and I:

*1) "Song without Words" No. 13; see Original. The 1st Phrase of Part II is an exact transposition of Phr. 1 of the First Part; the 2nd Phrase (Part II) is borrowed similarly from Phr. 5 of Part I; Phrase 3 (Part II) is also derived from the latter, but contains, besides, a new and rhythmically characteristic member.—The Second Part is simply a Sequence, or transposed reproduction, of Part I, in SCHUMANN, Jugend-Album, op. 68, Nos. 3 and 8; and mainly the same in BEETHOVEN, Pfte. Son. op. 26, *Marcia funebre*.—In SCHUBERT, Impromptu op. 142, No. 2, "Trio," the Second Part corresponds almost exactly to Part I, for a few measures, but *transposed to the minor mode*.—CHOPIN, Mazurka No. 51, meas. 1–32.—In MENDELSSOHN, "Song without Words" No. 42, the melody of Part I is reproduced in Part II, Phrase for Phrase, in variously transposed and somewhat modified form, and is extended by the reproduction of the last Phrase.*—See also No. 12, in which, again, every figure of Part II can be traced back to the First Part.—Also Nos. 39, 36, 20, and 10, where the thematic derivation of Part II from Part I can easily be traced. See also Ex. 72, note *2).

(b) Secondly, Part II derived from secondary members of the First Part:

80. 

---

*In using these references, and those which follow in this paragraph, the pupil must examine no more at present than Parts I and II, and only those points of the latter which reveal its thematic relation to the First Part.

*1) MENDELSSOHN, "Song without Words" No. 14. See the Original. The thematic derivation of the Second Part from the First is indicated by the brackets. It will be observed that the *second* member of Part I becomes the *first* (and therefore typical) member of Part II; as in Ex. 71, note *4), which review.

*2) "Song without Words" No. 29,—same as note *1). Here the derivation is cleverly disguised, but not sufficiently to arouse doubt of the composer's intention (or perhaps partly unconscious conception), in the mind of the closely observant student. This is one of the "secrets" of the true spirit of classical Form.

See also: "Song without Words" No. 21 (Part I is repeated; Part II starts out, in meas. 61, with measure 11 of the *repetition* of Part I); No. 28 (Part II based largely upon the last figure in the first Phrase of Part I); No. 25 (Part II utilizes at first melodic fragments of the first and 3rd measures of Part I,—to the exclusion of the *first* figure, in the preliminary half-measure; after a while this figure gradually reasserts itself, and finally the entire first Phrase of Part I is taken up twice in Part II, *of course in a different key*). See also MENDELSSOHN, op. 72, No. 1 (Part II starts out with measure 5 of the First Part); op. 72, No. 3 (the second half of measure 1 becomes the *first* half, in Part. II); op. 72, No. 5,—like note *1) above.

Sometimes Part II begins where (so to speak) Part I leaves off:

*1) This agrees with the last member of Part I (as found in the lower parts), but with nothing else that the Part contained.

*2) This figure corresponds to measure 6 of the First Part, in opposite direction ("contrary motion"; see Ex. 82).—See also Ex. 89; also

Haydn, Symphony No. 6 (Peters ed.), *Menuetto* (Part II is built entirely upon the last mel. member of the First Part); Symphony No. 9 (Peters ed.), *Menuetto* (Part II derived from last figure, in the Codetta to Part I).

SCHUBERT, Pfte. Son. 4 (op. 122), *Menuetto;* Son. 6 (op. 147), *Scherzo.*
SCHUMANN, *Papillons*, op. 2, No. 1.

(c) Thirdly, Part II constructed more or less in the direction opposite to that of the First Part,—similar to par. 39*b*; especially at the start:

See also Ex. 87.—MENDELSSOHN, "Song without Words" No. 9 (the first figure is in "contrary motion"; the remainder chiefly parallel); No. 8 (the same); No. 30.

BRAHMS, op. 76, No. 4.—SCHUMANN, Jugend-Album op. 68, No. 12, first 24 measures.

This thematic relation (or opposition) of Part II to Part I is one of the characteristic features of the old "Gigue-form," whether constructed in 2-Part or in 3-Part Song-form. See BACH, English Suites: No. 3, Gigue; No. 5, Gigue; No. 6, Gigue; "Well-tempered Clavichord" Vol. II, Prelude No. 5.

(d) Fourthly, Part II melodically different from the First Part, though similar or related in general style; the same vein of melodic conception simply runs on over into the Second Part, which, in this variety of the form, becomes thus more nearly coördinate with (less dependent upon) Part I:

83.

*1) In the Original (Nocturne 15, op. 55, No. 1) the repetition of Part I is written out and very slightly modified.

*2) The organic continuity of the Parts is upheld by similarity of general style, and uniformity of accompaniment.

*3) This is the only place in Part II where real thematic agreement with the First Part can be detected, though the resemblance between this and the very first member is probably only accidental.

See also: MENDELSSOHN, "Songs without Words," Nos. 37; 1; 40; 16; 4. SCHUBERT, Pfte. Son. No. 1 (op. 42), "Trio" of 3rd Movement.

(e) Finally, Part II may diverge still more widely from Part I, and be not only thematically "new," but even *somewhat* independent in character and style. But see par. 73*b*. For illustration:

84.

*1) Certain slight thematic coincidences exist between this Second Part and its First Part, but the impression conveyed is that of a more pronounced change of character than is exhibited in the examples preceding; though the difference between this stage and that of Ex. 83 may appear scarcely definable.

See Mendelssohn, "Songs without Words," Nos. 2; 4; 35; 41.

Greater independence of Part II is found in Mendelssohn, "Song without Words" No. 7;

And still more in Schumann, "Album-Blätter" op. 124, No. 8 (in which, on the other hand, the outward connection between the Parts, i. e., at the cadence, is closer than usual).

Grieg, Lyric Pieces, op. 12, No. 5 (Parts II and III repeated).

Chopin, Mazurkas 11; 24.

Examples of the 3-Part Song-form in which the diversity of character in Part II is carried to an extreme, are rare; and in no case, however rich they may be in imaginative contents, or superior in attractiveness, can they be regarded as *models* of logical structure, or as thoroughly genuine exponents of the tripartite *Idea*, as demonstrated in the foregoing paragraphs. See, for instance, Beethoven, Bagatelle op. 33, No. 2, up to the "Trio"; and Schumann, "Album-Blätter," op. 124, No. 3. For the more reasonable classification of such irregular forms, glance at par. 112*a*.

The introduction of new material into Part II is most easily accounted for and justified when the latter is "sectional" in form; see Ex. 86, and its notes.

Tonality of Part II.

88. As regards the modulatory design of the Second Part, it should, in general, *avoid the Tonic line of the original key;* for the impression of a Departure will depend as much upon a change of key as upon anything else; and the idea of a Return is realized when the original key is regained, after a more or less marked absence.

But the *Dominant* (or Subdominant) harmony of the original key may be introduced into Part II; and in some cases the Dominant furnishes the basis of the entire Part from beginning to end; see BEETHOVEN, Pfte. Son. op. 31, No. 3, "Trio" of the third Movement; Symphony No. 1, "Trio" of the third Movement.

Or the Tonic harmonies may be *touched* in passing into other chords or keys.

Or the entire Second Part may disport itself in other related (or even unrelated) keys. See Ex. 89; also

MENDELSSOHN, "Songs without Words" No. 1 (Part I, E major; Part II begins in E minor, passes into G major, and remains there nearly to the end); No. 7 (Part I, E♭ major; Part II, E♭ minor, G♭ major, E♭ minor); No. 25 (Part I, G major; Part II, E minor, F major, G major transiently, A minor, C major, A minor); Nos. 29; 31; 40; 42.

BEETHOVEN, Symphony No. 2, "Trio" of 3rd Movement (Part II all on the Dominant of the *Relative* key, up to the last chord).

For more specific directions in reference to Modulation, see par. 94.

As a rule, the Second Part should at least *begin* with some other than the original Tonic harmony, in order to distinguish itself immediately from the beginning of Part I. This need not interfere with the plan of derivation and relation illustrated in Ex. 81. When, as is the case in some rare examples, the Second Part starts out *exactly* as the First Part began, the member should diverge very soon into other chords or keys. For example:

*1) Part II is exactly identical with Part I, up to this f♮, which turns the melodic current from G into C. The keys through which the Second Part passes are indicated.

See also Schumann, op. 15, No. 7 ("Träumerei"); and Mendelssohn, "Songs without Words," No. 36; No. 20.

Structural design of Part II.

89a. In regard to the form and length of the Second Part, it is both unnecessary and impracticable to recommend any other law than that of sensible proportion, and balance; and this, as it will depend upon a variety of circumstances and conditions, must be left to the judgment or intention of the composer. The principle of approximate symmetry is apt to prevail, and therefore, as already stated, if Part I is a Period, Part II is somewhat likely to be a Period also, perhaps slightly extended.

Sometimes, however, the Second Part is so brief (only Phrase-form) and comparatively insignificant, that it assumes the character of a mere interlude,—a hasty (though genuine) Departure, introduced for no other purpose than to create the impression of a Return.

See MENDELSSOHN, Fantasie op. 28, 2nd Movement, first 18 measures (Part I, 7 measures; Part II, only 3 measures); op. 16, No. 1, *Allegro* movement (Part I, 34 measures and repeated; Part II, only 10 measures).

CHOPIN, Mazurka 47 (op. 68, No. 2) first 28 measures.

BEETHOVEN, Violin-Concerto, op. 61, *Finale* (Rondo), first 18 measures (Part II, only 2 measures).

Other examples of the small Second Part are cited in the footnote upon page 138. (BEETHOVEN, Pfte. Son. op. 49, No. 2, *Finale*, first 20 measures; etc.).

It is, perhaps, more common to make the Second Part a little longer than Part I. And, unquestionably, the peculiar nature of the *Chain-phrase* and the *Group of Phrases*, especially in *sequential succession*, adapts them in every sense more fully to the purpose and conditions of a Second Part than any other more regular and perfect structural design. Hence, the formation of Part II in Ex. 85 may be regarded as exemplary. See par. 31, first clauses, and the very last clause of par. 58.

See MENDELSSOHN, "Songs without Words" No. 35 (Part I, Period; Part II, Period extended); No. 28 (Part I, Period; Part II, Period, sequential construction); No. 19 (Part I, small Double period; Part II, group of 6 Phrases); No. 31 (Part II, a Group of Phrases); No. 10; No. 15; No. 40 (sequential construction).

SECTIONAL FORM OF PART II.

(b) In some, especially the larger, varieties of the 3-Part Song-form, the Second Part is SECTIONAL in form; i. e., it consists of two (or even more) "Sections," separated from each other by a complete cadence in the momentary key, and often so distinctly individualized that they would have to be regarded as complete "Parts" under ordinary circumstances; but their *location*, between Part I and its Recurrence, renders it possible, notwithstanding their independence, to preserve the impression that they are only the *subdivisions* of one broad Part,—just as the three-fold condition of Departure, Absence and Return may all be comprehended within the single idea of Digression. For illustration:

Part II. Section 1.
cresc.
f
p
cresc.
f
Extension
|| Section 2.
ff
p
tr
Extension

*1) Pfte. Son. op. 2, No. 2, *Scherzo*.—The subdivision of the Second Part into two independent sections is strongly marked; but they nevertheless constitute, together, only the *one Part* which represents the Digression, the interim between Parts I and III, whose identity is unquestionable. Still, if carried to an undue extreme, this subdividing process (like that mentioned in the very last clause of par. 87) destroys the legitimacy of the tripartite design, and gives rise to a "Group of Parts," such as appears in CHOPIN, Mazurka No. 14, the classification of which will be found in pars. 114, 115.

See also Ex. 89; also MENDELSSOHN, op. 72, No. 1.

SCHUBERT, Pfte. Son. No. 10 (B♭ major), *Scherzo*.

HAYDN, Symphony No. 11 (Peters ed.), *Menuetto*.

The most plausible variety of this sectional form is obtained by adding a Codetta to the body of the Second Part. This, while comparatively unusual, and somewhat out of place, can nevertheless be done without injuring the form, if the Codetta-section be chiefly a confirmation, or independent extension, of the Cadence-member of Part II, so manipulated as not to interfere with the purpose of the latter to prepare for the Recurrence of the First Part (as Third Part).

See MENDELSSOHN, "Song without Words" No. 30 (Part I, Double period, 15 measures; Part II, Section 1, Group of 4— or 5—Phrases, 20 measures; Section 2, Codetta of 4 measures; a 3rd Section follows, as Retransition, to which explanatory reference will be made in the next paragraph).

See also MOZART, Pfte. Son. 17 (Cotta ed.) *Finale*, first Subject (Part I, Period, 12 measures; Part II, Section I, Group of 3— or 4—Phrases, 18 measures; Section 2, Codetta of 2 measures, repeated; a 3rd section,—Retransition,—follows, as in the preceding quotation).

SCHUBERT, *Moment musical*, op. 94, No. 6 (Part I, large Per., 16 measures; Part II, Per. ext. at end, 17 measures; Codetta of 3 meas., repeated; a Retransition of 14 meas. follows).

BEETHOVEN, Pfte. Son. op. 13, *Adagio*, meas. 23–27.

THE CADENCE OF THE SECOND PART.

90a. As regards the CADENCE of Part II, it is evident that it must be made in such a manner as to foreshadow, prepare for, and lead with a certain degree of emphasis into, the first member of Part I as it recurs at the beginning of Part III. Hence, as shown in par. 83*a*, 2nd clause, it is most likely to be made upon the *Dominant Harmony* of the original key (or the Tonic Harmony of the *Dominant key*), because no other chord than this tends so urgently toward the tonic Harmony, with which Part I (and therefore Part III also) is supposed to begin. Sometimes the Dominant idea (as Dom. chord, or Dom. key, or Dominant Organ-point) runs through the entire Second Part, as in Ex. 78.

BEETHOVEN, Pfte. Son. op. 31, No. 3, "Trio" of the 3rd Movement; Pfte. Son. op. 2, No. 2, *Largo*, first Subject; MENDELSSOHN, "Song without Words" No. 2.

Or the Second Part is conducted into the Dominant a certain distance (one or more measures, or Phrases,) before its end, as in Ex. 83.

Often quite a persistent *extension* of the Dominant Harmony is made, in some form or other, to stimulate expectation of Part III, as in Ex. 84 and Ex. 85.

CHOPIN, Mazurka 18. MENDELSSOHN, "Songs without Words," Nos. 9, 19. BEETHOVEN, Bagatelle op. 33, No. 1.

Sometimes this expansion of the Dominant harmony is elaborated by transient alternation with other (most effectively with Subdominant) chords; the Dominant is reached in due time, but instead of passing immediately over into the Tonic, it sways a few times, generally at least twice, back and forth, like a pendulum before coming to rest.

See MENDELSSOHN, "Songs without Words" No. 1, measures 9–14 from the beginning of Part II; No. 10, meas. 26–38 from beg. of Part II; No. 27 (the expansion and elaboration of the Dom. differs so completely in character as to appear to be an Interlude or Retransition).

The hearer's anticipation of Part III is furthermore confirmed and emphasized, as a very general rule, by a relaxation of motion (*ritard.*) in ending Part II. This is seen in Ex. 83; also in Ex. 86, where the effect is further heightened by a rest of nearly two measures' duration,—the appropriateness of which, after so wide a digression in character and in key, the student will realize.

MENDELSSOHN, "Songs without Words," Nos. 28; 32; 8.

On the other hand, the Dominant ending is sometimes so brief, and the cadence so completely bridged over, that, but for its being in the proper measure, and followed by a particularly well-defined announcement of the original initial member, it could not fulfil its important purpose.

See Ex. 76; MENDELSSOHN, "Songs without Words," Nos. 23; 32; 38; 20 (very brief diminished 7th); SCHUMANN, op. 15, No. 1; CHOPIN, Mazurkas, Nos. 4; 11.

(b) But, while the Dominant termination of Part II is unquestionably the simplest, the most common, and (ordinarily) the most appropriate, other harmonic forms are quite frequently employed; chiefly because of their superior effectiveness, but also in consequence of a possible irregularity in the *beginning* of Part I (and Part III) which may call for special treatment of the cadence of the Second Part.

In Mendelssohn, "Song without Words" No. 25, Part I begins upon the Dominant, and consequently, the Second Part ends upon one of the Second-Dominant* Harmonies (the altered II^7); No. 46, though in G minor, begins upon the Dom. of F; Part II closes with a very prolonged exposition of this same chord, and leads into Part III very smoothly, though noticeably enough; No. 24 is similar, though more abrupt.

The most common substitute for the usual Dominant ending is the chord (or key) upon the Mediant,—the 3rd scale-step of the original key. This will appear less peculiar when the student recalls that the chord III is a *member of the Dominant harmonic family*, and that, in any event, it *contains the leading-tone of its key*, through which the safe transition back into the Tonic beginning is sufficiently assured.**

See Mendelssohn, "Song without Words" No. 22 (F major; the Second Part ends upon the Tonic of A minor, which corresponds to the III of F; the *e*, in Bass, is effectively treated, as Leading-tone); No. 11; No. 42.

Chopin, Mazurka No. 16 (A♭ major; the Second Part closes with an emphatic extension of the chord upon the 3rd scale-step, but in the *major* form, as actual Dom. chord of F minor; this merely adds to the effectiveness of the device, without impairing its legitimacy); Mazurka No. 29 (the same); Mazurka No. 22 (G♯ minor; Part II ends upon the Tonic chord of its 3d step, i. e., B,—but, naturally, as *major* Triad; this cancels the Leading-tone of the coming Part, it is true, but the transition is still far less abrupt than in many other cases).

More abrupt forms of transition from the end of Part II into Part III are found in Mendelssohn, "Song without Words" No. 45 (hinging upon the Leading-tone); No. 39 (Parts I and III beginning upon the Subdominant Harmony).

Another effective mode of closing Part II, in convenient preparation for the initial member of the Third Part, consists in employing some form of the *Subdominant* (or Second-Dominant) Harmony, i. e., the IV, II, II^7 or IV^7, either in their legitimate form, or (preferably) in any of their altered or mixed forms (with lowered 6th scale-step, raised 4th scale-step, etc.). These chords almost necessarily involve resolution into some *inverted* form of the Tonic Harmony, wherefore Part III will, in this case, usually be found to begin upon the *Tonic six-four chord*. For example:

---

* See the Author's "Material used in Mus. Comp." paragraph 6*c*.

** *Idem*, paragraphs 90–93.

*1) The Second Part closes upon the chord of the II^7 (with the raised 2nd and 4th, and then the lowered 6th, scale-steps); and Part III begins upon the accented $\frac{6}{4}$ chord of the Tonic. This latter differs slightly from the harmonic form of the beginning, but not enough to obscure the effect of Recurrence.

See also Mendelssohn, "Song without Words" No. 7 (Part II ends with an altered Subdom. chord; Part III begins with the Tonic $\frac{6}{4}$ chord); No. 12; No. 29; No. 43 (all similar).

Any such tampering with the beginning of Part I (as Part III) involves, of course, the danger of impairing or destroying the principal landmark of the tripartite form, i. e., the *distinctly recognizable Return to the beginning, in exactly its original condition.* Therefore, if any modification at this point be ventured, it must be very cautiously effected, with a view to preserving at least all the essential and characteristic elements of the initial member of Part I. To what such modification of the latter may lead, will be seen in par. 110.

See also MENDELSSOHN, "Songs without Words," Nos. 41; 40; 37; 21; in each case the initial *melodic* member is retained in Part III, but differently harmonized. No. 36 (the first measure of Part III is so disguised that full consciousness of the form is not aroused until the 2nd measure appears). CHOPIN, Mazurka 46, Principal Song; Nocturne No. 16, first 12 measures (already referred to as 3-Part Period).

The most irregular and confusing of all modes of terminating the Second Part, is to lead it into the *Tonic* Harmony; this, just before the announcement of Part III upon the same chord (Tonic), seriously endangers the identity of the Third Part as "Return" (comp. par. 88, first clause).

See Ex. 91; and MENDELSSOHN, "Songs without Words," No. 4; No. 31; BEETHOVEN, Rondo in C, op. 51, No. 1, first Theme; (Rondo in G, op. 51, No. 2, first Theme, is scarcely better).

THE RE-TRANSITION.

(c) It must be borne in mind that a full-fledged Second Part comprehends three successive phases, which, while their lines of demarcation may be almost imperceptible, are still distinct enough in their several purposes to give rise to three different courses of conceptive action. These are: (1) a Departure from the line of the principal Part; (2) an optional period of Absence, during which considerable individuality may be developed,—as, for instance, in the sectional form; and (3) the Return to the original starting-point. This third phase may justly be regarded as the most significant of all, for it is the ultimate aim of the entire Part, and an endless amount of ingenuity may be displayed in the effective formulation of the means employed in realizing this "return to the starting-point." The larger the form, the greater the likelihood and necessity of devoting a separate section wholly to this purpose. For such a "returning section" the term RE-TRANSITION appears most fitting.

In case the Re-transition thus forms a separate section, by itself, the *body* of Part II will usually have a complete Tonic cadence in whatever key it chances to have reached. The Re-transition then leads back, from that point, into the key, chord, style and melody of the beginning, in such a manner, and at such length, as seems most adequate and effective. It appears useless to undertake to give any more definite rules than this for the process; for it is governed by ever-varying circumstances. There is no better source of information than standard musical literature, and the student is therefore urged to make careful examination and analysis of the given examples, references, and whatever other illustrations he can find. In all essential respects the Re-transition partakes of the nature and purpose of the "Introduction," though infinitely richer in possibilities. For example:

89.

*1) The division of this Second Part into Sections is very recognizable. Section 1 is the "Departure," with just sufficient lingering recollection of Part I to emphasize the idea; Section 2 is a more decisive digression from Part I, and stands for the "Absence."

*2) Here the body of Part II terminates, with the perf. cadence in the key into which the 2nd section has strayed (G♭ major). The Re-transition which follows, consists: firstly, in an abrupt chromatic dash back into the original Dominant, accentuated by the isolated *forte;* and, secondly, in a 4-measure expansion of this Dominant, during which the Soprano and Bass converge smoothly but persistently toward the tones with which Part I began.

See also SCHUBERT, Pfte. Son. No. 4, *Menuetto.*

MENDELSSOHN, "Song without Words" No. 13, E♭ major; the body of Part II terminates in the 32nd measure, on the Tonic of G minor; the following 8 measures are Re-transition, *based entirely upon the first melodic figure* of Part I, which suggests, and is skilfully led into, the Third Part; the original Dominant is reached in the 5th measure of the Re-transition, and then sways, as seen in former references,—text following Ex. 87;—*it will be observed that when, in thus swaying, the original Tonic is touched, the composer is careful to use the minor form of Tonic Harmony*, in order to preserve, and even increase, the force of the original *major* form, when the latter heralds the beginning of the Third Part; this same significant trait will be found in many other major examples,—"Songs without Words," Nos. 1, 7, 19, 20, 31, 37.

See also "Songs without Words," No. 16; Part II virtually ends in the 19th measure, with a Dominant semicadence; a Re-transition of 2 measures follows, built upon the first melodic member.—No. 26; effective Re-trans. of 4 measures before Part III.—No. 34, measures 25–29.—No. 37, Re-transition of 4 measures.—No. 3; Part II is 16 measures long, ending with a firm cadence in the key of the original 3rd step; a Re-transition of 5 measures follows.

Such a separate Re-transition is very likely indeed to accompany (i. e., follow) a Codetta to the Second Part, when that somewhat rare factor is employed (see last clause of par. 89). The Re-transition, in this case, starts with the apparent intent of *repeating the Codetta*, but sooner or later "dissolves" the original form of the latter, and digresses into such a course as defines its re-transitional purpose.

See MENDELSSOHN, "Song without Words" No. 30, A major; Part II terminates with a Tonic perf. cad. in E major in the 35th measure; the 4-measure Section which follows is an independent and regular Phrase, with its own unmistakable cadence; it does not belong to the *body of the Second Part*, for that terminates with the utmost decision before this Phrase begins; nor is it in the *Third Part*, for obvious reasons; nor is it a *Re-transition* into the latter, because of its complete cadence; thus it proves to be an adjunct of Part II, in the capacity of a "Codetta." The measures which follow indicate for a time the intention of repetition, but then abandon this purpose and become a genuine, and exceedingly attractive and clever Re-transition.

The same treatment is found in "Song without Words" No. 17, measures 14–17 (Part I closes in the 4th measure with a vague form of cadence, explained in par. 93*a*).

See also CHOPIN, Nocturne No. 17, measures 21–28.

In the ordinary 3-Part Song-form, however, the Re-transition is somewhat more likely not to constitute such a distinct section, but to grow out of some later member of the Second Part, perhaps so imperceptibly that it is not easy to point out the exact beat where the purpose of re-transition is evident. Here, the persistent bent of the harmony toward the *original Dominant*, and the equally characteristic tendency of the melodic current to lead into and regain the *first tone and figure* of the First Part, is possibly more noticeable than in the separate Re-transition; *and*, *in any case*, *this two-fold tendency* (first toward the *key* and then toward the *melody*) *must be regarded as inherent in all re-transitional passages.* This is plainly shown in Ex. 89. In the following illustration, the bent of the Re-transition is concentrated upon the initial *melodic* member of Part III:

*1) "Song without Words" No. 33.

*2) The re-transitional purpose appears to assert itself here, but in such close keeping with the melodic line of the foregoing measure, that its actual bearing upon the coming Third Part is only gradually apprehended. It is left to the pupil to trace, in this particularly beautiful example, the slow but sure approach of the melodic delineation to that of the first figure of Part III, and to observe how the harmonic color of these re-transitional measures tinges the first tones of the Recurrence of the initial figure, until the C♮ puts a stop to the playful illusion, and restores the serious mood of the Third Part. "Song without Words" No. 41 is similar.

See also MENDELSSOHN, "Songs without Words," No. 11 (the re-transitional purpose is manifested in the 20th measure; the melodic figure of three tones corresponds to the beginning of Part III); No. 14, last 3 measures of the Second Part; No. 21, last 8 measures of the Second Part (built upon the first melodic member,—2 measures,—of Part III); No. 39, last 4 measures of the Second Part; No. 45, C major, last 4 (or perhaps 8) measures of Part II; No. 37; No. 36, last 3 measures of Part II (this re-transitional expansion of the Dominant flows over into, and slightly influences, the first figure of the Third Part). No. 47 (A major) is peculiar; Part II virtually ends at the beginning of the 37th measure; the measures which follow are partly a sequence of the two which precede, and partly an anticipation of the beginning of Part III.

The Third Part.

91. In the ordinary complete 3-Part Song-form, here under consideration, the Third Part is a SIMPLE RECURRENCE OR REPRODUCTION OF PART I.

If the First Part closes with a perfect cadence in the original key, then it may reappear *literally* in Part Third, as conventional "da capo."

But if the First Part cadences in some other key, or has any other imperfect form of cadence, then at least enough of the ending of Part III must differ from the original Statement to admit of its cadencing properly, in the principal key.

And, furthermore, any *purely unessential* modifications of Part I (affecting the harmonization, or the register, or ornamenting the Melody) may be introduced in the Third Part, to heighten its effect. But no more important changes than these are exhibited in the "Simple Complete Form." For example:

*1) Part II closes on the original Tonic; but the beginning of Part III is distinct enough. See par. 93*a*.

*2) Part III is essentially the same as Part I; the register of the melody is changed, and one measure is omitted.—In Chopin, Mazurka No. 49, Part III is not written out at all, but simply indicated by the words "da capo."

In Ex. 76 and Ex. 77, though a smaller species of the tripartite design, the *literal* agreement of Part (Phrase) III with Part (Phrase) I, is illustrated. In Mendelssohn op. 72, No. 1, and "Song without Words" No. 45 (C major) the Recurrence is literal.—Ex. 89 is concluded (in the Original) by reproducing the first 4 measures of the melody an octave higher than at first, while all the rest is left precisely as it was.—Ex. 84 is concluded in the Original (SCHUMANN, op. 68, No. 24) by reproducing Part I with very slight changes.—In the conclusion of Ex. 83 (CHOPIN, Nocturne 15, Principal Theme) a brief variation of Part I is made.

In BEETHOVEN, Pfte. Son. op. 2, No. 2, *Scherzo* (Ex. 86) the reproduction is literal. In Pfte. Son. op. 22, *Menuetto*, slight changes are made. In the F major Variations, op. 34, Theme, the Recurrence is literal.

In MENDELSSOHN, "Song without Words" No. 22, Part III is a little differently harmonized from its First Part; in No. 32, the single melody of Part I is transformed into a *duet* in Part III.

In HAYDN, Pfte. Son. No. 6 (Cotta ed.), 1st Movement, Principal Theme, there is, in addition to interesting variation in Part III, a change in the last member, necessitated by the circumstance of Part I having closed with a cadence in the Dominant key; the same in SCHUBERT, Pfte. Son. No. 1, 2nd Movement, Theme (Part I repeated); the same in BEETHOVEN, Pfte. Son. op. 2, No. 1, "Trio" of 3rd Movement.

CHOPIN, Étude in A♭ (No. 3 in the "Moscheles-Fétis" method), Part III slightly expanded at end. CHOPIN, Mazurkas 16; 22 (long Second Part); 24 (Part II quite distinct, and repeated); 40; 43 (Part II repeated, distinct re-transitional interlude; Part III, literal Recurrence of Part I); 44.

GRIEG, Lyric Pieces op. 12, No. 2; op. 38, No. 2; op. 43, Nos. 1, 4, 6 (extended at end).

BRAHMS, op. 116, No. 7, "Trio" (6-8 Time).—Op. 117, No. 1, first *tempo* (Parts I and II small Periods; Part III is extended to *Double* period, by reproduction; Codetta); compare with 3rd (last) *tempo*.—Op. 118, No. 2, meas. 1–25 after first double-bar.—Op. 118, No. 3, first 37 measures.—Op. 118, No. 6.—Op. 119, No. 1.—*Intermezzo*, op. 76, No. 4.

EXTRANEOUS MEMBERS.

92. The 3-Part Song-form may be, and, as a rule, should be, enlarged by the addition of a CODETTA OR CODA. More explicit explanation of the character, purpose and formation of these factors is given in par. 98, to which brief reference may be made.

The prefixing of an INTRODUCTION, while less significant than a Coda, is, however, barely less desirable; for it serves to emphasize, by mild contrast, the *body* of the Song-form, to which it stands in the same relation as the "margin" to a picture.

Turn, again, to MENDELSSOHN, "Song without Words" No. 12, and examine into the relation of the Introduction to the entire composition; also Nos. 15; 26; 29; and 32.

When a PRELUDE is substituted for the Introduction, or a POSTLUDE for the Codetta, its architectural and logical connection with the body of the form is less close, and its relation to the latter is more like that of the independent "frame" to the picture.

Examine, again, MENDELSSOHN, "Song without Words" No. 4 (both Prelude and Postlude; almost identical; here the simile of the picture with its frame is very fitting); also No. 9 (a Codetta of 4 measures is added to Part III, or, more accurately, to the body of the form, before the Postlude appears); Nos. 16; 28; 35; and 41 (in each, similar Prelude and Postlude). In No. 21 the Prelude does not recur at the end, and, in other respects also, it approaches the character of an Introduction.—In No. 3 the Prelude becomes the thematic basis of the entire elaborate Coda.

The insertion of INTERLUDES between the Parts is a more hazardous proceeding, as they tend to disrupt the structural continuity. But if carefully handled, with a view to avoiding this error, they may be very effective. They must either conform strictly to the limitations imposed upon the Introduction (in par. 28, second and third clauses); or they must prove their extraneous nature by agreement with a Prelude.

In MENDELSSOHN, "Song without Words" No. 23, the substance of the Prelude reappears after 9 measures, as Interlude between Parts I and II; then again 23 measures later, as Interlude between the second Division of the form (i. e., Parts II and III) and its repetition; and again as Postlude, at the end.—In No. 27 a similar recurrence of the substance of the Prelude appears between Parts II and III (quasi as Codetta or Re-transition), and again at the end.—In No. 29 there is one measure of Interlude between Part I and its repetition; in No. 46 the same (in each case borrowed from the Introduction). In No. 34 the brief introductory figure is utilized as Re-transition, both in the second Division (Parts II and III) and its reproduction; and again, as final section of the Coda.

EXERCISE 23.

A. Take one of the major Periods with perf. cad. in the original key, invented in Exercise 9; to this, as Part I, add a Second Part according to the directions given in par. 87*a*, in Period-form, with cadence as prescribed in par. 90*a*; and add a Third Part as *literal* Recurrence of Part I (the words "da capo" will suffice).

B. Some former minor Period with regular perf. cadence, as Part I; to this add a Second Part according to the directions in par. 87*b*, in Period-form; cadence as in par. 90*a*; Part III a literal *da capo.*

C. Some other former major Period as Part I; to this add a Second Part according to par. 87*c*, in Period-form with *extended* Dominant cadence. Part III a literal *da capo.*

D. Some other former (or new) minor Period as Part I; to this add a Second Part according to par. 87*d*, in Phrase-group design, with some form of cadence explained in par. 90*b*; Part III a *nearly* literal *da capo.* Review par. 88.

EXERCISE 24.

A. Some former (or new) Period in major, with cadence in some other than the orig. key, as Part I; to this add a Second Part according to par. 87*e*, in Phrase-group design, with optional cadence-form; Part III a literal *da capo*, excepting change of last member. Review par. 91.

B. Part I as minor Period (regular or extended), with cad. in some related key; Part II optional melodic construction, but sectional form, as explained in par. 89*b*; brief Re-transition, par. 90*c*; Part III a slightly modified Recurrence of Part I. Review par. 88; AND THE DIRECTIONS GIVEN IN EXERCISE 9.

C. Part I major, optional form, but with Introduction; Part II optional form and structure, but with Retransition; Part III a slightly modified Recurrence, followed by *brief* Codetta. Review par. 92.

D. Part I minor, Double period, Introduction or Prelude; Part III a slightly modified Recurrence with brief Codetta or Postlude.

EXERCISE 25.

A. Part I major, optional form, but with brief Codetta; Part II optional; Part III a modified Recurrence, including former Codetta, and with an *additional* brief Codetta. Review par. 23; 27; par. 30; 53; par. 40.

B. Minor, entirely optional in all save the essential requirements of the Simple Complete 3-Part Song-form.

CHAPTER XIII.

ADDITIONAL DETAILS OF THE SONG-FORMS.

1. IRREGULAR CADENCES.

93. There are a few peculiar conditions of the CADENCE, not yet explained, to which attention must now be drawn.

(a) The purpose of a Cadence is, to indicate a point of more or less complete separation between two contiguous members of the structure,—a "joint," where one member ends and another begins (par. 2*b*). There are two modes of fulfilling this purpose, namely:

(1) to mark *the end of the first* of these two members distinctly;

(2) to mark *the beginning of the new member* with equal distinctness.

The first mode is the simpler and more common, and consists in using a strong Cadence-chord, and making a pause in the audible rhythmic pulse, adequate to the degree of separation required. This is illustrated in nearly all of the foregoing examples; see Ex. 46, No. 3, and the *end* of any example from 25 to 37.

The second mode, while naturally less distinct and decisive at the moment, is nevertheless, when properly executed, ultimately quite as effectual, and, at the same time, smoother than the other. It consists in defining the beginning, at least, of the *following* member (Phrase, Period, Part, or whatever it may be) so distinctly that no doubt of its being a new member can exist; this defines the form, for where there is a beginning there must before have been an ending. This is precisely the principle which prevails in the mode of "phrasing" explained in par. 10, 3rdly (Ex. 15); while sometimes desirable even between "Parts," it is naturally most important in application to the arrangement of *smaller* members, because *frequent* complete stops (to define the "end" of every member) would entirely disrupt the design.

The more unmistakable the *outset* of the following member is, the less emphatic need the foregoing *Cadence* be. This accounts for all the vague, imperfect Cadences (often so brief and indefinite as to be scarcely discoverable at first *as Cadences*) hitherto seen, and those now to be examined.

For example, the *Semi-cadence at the end of Part First* in the Song-forms: See MENDELSSOHN, "Song without Words" No. 17, measure 4 (reg. Dom. Semicadence; but evidently the end of Part I, because what follows is sufficiently characteristic to be evidently the beginning of Part II); No. 38, measure 10 (Cadence of Part I on a $\frac{6}{4}$ chord! It is rendered sufficient by appearing in the 8th measure and being repeated in the 10th; moreover, the beginning of Part II is unmistakable); No. 47, measure 18, similar to No. 38; No. 39, Part I ends with chord-Fifth in Soprano. In Nos. 7, 8, 10, and 11, Part I ends with some imperfect form of Cadence (usually *extended*, however); but the identity of the Part is fixed by its repetition (see par. 77, last clause). In Nos. 30, 33, 41, and 48, the Cad. of Part I is unusually brief and "breathless," but still sufficient, under the thematic circumstances. These stand in marked contrast to the decision and frankness of the Cadence to Part I in Nos. 23, 12, 15, 27, 35 and others.

For other examples of an imperfect Cadence at the end of a complete member, see MENDELSSOHN, No. 15; at the beginning of measure 5 from the end, the Tonic Cadence-chord has the Third in Soprano; but the following member nevertheless constitutes a Codetta (without being preceded by a compl. perf. Cad. according to rule), because its outset is sufficiently distinct to indicate the beginning of a new member. The same trait is observable in No. 16, in the 4th meas. from the end; No. 31, five meas. from the end; and No. 33, six meas. from the end.

See also CHOPIN, Nocturne No. 9 (op. 32, No. 1), ending (the Codetta follows an Evasion of the Cadence); BEETHOVEN, Pfte. Son. op. 31, No. 3, *Menuetto* (Part I ending with Dom. Semicadence, but repeated); BEETHOVEN, Pfte. Son. op. 27, No. 1, *Adagio* (Part I ending with a Semicadence); HAYDN, Symphony No. 1 (Peters ed.), *Menuetto*, Part I; BRAHMS, Symphony No. 1, *Allegretto*, first 18 measures (probably a Two-Part Song-form, followed by a somewhat extended complete repetition; Part I ends in meas. 10 with a Semicadence); BEETHOVEN, Theme of 24 Variations in D major, Part I; SCHUBERT, Pfte. Son. No. 7, *Allegretto*, Part I; SCHUBERT, *Moment musical*, op. 94, No. 5, Part I; CHOPIN, Preludes op. 28, No. 11 and No. 22, Part I of each; MENDELSSOHN, Praeludium op. 104, No. 2, Part I.

To this category belong also all examples of the "Elision" (par. 60, which review), in which the "Cadence" disappears altogether by the overlapping of the contiguous members. See MENDELSSOHN, Prelude op. 35, No. 6 (Part II begins in the middle of measure 15, with an Elision of the expected Cadence); also the Praeludium of the "Praeludium and Fugue in E minor" (without opus-number), measures 22–23.

(b) Exactly the reverse of this peculiarity (that just explained being: a vague Cadence sufficing to separate independent members) is seen in those places where a *complete Tonic Cadence fails to sever the connection* between contiguous members, because the second one maintains so intimate a thematic relation that it necessarily still belongs to the section in question. Under such conditions it is possible for a regular perfect Cadence to occur *in the course of the First Part* (i. e. without terminating it). As contradictory of the strict rule given in par. 70 as this appears to be, it is not at all unusual,—*especially near the beginning*, where such an unlooked-for Cadence seems rather to serve the desirable purpose of establishing the tonality. For example:

92.

*1) This is a Tonic perf. Cad. of the most unequivocal kind; and yet it does not terminate the First Part, because the latter obviously runs on, in unbroken thematic connection, to the 8th measure. See also Ex. 62, 4th measure.

*2) In this unique example the Part *begins* with a genuine perf. Cadence! See the Original (Symphony in C, "Trio" of Minuet).

See also Mendelssohn, "Songs without Words" No. 39 (perf. Cad. in 2nd measure); No. 43 (Part I, extended Period, with perf. Cad. at end of Antecedent Phrase); No. 44 (Part I, the same; in the last two cases the unbroken thematic connection is established by parallel construction); No. 42 (Part I, contrasting Double period, with *Dominant* perf. Cad. in the center). A glance at the beginning of the other "Songs without Words," on the other hand, teaches how, as a rule, the composer aims to avoid this misleading use of an untimely perf. Cadence.

See further, Chopin, Mazurka No. 24, Part I; Schubert, *Moment musical* op. 94, No. 4, "Trio" (5-flat signature) first 12 meas. (group of 3 Phrases, repeated); Beethoven, Pfte. Son. op. 31, No. 1, *Adagio* (Part I a very broad Double period, *parallel*, with Tonic perf. Cad. in the center); Pfte. Son. op. 27, No. 2, 1st Movement, Part I (23 measures in length—including a 5-meas. Prelude,—and containing *two* perfect Cadences in its course).

This trait is very common in repetitions. See MENDELSSOHN, "Song without Words" No. 4 (the perf. Cad. in meas. 4 does not mark the end of the First Part, because the 4 following measures are a repetition); No. 11 (at the beginning of the 5th meas. from the end there is a strong perf. Cadence, but the following member is not a Codetta, because it belongs to the foregoing Phrase, as evident repetition of the 2nd half).

(c) It is clear that both of the above irregularities of Cadence are counteracted by the *thematic* conditions attending them. In each case it is the unmistakable import of the thematic arrangement (in reference to melody, rhythm, character, etc.) that overpowers the ordinary forcible agency of the Cadence, and renders it at one time unable to prevent, and again unable to effectuate, the "separation" of members, which is its chief purpose in form. This evident predominance of the Idea over the technical Detail is an additional corroboration of the justice of the classification defended in the footnote on p. 138.

2. MODULATION.

94. In addition to what was said in par. 88 about the modulatory design of the Second Part, the student must be reminded that changes of key are very important and necessary indeed, in *all* of the Parts (least, it is true, in Part I). This refers not only to complete, or lengthy, modulations, but particularly to *transient* digressions, which heighten the color of the Phrases, without cancelling the ruling effect of the principal, or dominating, tonality.

(a) These modulations (i. e., transient ones,) need not even be limited to the five Next-related keys,* but may extend to any of the Remotely-related ones,** at least occasionally, and, of course, on condition of returning immediately (or soon) to the original tonality, or to its close neighborhood. The Remotely-related keys are: (1) the Opposite mode of the same tonic (for instance, C major–C minor, and vice versa); (2) the Stride (C major–f minor, and vice versa); (3) The Mediant-keys C–E, C–A♭; C–E♭, C–A, etc.); and to these may be added, (4) all keys accessible through the coincidence of important pivotal tones.

A superb example of this quality of modulation will be found in SCHUBERT, Impromptu op. 90, No. 3 (G major) measures 26 to 10 from the end (first Phrase of Coda, and its repetition); the keys touched in close succession are G maj.–c minor–G maj.–c min.–a♭ minor–G.

---

* "The Material used in Mus. Composition," paragr. 266.

** The same, paragr. 267–269; par. 281, 282, 288; par. 289.

(b) In making more lengthy modulations, care must be taken *not to remain in any other key* (whether related to the original key or not) *long enough to create the impression of a central or primary tonality at that place.* The original tonality,—the principal key, in which the composition is written,—must be regarded as the AXIS, about which the entire structure revolves. Any *protracted* absence from this axis, or, more properly, any undue retention of some other key, would have the effect of shifting the axis, or of replacing it by a foreign one, and would thus tend to destroy the necessary centralization of the keys and chords.

On the other hand, a *temporary* shifting of the modulatory axis (subject to the above restriction) may constitute one of the best modes of individualizing certain Divisions of the architectural design,—for example, the Second or Middle Part in the tripartite forms. Hence, some other key (probably related to the principal one) may be chosen upon entering a new Part, or still larger Division, and be allowed to prevail as temporary axis of that section; and the extent of the new key, and its distance from the original key, will serve to determine the degree of independence and individuality of the section in question. See par. 88.

This is illustrated in SCHUMANN, Humoreske, op. 20, first Movement (3-Part Song-form with Coda; Part I, repeated Phrase in the key of "two flats"; Part II, a Group of three Phrases, throughout which the key of "six flats" prevails; Part III, literal Recurrence of Part I).

(c) Two very useful general rules of modulation in "Form" are:

(1) Avoid a series (especially a long series) of modulations in the same direction (i. e. successively increasing sharps, or flats; or successively decreasing the same, in more or less regular progression); *modulate* BEYOND *the desired key*, if possible quickly, by some extraneous transition, *and then turn back into the latter.* For instance: if aiming for four sharps, from C major, modulate into *five* sharps, and then turn back to four.*

(2) After any remote modulation, it is better to *turn back into some intermediate key*, than to remain upon the new key, or to pass on beyond it.

---

*It is well for the student to bear in mind that the fundamental modulatory movements are best defined by SIGNATURE, not by key-note.

Both of these must be accepted as general rules only, subject to many exceptions. As usual, the best source of information for the student on this point is classic or standard musical literature, to the analysis of which he should devote himself most assiduously.

(d) The *general modulatory design* of an entire composition, almost regardless of its size, is as follows:

At the beginning, a sufficient pause in the original key to establish the principal tonality; then a general tendency *upward* (toward the Dominant keys: those whose signatures contain one sharp more or one flat less than the original signature),—extending approximately one-quarter or one-third of the entire distance; then a more or less ample digression, or a modulatory oscillation between various keys in optional direction and measure; and finally, somewhere during the last sections, an inclination toward the *Subdominant* keys (those whose signatures contain one sharp less or one flat more than the original). See par. 73*c*, 2nd clause.

This plan is quite accurately followed in HAYDN, Symphony No. 3 (Peters ed.), *Finale*, first 20 measures.

See also MENDELSSOHN, "Song without Words" No. 48 (Part I, C major, passing into "one sharp"; Part III, "natural scale"; Coda, largely "one flat"); also Ex. 28 (4 measures) where it is exhibited on a very small scale; Ex. 47, No. 1; Ex. 71; 72; 75. There is scarcely an example to be found in classic music, in which this general modulatory line is not *more or less* completely and emphatically traced, not only in the whole, but in each independent Division.

For examples of peculiar modulatory design, see MENDELSSOHN, "Wedding-March" (in C; Part I *begins* with a distinct exposition of e minor); BEETHOVEN, Pfte. Son. op. 26, *Scherzo* (A♭; Part I begins with exposition of E♭); op. 27, No. 2, *Allegretto* (the same idea); Pfte. Son. op. 90, 2nd Movement (unusual prevalence of principal key throughout entire Principal Theme); Violin-Concerto, op. 61, 2nd Movement (the same idea); Symphony No. 3, 3rd Movement (strangely meagre representation of the principal key, up to the *ff* in the course of Part III). Ex. 91 contains no modulation whatever.

3. THE DYNAMIC DESIGN.

95. The dynamic design refers to the use and disposition of the various grades of tone-power, i. e., *pianissimo*, *piano*, *forte*, *fortissimo*, with all their attendant shades of force, and all the auxiliary tone-effects to which these distinctions may give rise (*crescendo*, *diminuendo*, *sforzando*, etc.).

(a) While it is quite certain that no definite rules for a dynamic design can be, *or should be*, given, it is equally certain that some such design nevertheless exists in every good composition, whether defined beforehand, or in the course of conceptive action; and it is necessary for the student to realize and correctly estimate the importance of these factors as a means of adding life to the musical image, and of emphasizing essential traits of the architectural design,—just as the effects of light and shade add vitality and distinctness of character to a picture, a landscape, or a theatrical scene. And, furthermore, there is an element of suggestion in the definite purpose of making a *crescendo* or *diminuendo*, a *pp* or *ff*, which acts as a stimulus upon the imagination, much more powerfully than might be suspected before putting it to the test.

The general effect of these dynamic distinctions is fully enough understood. Attention is simply called to the change in power as a means of increasing the interest in a *repetition* (as seen in Ex. 56); and as a means of accentuating the beginning of a new section by a sudden change from *p* to *f* or *ff*, or from *f* to *p*; see BEETHOVEN, Pfte. Son. op. 2, No. 3, first Movement, measure 13; also measures 25–27; Ex. 65, note *1); Ex. 95, note *1); Ex. 72; Ex. 73; Ex. 75; Ex. 88, beg. of Part III; Ex. 89, note *2).—Observe, also, the dynamic traits of Exs. 64, 74, 76, 83, 86, 91 and 99; and of all future quotations.

(b) Hand in hand with these factors, often almost inseparably, go those shades of expression which refer to the rate of motion, (i. e., *ritardando*, *accelerando*, *sostenuto*, *meno* or *più mosso*, etc.).

See Ex. 83; Ex. 86; the 𝄐 in Ex. 56; Ex. 76; MENDELSSOHN, "Song without Words" No. 39, last 11 measures. Compare par. 97*b*.

4. CONTRAST.

96. In paragr. 40, which review, the significance of Unity and Variety was demonstrated, in their bearing upon the smaller factors of creative structure.

As the dimensions increase, these same elements are more apt to be recognized as the attributes of SYMMETRY and CONTRAST; and while variety and unity are originally of equal importance, they gradually and steadily diverge, so that *in proportion to the magnitude of the design, the necessity for Symmetry decreases, and the need of the element of Contrast becomes more and more imperative.*

It is so obvious that Symmetry is of less importance in musical form than Contrast, that some composers deny its claims altogether, and labor to avoid all evidences of symmetrical structure in their works. But any such extreme conception must be condemned. It is more just to moderate this aim by merely avoiding the *obtrusive* evidences of Symmetry; and, at the same time, to restrain all exaggerations of Contrast by constant and serious regard for the vital condition of Unity.

This law is clearly recognizable in all the given details of the Part-forms, whence, for instance, the inference may be drawn that it is not nearly as necessary to preserve equality of size in successive *Parts*, as it is in successive *Measures;* and that contrast in style and character will be more pronounced between consecutive *Parts* than between consecutive *Phrases*. Hence it is that the student should now begin to devote a part of his attention to the elements of variety and contrast; and while he must scrupulously observe moderation, Unity, and a rational degree of formative and logical agreement, he must not forget that

THE BANE OF ALL ART-CREATION IS MONOTONY.

Glance at the evidences of Contrast in Ex. 48, No. 2; Ex. 53; Ex. 60 (BEETHOVEN, Pfte. Son. op. 2, No. 1, *Finale*, 1st Theme); Ex. 83; Ex. 86.—Observe, in MENDELSSOHN, "Song without Words" No. 1, how welcome the change in the 5th measure of Part II, in a composition where uniformity of style becomes almost oppressive. Note the brilliant effect of the Coda in No. 3, with its change in rhythmic style. Also the interludes in No. 23.—But observe, too, how wisely the unity of the *whole* is guarded, in each case.

5. STYLE.

97. The germs of those distinctions in Style which concern the harmonic (and, to a certain extent, the rhythmic) *details* of a musical sentence, are enumerated in par. 14 and 15, and have been unavoidably involved in all the foregoing Exercises. But STYLE, in the broader sense of the term, depends upon certain *general* characteristics, to which the attention of the student must now be directed; namely:

(a) Upon the choice of TIME; i. e., the use of the Duple or Triple rhythmic group (as respectively embodied in the $\frac{2}{4}$ or $\frac{4}{4}$ Time of the March, etc., and in the $\frac{3}{4}$ or $\frac{6}{8}$ Time of the Waltz, Barcarolle, etc.). The characteristic effect of each of these two fundamental classes is so generally appreciated, that it suffices here to observe that duple measure is the more vigorous, and triple measure the more graceful species. There are no other species, unless the peculiarity of $\frac{9}{8}$ (or $\frac{9}{4}$) Time, and of $\frac{5}{4}$ (or $\frac{7}{4}$) Time, be regarded as a radical metrical difference.

(b) Upon the choice of TEMPO; i. e. rate of speed, from *Adagio*, through *Largo*, *Larghetto*, *Andante*,* *Allegretto*, *Allegro* and *Presto*, up to *Prestissimo*.

The deep significance of this distinction will appear upon comparing MENDELSSOHN, "Song without Words" No. 22, with No. 10, and these again with No. 36; or the 4 Movements of Beethoven's Pfte. Son. op. 2, No. 2, one with another.

In indicating the *tempo*, it should be borne in mind that the given rate—for instance, *Allegro*—refers to the *beat in the adopted Time-signature:* in $\frac{6}{8}$ Time it must mean that the *8th-notes* pass at an *allegro*-rate of speed; in $\frac{6}{4}$ the same rate would apply to the *quarter-notes*. The uncertainty which prevails, because of a general misunderstanding or violation of this rule, can be dispelled by employing the metronome-marks,—e. g. ♪ or ♩ or 𝅗𝅥 = 60, etc.

(c) Upon the choice of PRINCIPAL MODE, i. e., major or minor, the characteristic distinctions of which are doubtless sufficiently palpable to every musical sense.

(d) Upon certain RHYTHMIC peculiarities, which, while available at any time and in any consistent connection, have become chiefly characteristic of certain conventional varieties of composition; for example, the respective typical rhythms of the Polonaise, the Bolero, the March, Minuet, Mazurka, etc.

It would, however, be a deplorable limitation of the student's resources, were he to confine his experiments in "rhythmic style" to those popular forms of which a certain (permanent) rhythmic figure is the ruling element. Unity, on the one hand, will dictate close adherence to the adopted rhythmic figure throughout the section, and even on to the end of the Song-form,—as in MENDELSSOHN, "Songs without Words" Nos. 1, 8, 14, 21, 23, 36, 43; but Contrast, with its equally just and persistent claims, must not be disregarded, in planning and executing the rhythmic design. Of the "Songs without Words" cited above, Nos. 8, 21, and 23 bear more or less frequent and striking traces of the writer's intention of occasionally abandoning the predominant rhythmic motive.

See BEETHOVEN, Symphony No. 7; observe how, in each one of the 4 Movements, the prevailing rhythmic figures fix the general character or style. Also SCHUBERT, Fantasie, op. 78, 3rd Movement (*Menuetto*); *Momens musicals*, op. 94, No. 2; No. 4, "Trio" (5-flat signature); No. 5; and ponder upon the resources of interest and variety suggested by the following manipulations (*in different Divisions*, however, be it understood) of a primary rhythmic figure:

---

* "*Andantino*" should be used with discrimination. For the definition of this frequently misinterpreted term, see BAKER, "Dictionary of Musical Terms."

The systematic demonstration of this fertile rhythmic process must be deferred until the pupil has undertaken the study of "Applied Counterpoint;" but he is already entitled to such uses of it as his stimulated imagination may achieve. (It is somewhat akin to the processes described in par. 29*c* and 32.)

There is one general rule, in reference to rhythmic style, which must be respected, namely:

The less striking (i. e., less irregular) a rhythmic figure is, the longer may it be adhered to without incurring monotony; and, inversely, *the more irregular a rhythmic figure is, the sooner should it be exchanged for a simpler figure.*

(e) The well-nigh infinite combinations of the above distinctions, including those given in par. 95 and 96, afford that complex of resources out of which the scarcely definable (for convenience called EMOTIONAL) elements of musical thought are evolved. These resources cannot, and should not, be theoretically classified; it is the duty of the individual student to investigate them for himself and develop his taste and *individual style* according to what he may discover.

But against one very popular, and unquestionably mischievous, fallacy he must be earnestly warned, namely: *the error of supposing that Music can definitely indicate any object, tell a story, express any idea clearly, portray any incident, or transmit emotional conditions with even approximate distinctness.* THIS IS NOT THE MISSION OF THE TONE-ART. And insisting upon its use in the service of other than intrinsically *musical* ideas, is a degradation of its ethereal and lofty calling.

At the same time, the student must quite as fully realize what Music *can* do: Music can *arouse* and can *reflect* emotional states, sometimes with greater power, and always with more searching keenness, than other arts. But it is not possible to foretell *which* emotional state will be aroused, save in an extremely general way; and the subtility of musical impressions is the very attribute which distinguishes the emotional magnetism of Music from all other emotional stimuli, and robs these impressions of all definiteness.

Further, Music can also roughly *delineate* and *imitate* (by its melodic "lines," its rhythmic "movements," etc.) certain primary motions of the material world; but with only just enough clearness to *suggest*,—and *only* suggest,—any one of a thousand similar material motions.*

This imposes the undeniably binding duty upon the composer, of so choosing these accidental elements of suggestion as to *avoid incongruity.* For example, in a "Slumber"-song constant or frequent *fortissimi* would be inappropriate,—except as an exposition of "Humor in Music." For an exquisite example of appropriate musical suggestiveness, see SCHUMANN, op. 15, No. 12 ("Child falling asleep"); especially the last 6 measures, in which the extraordinary widening-out of the chord-forms suggests the distorted fancies of half-slumber, while the tired little soul floats out into oblivion upon the unresolved $\frac{6}{4}$ chord of the Sub-dominant. He who can play or hear this passage without deep emotion, has not learned the power of the gentle Art of Tone!

The pupil need make no definite effort to apply these general truths. He should "bear them in mind" and ponder over them,

---

*See the *Revue philosophique* for Febr., 1893, pages 124–144 (translated in the "Music Review," July and August, 1894).

and leave the issue to the absorbing and assimilating processes peculiar to his own mental organism. In the meantime *he is to follow all the given* RULES *to the very letter.*

Coda and Codetta.

98. The difference between these two terms is solely one of extent,—"Coda" being the original designation for an independent ending, and "Codetta" signifying "a small Coda." The distinction may be formulated with greater accuracy by calling every SINGLE addition at the end (even when repeated and extended) a CODETTA, and defining the CODA as a SERIES OF CODETTAS.

The latter (a series of Codettas) is extremely unlikely to appear anywhere in the *course* of a composition; hence it is safe to say that the term Coda will be applied only to the ending of the whole, whereas *a Codetta may be added to any sufficiently definite member or Part*, even in the course of the design.

(a) The object and character of the Codetta are defined in par. 51, which carefully review, with all the illustrations; and see also par. 27 and par. 32.—The primary purpose, which corresponds to the "Extension of a Phrase-cadence," remains the same through all the grades of dimension in which it is achieved; and the dimension, or length, of the Codetta will increase in a more or less regular ratio to the size of the body of the design to which it is affixed.

These proportions may be approximately graded, as follows,—it being remembered that *a complete perf. cadence usually precedes the Coda or Codetta*, to mark the limit of the body of the design.

(1) The shortest cadence-extension is the reiteration (perhaps 2, 3, or 4 times) of the *single final Tonic chord.*

(2) The next larger extension consists in a repetition (perhaps 2 or 3 times) of the *two cadence-chords* (V–I).

(3) The next larger formation is somewhat apt to be a brief Codetta (i. e., not an extension of the given cadence, but an "appendix," independent of the latter), about *two measures in length;* generally repeated, and possibly extended as at (1) or (2).

(4) The next larger independent ending would be a Codetta of *four measures*, probably repeated and extended.

(5) The next larger formation might be such a 4-measure Codetta (repeated), followed by another of 2 measures (repeated and extended). This series of Codettas would be termed a *Coda*.

(6) A still broader Coda would consist of an 8-measure Codetta (possibly repeated), followed by one of 4 measures (probably repeated), and another of 2 measures (almost certainly repeated and extended). No larger form of Coda would be appropriate in the present grade of forms.

Nos. 2 and 1 of this schedule will suffice, as a rule, for the "Phrase"; Nos. 3, 2, and 1 for a large Phrase, or "Period"; Nos. 4, 2 and 1 for a large Period, Double period, or "Part"; Nos. 5, 2 and 1, or No. 6, for an entire 2-Part or 3-Part "Song-form." It will be observed that the proportionate length is obtained by adding a higher (larger) grade, and not by singling out any special grade; in other words, the smaller grades are all expected to follow, in order to preserve the tapering form. *But it must be distinctly understood that this entire schedule is only an approximate theoretical table, and not necessarily practically binding, save as it illustrates an important and generally valid principle.*

An exact illustration of this tapering form is found in Chopin, Mazurka 35 (op. 56, No. 3), last 32 measures (Coda of 5 sections: an 8-meas. section, with repetition; then a 4-meas. Phr. with repetition; then a 2-meas. Codetta, with repetition; then one measure, repeated, and a final reiteration of the last chord).

Chopin, Nocturne No. 8 (op. 27, No. 2), last 15½ measures (4-meas. Codetta, repeated; 2-meas. Codetta, repeated; Tonic extension).

Mendelssohn, "Song without Words" No. 30, last 19 measures (4-meas. Codetta, repeated; 2 measures, repeated; one measure, 4 times; final chord through 3 measures).

Beethoven, *Bagatelle* op. 33, No. 2, last 28 measures (similar); *Bagatelle* op. 33, No. 1, last 13½ measures (4 measures, repeated; 2 measures, repeated twice; one measure); *Bagatelle* op. 33, No. 6; see also op. 33, Nos. 3, 4 and 7.

Mendelssohn, "Songs without Words," No. 11 (last 8½ measures); No. 12 (last 12 measures); No. 14 (last 11 meas.); No. 19 (last 15½ meas.); No. 34 (last 17 meas.); No. 42 (last 15 meas.).

In the "Songs without Words," Nos. 1, 13, 25, etc., the entire "Song" has no more than a brief Codetta. In No. 24 the Coda is very long (44½ meas.). In No. 6 there is first a Codetta, and then a Postlude corresponding to the Prelude. In Nos. 7, 8, 10, etc., the formation of the Coda is irregular, i. e., not agreeing with the above schedule.

(b) It has already been stated that a Codetta, being somewhat independent of the body of the design, may also be independent in its *thematic* structure. This is a little more likely to be the case with larger Codettas, and Codas, whereas the smaller appendages are less likely to contain new motives. The following examples will sufficiently illustrate the derivation and thematic character of the Coda:

MENDELSSOHN, "Songs without Words" Nos. 3, 6, 7, 14, 21, 25, 26, 31, 37; here the Coda or Codetta is in each case derived from the first Phrase of Part I; often by "Melody-expansion" (par. 32). In No. 15 it is developed out of the end of Part III.

In Nos. 29, 32, 44, 46 it is a reflex of *Part Second*. This is more logical than it is usual, in composition; for the Coda will follow Part III most naturally in the same way that Part II followed its First Part; and Part II, if independent of Part I, may need just such corroboration (see par. 103). It will be observed that in this case the melodic member used will appear in two different tonalities; at first in the key or harmony of the Second Part, and in the Coda,—of course,—transposed to the *principal* key.

In Nos. 22 and 43, and in op. 72, No. 4 (MENDELSSOHN), the Coda is a contracted recapitulation of Parts II and III. In Nos. 11, 12, 19, 36, 48, it contains more or less new melodic material.

(c) The most appropriate place for a Codetta is at the end of the entire structure, where, according to the dimension of the body, it may, if necessary, expand into a Coda.

But the possibility of thus rounding off an earlier section of the form has been touched upon, and examples of a Codetta to the *Second Part* have already been seen (par. 89*b*, last clause).

Far more natural and customary than this, however, is the addition of a brief Codetta to the *First Part*, usually with repetition and extension. This presupposes that the design of the entire Song-form is somewhat broader than usual.

See MENDELSSOHN, "Song without Words" No. 39, last 2 measures of Part I.

HAYDN, Symphony No. 3 (Peters ed.), *Menuetto*, Part I; Symph. No. 4, *Menuetto*, Part I; Symph. No. 8, *Menuetto*, Part I; No. 9, *Menuetto*, Part I.

EXERCISE 26.

A. An example in major, (ordinary Complete 3-Part Song-form as in former chapter,) with such application of the irregular Cadence-conditions (par. 93) as may be appropriate; with greater modulatory freedom (par. 94); and with *some dynamic design*,—the Song to contain at least one *pp* and one *ff*, disposition optional (par. 95). A Coda is to be added (par. 98).

Also a similar example in minor, with Coda.

B. A similar example in *Adagio tempo* (par. 97*b*), with some regard to the conditions explained in par. 96; and with a Coda.

An example in *Presto tempo*, with a Codetta to Part I, and a Coda to the whole.

C. Optional, (but simple 3-Part form). See par. 137.

CHAPTER XIV.

The Incomplete 3-Part Song-form.

99. In the Incomplete (or abbreviated) form, the Third Part is considerably *shorter than Part I*, in consequence of reproducing only a portion, instead of the whole, of the latter.

It is evident that this reproduced portion must, however, include the *very first member* of Part I, at least, in order to fulfil the essential condition of the tripartite design, i. e., the return to the *beginning* (par. 81*a*; par. 84*b*, 4th clause). A single measure, if of somewhat striking character, may be sufficient to establish this distinction; but, as a rule, no less than an entire Phrase of Part I recurs, as Part III.

(a) If the First Part is a Period of parallel construction, Part III may appear to be the Consequent Phrase; or it may be combined out of the essential members of both Phrases. But if the construction of Part I is contrasting, or if it consists of a Group of dissimilar Phrases, then the *first* of these Phrases must constitute the body of Part III.

The difference between the "Incomplete" and the "Incipient" 3-Part Song-form is discoverable in the extent (or form) of the *Second* Part. In the Incipient form, both Part III *and Part II* are so brief as to constitute together, apparently, no more than the equivalent of Part I; in the Incomplete form, on the contrary, Part II is a full-fledged "Part," about the identity of which there can be no question, not even of quantity, while Part III is a decidedly contracted recurrence of the First Part. Thus:

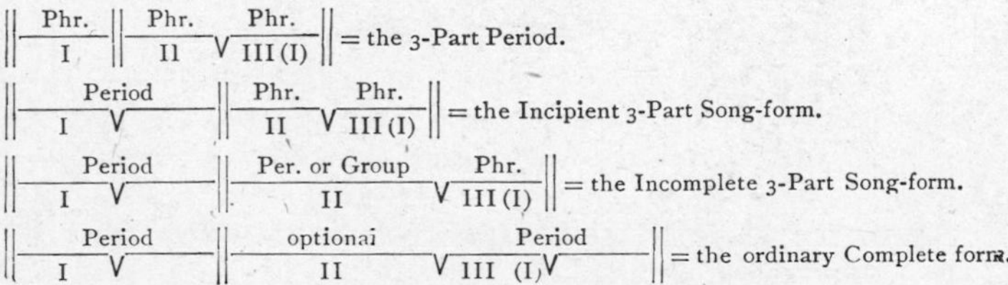

For illustration :

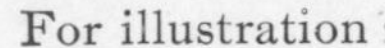

94.

Assai allegro.

p

Part II.

sf *1) *p*

crescendo

Part III.

sf *p*

BEETHOVEN.

*1) The First Part is a full parallel Period, of 8 measures; Part II is also 8 measures in length; Part III contains only six measures, in Phrase-form. At first glance, 3 or 4 of these last measures may seem to be derived from the *Consequent* of Part I; but, while they correspond to the latter in register only, their *thematic* agreement with the first Phrase is complete. The 5th measure is derived from the last measure of Part I, and a 6th measure is added for the sake of symmetry.

See also: MENDELSSOHN, op. 82, Theme; op. 83, Theme; op. 72, No. 4;—in each case Part III is just one-half the contents of the First Part; apparently the 2nd half, but always including the *beginning*.

MENDELSSOHN, "Songs without Words" Nos. 12; 20; 15; 43. In No. 3, the First Part is a Group of six Phrases; Part III contains the 1st, 2nd and 6th of these Phrases, besides 3 other (intermediate) measures.

CHOPIN, Mazurka No. 11; No. 32, first 44 measures; No. 51, first 40 measures (Part II an exact reproduction of Part I, but in a different key). CHOPIN, Nocturne No. 3 (op. 9, No. 3), "*Agitato*,"—Part III derived from second half of First Part, but including the beginning.

MOZART, Pfte. Son. No. 1 (Cotta ed.), *Andante*, (Part III corresponds exactly to 2nd half of Part I, but the construction of the latter is parallel.

HAYDN, Symphony No. 5 (Peters ed.), *Finale*, Principal Theme (model Second Part, sectional form; Part III like 2nd half of Part I, but including beginning).

SCHUBERT, Pfte. Son. No. 6 (op. 147), "Trio" of 3rd Movement.

BEETHOVEN, Pfte. Son. op. 2, No. 3, *Scherzo* (Part III about one-half the contents of First Part, and followed by two Codettas of 8 and 9 measures).

SCHUMANN, op. 82 ("Waldscenen"), No. 5.

GRIEG, Lyric Pieces, op. 43, No. 2 (II and III repeated).

BRAHMS, op. 116, No. 3, "*un poco meno Allegro*."—Op. 118, No. 2, up to first double-bar (Part I a reg. Period, repeated; the first member of Part III is in the "contrary motion" of Part I; Part III a Phrase, followed by Codetta, rep. and extended). Op. 118, No. 4, up to double-bar (both Part I and Part III close with a semicadence).—Op. 119, No. 2, second tempo (4-sharp signature).

(b) In some cases the Third Part is only a *slightly* contracted version of Part I,—as, for instance, in Ex. 91 (only one measure omitted). Such examples, where Part III does not omit any essential portion of Part I, should be classed among the Complete forms.

This may seem to place Ex. 94 in a somewhat doubtful position, though its Third Part is an indisputable contraction in *form*, from Period to Phrase.

See also CHOPIN, Nocturne No. 19 (op. 72, No. 1); Part I, 21 measures, Part III, 16 measures.

MENDELSSOHN, Præludium op. 35, No. 1 (Interlude betw. Parts I and II; elaborate Coda).

(c) On the other hand, as already intimated, a *very few* of the first beats of Part I, if fairly striking in character, will suffice to establish the tripartite design. But, unless this meagre indication of a "Return to the beginning" be followed by enough consistent material to fill the just measure of a full-fledged "Part" (in the manner to be seen in the 2nd and 3rd stages of the fully developed form, par. 102*b* and *c*), it will not, of itself alone, entirely overcome the impression of a *Two*-Part design. For illustration:

*1) There may be some doubt as to whether this last 4-measure sentence suffices to represent a definite Third Part, but the doubt is scarcely reasonable. It contains, to be sure, less than one-half of its First Part; but, firstly, it is a complete 4-meas. Phrase; and, secondly, the peculiarly effective dynamic conditions with which it is ushered in (*cresc. molto* ⸺ *pp*), emphatically mark one of the vital "angles" of the structural design. Almost precisely the same conditions prevail in the same opus (7), No. 1.

In MENDELSSOHN, op. 14, *Andante* (Introduction to Rondo), the recurrence of the first member, 5 measures from the end, is barely more than an *intimation*, and therefore the form is probably only 2-Part.

In CHOPIN, Prelude, op. 28, No. 21, the intimation of the Recurrence is also vague, but the form is surely 3-Part, on account of the individuality of the Second Part. In the following Prelude (No. 22), a Third Part can hardly be proven.

In BEETHOVEN, Symphony No. 8, "Trio" of 3rd Movement, there is a fairly convincing intimation of a Third Part, in meas. 9 of Part II.

In HAYDN, F-minor Pfte. Variations, the intimation of a Third Part is very vague in the Principal Theme, but quite distinct in the F-major Division which follows. Consequently, the former is probably 2-Part, the latter Incipient 3-Part form.

In BACH, Well-tempered Clavichord, Vol. II, Prelude 12, a Third Part is "intimated"; the same in BACH, English Suite No. 1, *Sarabande*.

In SCHUMANN, *Jugend-Album*, op. 68, No. 7 (F major), the intimation is so vague that the form is obviously only 2-Part; the same is true of MENDELSSOHN, *Scherzo a capriccio* (F♯), Principal Theme; BEETHOVEN, 7 Variations in F (P. v. WINTER), Theme; HAYDN, Symphony No. 6 (Peters ed.) *Andante* (32 measures; 2-Part form, each Part repeated).

EXERCISE 27.

Two examples, one in major and one in minor, of the Incomplete 3-Part Song-form.—Choose a different kind of Time, grade of Tempo, dynamic design and rhythmic style for each. Review the directions given in Exercise 9, last clause.—Add a Codetta or Coda, and an Introduction, if appropriate.

The Augmented Two-Part Song-form.

100. The occasional inclination of a Second Part to revert, in its later course, more or less emphatically to the *first member* of Part I, as seen in the preceding paragraph, is scarcely less likely to involve *some other*, *later*, *fragment of the First Part*.

If the fragment thus borrowed from Part I is *any other than the first* member, every suspicion of the genuine tripartite form vanishes, because it is no longer a return to the beginning: the form is unquestionably Two-Part.

If, again, the borrowed fragment is merely a corroboration of the *ending* of Part I, as ending of Part II, without causing any palpable check in the current of the latter, there is quite as evidently no essential change or enlargement of the Two-Part design (see Ex. 73).

If, however, finally, the Second Part has been sufficiently individualized, and, in consequence, a disposition to "return" asserts itself, but, in thus evidently returning, choice chances to fall upon some *later* (though equally characteristic) member of the First Part, it is certain that the form has become richer than the ordinary Two-Part design, though without reaching the lowest limits of the *Three*-Part form. (Review par. 65, and par. 77, first clause.) For this intermediate design the term "AUGMENTED 2-PART FORM" seems most appropriate.

The form is strictly only bipartite, because the vital distinction of the tripartite form is wanting, excepting as its presence is to a certain degree "understood" through the act of *substitution* which takes place, whereby an inferior agent is accepted as the representative of the expected one. If "distinct evidence of a return to the *beginning*" is to be upheld as an inviolable condition of the genuine Three-Part Song-form, then the following Example (96) is only a bipartite design; and such other, still larger specimens as may be found, consisting unmistakably of *three distinct Parts*, but lacking this evidence of a return to the beginning, must be classified among the "Group-forms" (par. 114). For illustration:

96.

*1) Old-German love-song (harmonized by L. STARK).

*2) Part II is a full Period, up to this point, equivalent in length and form to the First Part. The Phrase which follows is not derived from the *beginning* but from the *ending* of Part I, and therefore it is not a genuine Third Part. Under other circumstances, such an example as this, especially if broader in dimensions, might be called a Group of (3) Parts; but, considering the close affinity between this final Phrase and all the rest of the Song, it appears most accurate to speak of it as an AUGMENTATION of what is actually no more, in substance, than a TWO-PART FORM. The confusing resemblance between this example and Ex. 73 cannot be denied; but *there*, the Second Part reverts to the ending of Part I without checking its course, or augmenting its formal design; while *here*, the Second Part might seem complete without the addition; therefore the latter is really an augmentation of the design.

An excellent illustration is to be found in MENDELSSOHN, "Song without Words" No. 18; in measures 30–32 the Second Part evinces all the symptoms of coming to an end, and in meas. 32 a motive sets in (with strong dynamic emphasis and every other indication of a "new Part") which probably any one, at a first hearing, would accept as a genuine Third Part;—on examination it proves to be the *second* member of Part I, and not the initial one at all. The formal proportions are almost exactly the same as in Ex. 96, so the same reasons prevail for calling it an Augmented Two-Part form.

See also BRAHMS, *Rhapsody*, op. 79, No. 1, "Trio" (signature of 5 sharps). In meas. 8–9 of the Second Part there are strong indications of a regular Dominant-ending; but the Phrase which follows is not sufficiently convincing of a return to the *beginning*.

BRAHMS, op. 116, No. 6 (Intermezzo) first 24 measures; Part II contains a reproduction of all the First Part, *excepting its first Member* (2 measures); one is tempted, therefore, to call this "3-Part Song-form." BRAHMS, Pfte. Ballad, op. 10, No. 2, first 23 measures (excellent illustration).

See also CHOPIN, Nocturne No. 3 (op. 9, No. 3), Principal Song (Part I 20 measures and repeated; Part II 16 measures, followed by an Augmentation, consisting in the *last* Phrases—8 measures—of Part I).

In CHOPIN, Mazurka No. 28, the design must be called Incomplete 3-Part Song-form, because the first member of Part I—omitted in Part III—is much like an unessential Introduction; and because every other essential condition points to *three distinct Parts*, the third of which is an almost exact recurrence of Part I, contracted, and without the "Introduction."

EXERCISE 28.

An example of the Augmented Two-Part form, all details optional.

CHAPTER XV.

THE FULLY DEVELOPED THREE-PART SONG-FORM.

101. The complete development of the resources of the 3-Part Song-form depends, finally, upon the treatment of the THIRD PART, which, after having fulfilled the necessary condition of the tripartite design by reproducing the *first member of Part I*, may thereafter be elaborated into a more or less individual Part, independent enough (in its later conduct) of its original First Part, to constitute a coördinately interesting and essential section of the form. In this line of progressive development, four stages may be distinguished.

102a. STAGE 1 is represented by Ex. 91 and its context (par. 91); here Part III is either a *literal* recurrence of the First Part, or contains no other than such *unessential* modifications, and *brief* extensions, as add to its attractiveness without affecting the form, or any other essential feature of the Part. (MENDELSSOHN, "Songs without Words," Nos. 45, 22, 32, 35.)

(b) In STAGE 2, the Third Part is an *extended* version of its First Part, or, more commonly, of a portion of the same. As a rule, it reproduces only a certain fraction or section of Part I *literally;* generally no more than the first Phrase, or such a portion of the "beginning" as suffices to establish the tripartite design; and then, after doing this, fills out the remainder of its allotted length (usually at least equal to, if not beyond, the length of Part I) by an *extension or expansion of this member*, along lines approximately parallel with its First Part. For illustration:

*1) HAYDN, Symphony No. 1 (Peters ed.), *Andante*. The principal melody of Part I is transferred, in Part III, to the lower part, and is retained almost literally for 4 measures.

*2) From here on, Part III abandons the line of the First Part, and carries out an interesting extension of the melodic figure of its 4th measure, followed by a somewhat independent Cadence-member. The Third Part exceeds Part I in length by 2 measures.

See also: HAYDN, Pfte. Son. No. 9 (Cotta ed.) *Presto*, Prin. Theme.

BEETHOVEN, Pfte. Son. op. 7, 3rd Movement, up to the "Minore" (Part III very elaborate,—perhaps passing beyond this 2nd Stage; a Codetta is added); the same Sonata, *Largo*, Prin. Theme (similar).

MOZART, Pfte. Son. No. 9 (Cotta ed.) "Trio" of *Menuetto* (peculiar example; Part III contains no more than the first 1½ measures of Part I, exact; the rest of the way—15 measures—not a single member agrees literally with the original Part, but the general parallelism is so perfect that the actual difference would not be suspected).

CHOPIN, Mazurka 18; Nocturne 18 (op. 62, No. 2), 32 measures (also Incomplete Form, i. e., Part III decidedly shorter than I); Nocturne 13 (op. 48, No. 1) Prin. Theme (somewhat beyond the 2nd Stage).

MENDELSSOHN, "Songs without Words," No. 42; 46; 31; (compare, in every instance, Part III *very minutely* with Part I).

GRIEG, Lyric Pieces, op. 43, No. 5.

BRAHMS, op. 117, No. 2; op. 118, No. 1.

(c) STAGE 3 is characterized by the presence of more or less radically *new melodic material* in Part III. It emerges naturally out of the 2nd Stage, and is sometimes scarcely distinguishable from the latter, because it is not always possible to determine just when the "extension" of the initial portion of Part I digresses far enough from its original object to become "new" in effect. But usually the evidence of really *new* (though, of course, strictly kindred) members in the Third Part is unmistakable, as in the following:

*1) Up to this point, Part III is a literal reproduction of the first Phrase of the First Part; then the line of Part I is abandoned, and in its place stands, first, a 4-meas. extension of the first figure, and then an entirely new, but sufficiently homogeneous, member, which is confirmed by reproduction.

*2) In connection with this reproduction of the new member, see par. 103.

This 3rd Stage represents the most perfect, richly developed, and beautiful variety of the genuine 3-Part Song-form; and it is, therefore, quite commonly adopted, especially by modern writers. Examples of it are very numerous, but its resources are not, and cannot be, exhausted. (Stage 4, as will be seen, contains one further trait of structural coherency, but is, on the whole, a trifle less genuine than the 3rd Stage.)

See also: MENDELSSOHN, "Songs without Words," Nos. 37, 40 (between the 2nd and 3rd Stages); Nos. 25, 26, 36, 47 (all 3rd Stage). In No. 2, the Third Part has a somewhat suspicious break in its 16th measure, upon an imperfect Tonic cadence, but the following 16 measures are so intimately related to the preceding members, that they can hardly be called a Coda (comp. par. 93*b*).

SCHUBERT, Pfte. Son. No. 6 (op. 147), *Andante*, Prin. Theme.

CHOPIN, Mazurka 32 (op. 50, No. 3) last 100 measures (comp. with Principal Song, at the beginning),—Part I 16 measures, Part II 16 measures, Part III 33 measures, 17 of which are "new."

BEETHOVEN, Pfte. Son. op. 10, No. 2, *Allegretto*, first Song (codetta added); Pfte. Son. op. 10, No. 3, *Menuetto*, first Song; op. 14, No. 1, *Allegretto*, first Song; Symphony No. 1, "Trio" of 3rd Movement; Symphony No. 3, "Trio" of 3rd Movement.

BRAHMS, op. 118, No. 3, Subordinate Theme (5-sharp signature). This example might be called a Quadruple Period, but the 4th Phrase is so distinct in style as to tempt the assumption of a "Second Part," brief and Interlude-like though it is. Op. 119, No. 3 (Part I 24 meas., Part II 16 meas., Part III modified at beginning, and extended). *Capriccio*, op. 76, No. 8.

SCHUBERT, *Momens musicals*, op. 94, No. 6, first Song.

SCHUMANN, op. 82 ("Waldscenen") No. 1; Part III very elaborate and followed by a Codetta, after an imperfect Cad. on a $^6_4$ chord.

(d) In STAGE 4, the Third Part contains, besides its own rightful material, *some characteristic member of the Second Part.*

The portion thus borrowed from the (foregoing) Second Part may be of any extent, from a single melodic member up to a Phrase, or an entire Period; but it must be something *peculiar to Part II*, and not a passage which found its way into that Part from Part I,—as is more likely to be the case; hence, this device is more liable to be adopted when Part II is partly "new" in construction (par. 87*e*). In no case will Part III include the whole of Part II, but only some characteristic *portion*.

The borrowed member will almost invariably be subjected to a transposition; for, while likely to appear at first in some key conforming to the modulatory design of the Second Part, it will, in Part III, be transferred to the *principal* key.

Finally, the member borrowed from Part II, must, in order to affect the design, recur during the *course* of the Third Part, i. e., before its final cadence. Otherwise it will only become a part of the Codetta or Coda (as seen in par. 98*b*, last two clauses, which review). For illustration:

*1) Up to this point, Part III pursues the line of the first Phrase of Part I closely; what follows is neither a continuation of Part I with unessential changes (as in Stage 1), nor a mere extension of the foregoing member (as in Stage 2), nor is it new (as in Stage 3), but is borrowed from the foregoing *Second Part*, to the Consequent Phrase of which it almost exactly corresponds, save in key. This is an unusually striking example; so characteristic, in fact, that the Third Part might be called a contracted recurrence, or "Recapitulation," of both Parts I and II. Compare it carefully with the text (par. 102*d*), all the conditions of which it fulfils.

See also: MENDELSSOHN, "Songs without Words," No. 41 (similar to the above; Part III further enriched by an additional "new" member); No. 38 (meas. 10–19 of Part III are derived from meas. 6–8 of Part II); No. 30 (meas. 15–22 of Part III borrowed from Part II); No. 13 (meas. 13–15 of Part III taken from II); No. 1 (meas. 5–6 of III borrowed from II). In Nos. 10, 33, 28 the coincidence between portions of Parts III and II is more *general* than detailed.—MENDELSSOHN, Præludium op. 35, No. 5. In Præludium op. 35, No. 4, there is a suspicion of the borrowed portion constituting the beginning of the Coda. See also op. 7, No. 2 (very broad; large Second Part); *Andante cantabile* in B major.

CHOPIN, Étude No. 2 ("Moscheles-Fétis" Method).

BRAHMS, op. 116, No. 4.—SCHUMANN, *Jugend-Album*, op. 68, No. 2.—BEETHOVEN, Symphony No. 2, *Scherzo*, Principal Song.

CORROBORATION.

103. According to the law of Corroboration,—which becomes more imperative in proportion to the increasing dimension of the musical design,—every member which assumes a sufficiently striking or impressive individuality to attract more than passing attention, should *recur* more or less exactly, sooner or later, (it does not much matter when or where,) for the sake of thematic confirmation and structural balance. Or, negatively expressed, it is necessary *to avoid the isolation of any conspicuous passage or member;* the law of Unity demands its corroboration somewhere or other within reasonable limits.

This rule is involved by the law of Contrast (par. 96, which review), the action of which must be counterbalanced by that of Corroboration. The greater the Contrast,—be it in quantity or quality,—the greater the need of Corroboration; hence, these two equally important conditions of rational Form are mutually dependent.

This very strongly emphasizes the principle of Repetition, and of Reproduction, as fundamental structural law; see par. 17, 23, Ex. 46, par. 41, 42, 43, 54, etc.

It demonstrates the logical justice of the tripartite designs; see par. 81*a*, 91.

It accounts for the occasional similarity between the ending of Parts I and II (par. 75).

It is often the direct cause of the Third Part reverting to some *characteristic* motive of Part II (par. 102*d*); or of the derivation of the Coda from Part II, when the latter is somewhat independent of its First Part.

And, finally, it resolves itself into a more general (though not rigid) rule for the treatment of *any single member* which, being *new*, *or striking*, (in obedience to the demands of Contrast,) rises above the level of its surroundings and becomes a salient feature of its Division; such a member should, in well-balanced Form, *reappear* somewhere, further on,—perhaps in the Coda.

For illustrations of this law, see Ex. 98, Note *2).

MENDELSSOHN, "Songs without Words," No. 4 (the independent Prelude, recurring as Postlude, at the end); No. 38 (the independent rhythmic figure in measures 6 and 7 of Part II, reappearing in Part III).

BEETHOVEN, *Rondo* in C, op. 51, No. 1 (Cotta ed., wherein all the Themes are marked); the triplet treatment of the principal motive, in measures 8–9 of the Retransition after the 2nd Subord. Theme, recurs in the following Prin. Th., measures 4–5; the ascending chromatic run in 𝅘𝅥𝅯-sextolets at the end of the same Retransition, reappears near the end of the Coda; the ascending arpeggios in measures 1–2, 5–6, of the 2nd Subord. Theme, are corroborated in measures 6–11 of the Coda.

MOZART, *Rondo* in A minor (Cotta ed. No. 20); meas. 5 of the 1st Sub. Th. is developed at the beginning of the 1st Retransition; meas. 16–18 of the 1st Sub. Th. reappear later on in the same Retransition; the 𝅘𝅥𝅯-figure in meas. 5–6 of the 2nd Sub. Th. reappears near the end of the Coda; meas. 5–10 of the 2nd Retransition are reflected at the end of the Coda.

Many other proofs might be adduced, of an equally convincing character, in confirmation of the classic rule: "*Shun the isolation of any significant or striking member.*"

EXERCISE 29.

An example (major) of the *2nd Stage* of the Fully Developed 3-Part Song-form (par. 102*b*.). Review par. 93 to 97. Add Coda or Codetta, and Introduction, if appropriate. Par. 130 may be referred to, and utilized if desirable.

EXERCISE 30.

Two examples (minor and major) of the *3rd Stage* (par. 102*c*). Review par. 103. See par. 137.—Par. 133 may be referred to, and utilized if desirable.

EXERCISE 31.

An example (all conditions optional) of the *4th Stage* (par. 102*d*).—Par. 135 may be referred to, and utilized if desirable.

The Large Phrase-Group.

104. Notwithstanding the distrust which the Group-forms arouse, and the caution enjoined upon the beginner in their conception and employment (par. 58, final clause), their peculiar importance among the architectural purposes of musical Form is undeniable, and their value (if for no other aim than that of variety, and a relaxation of the rigid lines of the primary designs) is positive enough, when used in the proper place, and in judicious proportion.

How easily possible it is to obtain a *long line* of Phrases,—for which the term "Chain" might be more fitting than "Group,"—by adding Phrase after Phrase, without pausing to sever the connection, and without diverging from the original character to such an extent as to indicate a new "Part," may be tested in such examples as the Pfte. Études of Cramer, and other similar compositions.

But, the longer the "Chain" becomes, the stronger will the inclination assert itself to mold it into a general agreement with one of the regular designs, and thus to give to the otherwise almost inevitably incoherent series a more recognizable shape, at least *approaching* the design of the Song-forms, or a broadly magnified Double or Quadruple period.

See Cramer, Étude Nos. 1, 2, 6, 13 (original *complete* edition, Peters);—these are simply Phrase-Chains, with little or no indication of any higher structural purpose or disposition; Nos. 8, 10, 14, 78 (quasi 2-Part Song-form); No. 5 (quasi Double period); Nos. 4, 7 (quasi 3-Part Song-form).

Haydn, Pfte. Son. No. 6 (Cotta ed.) *Finale* (an introductory Period, answering roughly for a First Part; then 15 Phrases in Chain-form, followed by two Codettas).

Chopin, Étude No. 1 ("Moscheles-Fétis" method), quasi 2-Part Song-form.

BACH, Well-tempered Clavichord, Vol. I, Preludes 1, 2, 5, 6, 13, 15, (simple Chain of Phrases); Vol. I, Prelude 10 (probably 2-Part Song, with long and distinct Coda); Vol. I, Prelude 20 (quasi 3-Part); 21 (quasi 2-Part); Vol. II, Prelude 6 (quasi 2-Part).

GRIEG, Lyric Pieces op. 38, No. 5 (quasi Double period; Coda).

BRAHMS, op. 116, No. 2 (Intermezzo) *non troppo presto* (6 Phrases, quasi Double period, extended). BRAHMS, op. 116, No. 4, Part I (7 Phrases, quasi Double period).—Op. 119, No. 2, first tempo (quasi 3-Part Song-form; a brief thematic Phrase reappears several times, in various keys and styles).

CHAPTER XVI.

THE EVOLUTION OF THE FIVE-PART SONG-FORM.

1. SIMPLE REPETITION OF THE PARTS.

105. The growth of the ordinary tripartite Song-form into a correspondingly legitimate form of FIVE PARTS is initiated by the simple condition of REPETITION, applied to the Divisions of the 3-Part form.

(a) The general rule for these repetitions is as follows:

Part I may be repeated alone;

Part II should not be repeated alone, but only in company with Part III.

In other words: the 1st Division (consisting of Part I) may be repeated, and the 2nd Division (consisting of Parts II and III *together*) likewise; thus:

||: I :||: II V III :|| (See par. 83*a*.)

Either one alone, or both, of these Division-repetitions may occur; and the repetition may be *exact* (in which case repetition-marks :|| will be used, possibly with 1st and 2nd ending), or it may be *unessentially modified.*

The questions: Whether to repeat or not? Whether to repeat exactly or not? and, if the latter, How little or how much unessential variation to introduce? are touched upon in par. 23, *which review.* See also par. 103. From these, the general principle will be inferred that the advisability of repetition depends: (1) upon the simple requirement of *dimension* or proportion, and (2) upon the necessity of emphasizing or confirming *a somewhat complex*, or *a sufficiently attractive*, sentence. Furthermore, a simple sentence will call for more elaborate alteration than a complex one.

(b) The rule against the repetition of the Second Part alone, while quite strict, is not infrequently disregarded when the Part is *small* (as in Ex. 78 and Ex. 91); or when the repetition is followed by additional retransitional material (as in Ex. 84); or when the repetition, for any other evident reason, does not tend to *sever the connection* with Part III. Other, distinctly irregular, cases of the repetition of Part II alone, are shown in par. 112*b*.

(1) For illustrations of *exact rep. of Part I*, see Exs. 81, 84, 85, 89; MENDELSSOHN, "Songs without Words," Nos. 1, 3, etc.; GRIEG, Lyric Pieces, op. 43, No. 5.

(2) An exact repetition of *Parts II and III* takes place in MENDELSSOHN, "Songs without Words," Nos. 12, and 45; GRIEG, Lyric Pieces, op. 12, No. 5, No. 7; op. 38, No. 3, No. 6; op. 43, No. 3 (final extension added).

(3) *Both* Divisions are literally repeated in BEETHOVEN, Pfte. Son. op. 2, No. 1, both *Menuetto* and its "Trio"; MENDELSSOHN, "Songs without Words," No. 7; GRIEG, Lyric Pieces, op. 12, No. 4; op. 38, No. 4.

(4) For illustrations of the repetition of Part I *with unessential modifications*, see MENDELSSOHN, "Songs without Words," Nos. 4, 9, 16, 21, 27, 31, 46; BEETHOVEN, Pfte. Son. op. 26, *Scherzo;* SCHUBERT, *Momens musicals* op. 94, No. 6, "Trio"; CHOPIN, Mazurka No. 37; HAYDN, Pfte. Son. No. 15 (Cotta ed.), *Adagio;* BRAHMS, op. 118, No. 2, first 48 measures; op. 118, No. 6.

(5) Modified repetition of the second Division (Parts II and III) will be found in MENDELSSOHN, "Songs without Words" Nos. 19, 23, 48, 8; BEETHOVEN, Pfte. Son. op. 53, *Finale* (Rondo) first 62 measures; SCHUBERT, *Momens musicals* op. 94, No. 2; CHOPIN, Nocturne No. 11 (op. 37, No. 1) Principal Song; Nocturne 13, second tempo (C major); Polonaise No. 5 (op. 44) first 78 measures (introd. 8 meas.); SCHUMANN, op. 99, No. 5 (*b* minor).

(6) Finally, *both* Divisions are repeated *with modifications*, in MENDELSSOHN, "Song without Words" No. 29; HAYDN, Pfte. Son. No. 14 (Cotta ed.) *Adagio*, first 56 measures; CHOPIN, Nocturne 2 (op. 9, No. 2); Nocturne 3, first tempo; Nocturne 15 (op. 55, No. 1), first 48 measures; MOZART, Pfte. Son. No. 11 (Cotta ed.) *Andante*.

EXERCISE 32.

An example of the 3-Part Song-form, *each Division* (Part I alone,—Parts II and III together) *repeated, with unessential variations*. See par. 130, which may be applied here, if deemed desirable. See par. 137.

---

2. MORE ELABORATE REPRODUCTIONS OF THE SECOND DIVISION.

106. The entire line of development, beginning with the simple tripartite form and leading up to the genuine 5-Part Song-form, does not, in any sense, concern the manipulation of the First Part; but *refers exclusively to the reproduction of Parts II and III.* It runs through five successive and clearly distinguishable Stages, definable as follows, according to the method of treatment adopted IN REPRODUCING THE SECOND PART:

(a) The 1ST STAGE in the evolution of the 5-Part form is represented by the exact, or unessentially modified, repetition of the *second Division* (irrespective of the treatment of Part I), as indicated in par. 105, and illustrated in the fifth set of references given above. As nothing beyond the idea of simple Repetition is herein embodied, and as "repetition effectuates no actual advance in structural design," whether modified (*unessentially*) or not,—see par. 21, last clause,—the term "3-Part" form must be adhered to in this 1st Stage.

(b) In STAGE 2, a more significant alteration of the original Second Part is made (upon the reproduction of the latter as Part "Four"), consisting in its recurrence *in a different key.* Here, already, the term "Five-Part" Song-form may be adopted.

This transposition of the Second Part may be partial, or complete. In the latter case, the Part is transferred bodily, with little or no further change, a certain interval upward or downward; usually, though not necessarily, into some *closely related key.*

There will be no difficulty in making the modulation *into* the new plane, because of the (presumably) complete cadence at the end of the Third Part,—which the transposed version of Part II is to follow. And the *return to the original key* can easily be accomplished during the usual,—possibly special,—Retransition. Par. 90*c*. For illustration:

Extension
G I
Retransition.
G I
Part III. (Group of 3 Phrases).
etc.; see Original.
Part IV. (transposed recurrence of Part II, complete). *2)
A Minor.
Extension
E I
Retransition.
f
*3)
pp
f
*4)
p
Part V.
(recurrence of III).
Mendelssohn.
pp
etc.; see Original.

*1) MENDELSSOHN, "Song without Words" No. 34.

*2) The entire Second Part is transferred bodily *downward a 3rd;* and the transposition is literal, only excepting in measures 8 to 10 (chiefly during the "extension").

*3) At this point, the purpose—and the method—of regaining the original modulatory line, are displayed. The Fourth Part ends upon *E*, a 3rd lower than before; here the same Retransition is again utilized, but it gradually *shifts upward*, in admirable keeping with the nature of the figure, until, at Note *4), the original location, upon *G*, is reached.

See CHOPIN, Mazurka No. 33; the transposition is not literal, but constant.

RUBINSTEIN, *Le Bal*, op. 14, "Contredanse," No. 3 (*Allegretto*, $\frac{6}{8}$ time); transposition not literal, but affecting the entire Part.

SCHUMANN, *Bunte Blätter* (op. 99) No. 12 ("Abendmusik"), Principal Song; Part II distinct and repeated; Part III also repeated, alone.

If, as is somewhat more likely to be the case, the transposition of Part II (as Part IV) is not to extend uniformly through the entire Part, then the melodic line of Part IV may either be so conducted as to return at some point (gradually or abruptly, as proves most convenient) to the original line of Part II; or Part IV may be abbreviated, or otherwise so manipulated as to lead properly into the key of Part V.

See MENDELSSOHN, "Song without Words" No. 24; Part IV sets out a step higher than Part II; the transposition is not literal, but constant, so that the Parts are of exactly similar length; in meas. 13 of Part IV, the original melodic line is regained, then again abandoned for 1½ measures, and then so guided as to close precisely as Part II did.

In "Song without Words" No. 14, Part IV begins a fifth lower than Part II does, and adheres to this interval of transposition up to the 9th measure, whereupon a *skip of four measures* occurs, leading abruptly back into the original melodic line of Part II, the last 3 measures of which recur literally.

In No. 44, the transposition is only partial, affecting the *second half* (two measures) of Part IV, which is a 3rd higher than the corresponding measures of Part II; the change of key spreads slightly beyond the limit of the Part, however, and involves the first chord of Part V. (See par. 110.)

(c) In the 3RD STAGE, the idea of "transposition" still prevails, for a longer or shorter period, at the beginning of Part IV; but the change of key gives rise, naturally, to *other*, *more radical*, *changes in the thematic structure of the Part*, which sometimes assume significant proportions.

See MENDELSSOHN, op. 72, No. 5; Part IV begins a step higher than the Second Part does, and pursues the melodic line of the latter quite closely for 5 measures; then digresses, and expands, but closes just as Part II did.—"Song without Words" No. 43; Part IV lies a 4th above the Second Part for 4 measures; then diverges, adds 3 "new" measures, and leads into an *intimation* of the First Part (as Part V). This intimation is almost vague enough to justify calling these two "Parts" a *Coda*.—"Song without Words" No. 17; Part I is a small Period, 4 meas., closing with an imperfect cadence; Part III has exactly the same melody, but modulates into a similar imperfect cadence, thus inaugurating the *transposed* recurrence of Part IV, as a natural consequence; Part IV utilizes two measures of Part II, then diverges, extending the given material in an independent manner, and, omitting all the rest of Part II, closes in the 7th measure; a long Retrans. follows.

CRAMER, Étude 17 (orig. compl. edition); Part IV is much longer than Part II, and consists of two similar Sections, both ending with the same complete cadence. This last example might, perhaps more accurately, be classed among those of the 4th Stage.

CHOPIN, Nocturne 8 (op. 27, No. 2); Part I 9 measures, imperfect cadence; Part IV follows the melodic line of Part II quite closely for 8 measures (at first a 6th above, then a 2nd below), and then leads back to the beginning with a shorter and more emphatic Retransition.

SCHUBERT, Pfte. Son. No. 10 (B♭ major), *Finale*, first 73 measures; Part I repeated; Part IV begins exactly as Part II does, but soon diverges, transposes, extends and adds new material, to considerable length.

(d) In the 4TH STAGE in the evolution of the 5-Part Song-form, the Fourth Part no longer adheres strictly to any portion of the melodic line of Part II (in the same key, or a different one), but is a *completely "reconstructed" recurrence* of the latter. This reconstruction, however, is conducted along lines corresponding generally to the former contents and style of Part II, so that a more or less palpable *resemblance* between the two versions is preserved.

This is admirably illustrated in CHOPIN, Prelude op. 28, No. 17; Part II begins, in meas. 19, with an enharmonic change; Part III contains only the first half of Part I, and ends with the semicadence at that point; Part IV also starts out with an enharmonic change, imitates the conduct of the Second Part for a while, but is longer and more elaborate than the latter. Observe, particularly, the *dynamic design*, also, of this composition (par. 95*a*).

See further, MENDELSSOHN, Præludium op. 35, No. 2 (D major); Part IV is very much longer than Part II, and resembles the latter most closely in its later course.—SCHUMANN, *Arabesque* (op. 18), "Minore I."

(e) In STAGE 5, finally, all palpable resemblance disappears, and Part IV becomes a *distinct and individual* member of the form,—independent of the Second Part, notwithstanding their coincidence of purpose. For this, the fully developed, 5-Part Form, a new title might be adopted, indicative of its characteristic and inviolable derivation from the tripartite design, namely: A

3-Part form with two different "second" (or "middle") Parts, or "Departures" (par. 81*a*). It is the type of the Form explained in par. 124.

See SCHUMANN, *Kreisleriana* (op. 16) No. 6; *Humoreske* (op. 20), "Einfach und zart"; same work, "Innig"; *Nachtstücke* (op. 23), No. 4.

BEETHOVEN, Pfte. Son. op. 13, *Adagio;* Parts I and V repeated.—MOZART, "Fantasie and Sonata" in *c* minor, *Adagio* of the Sonata (Cotta ed. No. 18). These two examples are both unusually broad in design, and approach a certain grade of the Higher Forms, in connection with which they will again be cited, in another volume.

CHOPIN, Mazurkas, Nos. 1, 2, 5, 8, 15, 30 (long Coda), 48.—Pfte. Son. No. 2 (op. 35), "Più lento" of *Scherzo* (Parts IV and V repeated).

RUBINSTEIN, *Le Bal* (op. 14), "Contredanse," Nos. 1, 2, 4.

TREATMENT OF PART FIVE.

107. In all of the above cases of modified reproduction of the second Division, the Fifth Part is an *additional "return" to the beginning* (or *da capo*), and therefore it is likely to corroborate Part III. But it is not necessary that it should correspond exactly to the latter. All the various modes of treating the Third Part,—the several stages of divergence from, and elaboration of, the First Part, enumerated in par. 102*a*, *b*, *c*, and *d* (and par. 99*a*, *b*, *c*),—may be exhibited in Part V, irrespective of the species of manipulation previously chosen for the Third Part. Hence it is possible that Parts I, III and V, while *essentially* corresponding in contents, may all differ in treatment, each representing a comparatively independent version of the original "Statement" (par. 81*a*); perhaps in progressive ratio,—Part V becoming the longer and more elaborate of the three versions (comp. par. 53); but, on the other hand, it is equally consistent, though less usual, to *abbreviate* the third "return," especially in lengthy compositions, for obvious reasons.

In MENDELSSOHN, "Songs without Words," Nos. 19 and 24, Part V is *exactly* like Part III; in No. 48 it is a slightly variated recurrence; in Nos. 34 and 23 it is extended a trifle at the end; in No. 14 it is considerably changed and extended; in No. 8 it is enriched by the addition of new material.

In MENDELSSOHN, Præludium, op. 35, No. 2, Part V reproduces a larger portion of the First Part than the Third Part does (which is unusually brief), then adopts the whole of Part II, and then adds new material,—but without disturbing its own continuity.

In SCHUMANN, *Kreisleriana* (op. 16) No. 6, Part III is an extended version of Part I, while the Fifth Part returns to the original form and reproduces Part I almost literally.

In SCHUBERT, Pfte. Son. No. 10 (B♭ major), *Andante* Movement, Subordinate Theme (3-sharp signature), the First Part is repeated with a characteristic change of style; after Part III is closed, a similar repetition of the second Division is *started*, with the same change of style, and with every indication of genuine purpose; but upon approaching the end of Part II (IV) the purpose is abandoned, for reasons incidental to the Higher Form of which it is a portion, and, consequently, Part V does not appear at all.

In SCHUMANN, op. 82, Nos. 6 and 9, a somewhat similar omission of Part V (the final *da capo*) occurs, though here it is less convincing, because, unlike the SCHUBERT example, Part IV differs from Part II. These examples will be cited again, in par. 115.

THE OLD-FASHIONED RONDEAU, AND THE 7-PART FORM.

108a. The 4th and 5th Stages of the Five-Part Song-form, explained in par. 106*d* and *e*, correspond in design to the most common species of the "Rondeau,"—a form that was in vogue in the 17th and 18th centuries, and subsequently developed into the more elaborate modern "Rondo."

Illustrations may be found in "Les Maîtres du Clavecin" (Litolff ed.), Vol. II, pages 142, 148, 158, *Rondeaus* by J. PH. RAMEAU.

(b) The fundamental idea that has been seen to result in the enlargement or growth of the tripartite design into one of five Parts, is, plainly, that of *multiplying the "Departures"* from the original Statement (Part I), in connection with each ensuing "Return." This idea was quite frequently carried still farther, by older writers; more,—it must be observed,—with an eye to mere length, than to compactness and true beauty of form. Thus, the old-fashioned Rondeau often embraced three and even more different, but kindred, "Departures" (or "Counter-themes"), each in One-Part form, followed by as many recurrences of the First Part ("da capos").

See J. S. BACH, *Partita* II, "Rondeau" (three departures); J. PH. RAMEAU, "Les Maîtres du Clavecin" Vol. II, p. 144 (three departures); FRANÇOIS COUPERIN, same publication, Vol. II, pages 116, 126 (three departures).

In its application by later, and by some modern, composers to the system of musical designs, it has given rise to a form which, by analogy with the above, must be denominated the "SEVEN-PART SONG-FORM." Fortunately for the purity, concentration and stability of musical architecture, these attenuated, restlessly revolving structural designs, whose only logical justification is that of alternation, are very rarely adopted. The student of musical FORM should shun their imitation.

See SCHUMANN, *Nachtstücke* (op. 23), No. 1; 7-Part Song-form (i. e. a principal Part,—parallel Period,—with 3 different and distinct "departures," and as many *da capos*), followed by a long Coda in which even Parts VIII and IX are intimated.—Same opus (23), No. 2, measures 25 to 51; 7-Part form on a diminutive scale (Part I, 4 measures; II, 2 measures; III, 4 measures; IV = II transposed; V, 6 measures; VI, 5 measures; VII, 4 measures, followed by Retransition into the Principal Song).—SCHUMANN, op. 15, No. 11; 7-Part form, the 3rd departure (Part VI) identical with the first one (Part II).

EXERCISE 33.

A. An example of the 5-Part Song-form, *Stage 2* (par. 106*b*); all detailed conditions optional. Reference may be made to par. 132. See par. 107.

The pupil should, hereafter, endeavor to SKETCH HIS WORK RAPIDLY, especially the PRINCIPAL MELODIC LINE OR LINES,—unless his musical disposition be such as to render such a desirable process impracticable or insurmountably difficult. In any event, it is wise to fill out as much of the details as possible with all necessary accuracy *at leisure*, after the main design is fixed. See par. 137.

B. An example of *Stage 3* (par. 106*c*). See par. 107.—Application of par. 129, or 130, may be made, if desirable.

C. An example of *Stage 4* (par. 106*d*). See par. 107.—Application of par. 133 may be made.

D. An example of *Stage 5* (par. 106*e*). Review pars. 87, 88, 89, 90; pars. 95, 96; par. 107.—Application of par. 134, or 135, may be made.

CHAPTER XVII.

THE IRREGULAR PART-FORMS.

109. There are a few other varieties of these musical designs (consisting in the association or compounding of "Parts") which violate one or another of the essential conditions of the *regular* structural plan, and must, therefore, while being accepted and sanctioned, be qualified as "irregular." The pupil can not afford to remain in ignorance of them, but must estimate them as very rare, and abstain from their too frequent use.

1. The transposed Third Part.

110. A *da capo*, or recurrence of the First Part, beginning in any other than the principal key, is naturally hazardous, because the resumption of the *original key* (after probable absence from it during Part II) is quite as vital an indication of the Third Part, as is the recurrence of the *first melodic member*. But a harmless transposition is nevertheless conceivable under the following conditions:

(1) That the beginning of Part I is of *so striking a character* in melodic, rhythmic or harmonic respect, that its recurrence is sufficiently convincing, despite the change of key;

(2) That Part III appears just where it is *expected;*

(3) That it appears at nearly, or quite, its *full length;* and

(4) That a decided *return to the principal key* is effectuated during the course of the Third Part.

Further, the end of Part II should be plainly recognizable.

The transposition may extend through the entire Third Part, or through only a portion of it; but will always, in this phase of irregular form, affect its *beginning*.

Illustrations of such "tampering with the beginning" of Part III as paves the way to the deliberate transposition of a section, or all, of the Part, have been cited in the notes to Ex. 88, and context, and are repeated here for renewed reference: Mendelssohn, "Songs without Words," Nos. 40, 41, 36, 37 (first measure of Part III); Chopin, Mazurka 46 (meas. 24–25); Nocturne 16 (op. 55, No. 2, meas. 9); Schumann, *Waldscenen* (op. 82) No. 4,—*d* minor, meas. 23 (comp. with meas. 1); Brahms, *Balladen* op. 10, No. 4, meas. 27–28 (comp. with meas. 1–2); Pfte. Pieces, op. 117, No. 2, meas. 51–54 (comp. with meas. 1–3); op. 118, No. 2, meas. 34–36 (comp. with meas. 1–2, of which they are the "contrary motion"); op. 118, No. 6, meas. 59–62 (comp. with meas. 1–4); op. 119, No. 2, second tempo (4-sharp signature), measures 25–26 (comp. with meas. 1–2); op. 119, No. 3, measures 41–42 (comp. with first measure, of which they are an "augmentation").

In some cases the transposition of Part III does not affect the original *Tonic*, but simply changes the *mode* from major to minor, or vice versa. But usually some other (almost invariably *next-related*) Tonic is chosen; most frequently the Subdominant. These various conditions, concerning the manner, the extent, and the modulatory relation of the transposed Third Part, are illustrated in the following:

Schumann, *Bunte Blätter* (op. 99), No. 11,—March in *d*-minor, meas. 27–30 (a third higher than first Phrase of Part I); same work, No. 3 (Part III in Subdom. key); *Arabesque*, op. 18, "Minore II" (Part II very independent).

BRAHMS, op. 116, No. 5; (Part II ends on Dom., as usual; Part III begins in Subdom. key, and follows the First Part closely for four measures, then becoming more independent).

GRIEG, op. 38, No. 8, first tempo.

BEETHOVEN, Symphony No. 3, *Funeral March*, first Theme; (Part III begins in Subdom. key; Parts II and III repeated; Codettas).—Pfte. Sonata, op. 14, No. 1, *Finale*, one-sharp signature. Pfte. Sonata, op. 22, *Finale*, measures 72–103.

BACH, Well-tempered Clavichord, Vol. I, Prelude 9; Vol. II, Prelude 19 (in each case, Part III begins in the Subdominant key); Vol. II, Prelude 22 (the same; Part II begins in meas. 16, Part III in meas. 55).

SCHUBERT, *Momens musicals* op. 94, No. 1, "Trio" (one-sharp signature; Part III the Opposite mode of Part I for 4 measures); *Impromptu* op. 90, No. 4, "Trio" (four-sharp signature; similar); Fantasie in *G*, op. 78, "Trio" of *Menuetto;* String-quartet in *A*, op. 29, *Menuetto*.

CHOPIN, Nocturne 12 (op. 37, No. 2), meas. 30–69.—*Impromptu*, op. 36 (*F*♯-major); a unique example, the Parts very broad, very elaborate Coda.

Sometimes this transposed recurrence is applied to the *Fifth* Part (par. 107).

And it is not infrequently involved by some modulatory design extending through an entire 5-Part Form.

HAYDN, Symphony 12 (Peters ed.), *Adagio;* (Part V transposed, extended, and reproduced in original key; quasi 7-Part form, with Coda).

CHOPIN, Étude op. 25, No. 3 (Parts III and IV transposed; Part V again in original key; quaint modulatory design).

SCHUMANN, *Faschingsschwank* op. 26, movement IV, "Intermezzo" (key-scheme: Part I, *e*♭–*e*♭–*F*; Part III, *e*♭–*a*♭–*B*♭; Part V, *a*♭–*d*♭–*E*♭). These last two unique examples should be carefully examined.

2. The Group of Parts, Incipient Stage.

111. The distinction made in chap. VII (particularly pars. 57, 58, 59) between the regular, coherent forms, and the more loosely connected group-formations, may be extended to the Part-forms also. Thus, the "Parts," even in the 3-Part form, are sometimes so loosely *associated*, with so little regard to the principles of logical continuity and cohesion, that only the term "Group" may justly be applied. This disintegration of the form is initiated by all such liberties in the structure of the *Second Part* as tend to isolate it from its fellows, either in consequence of thematic independence and diversity, or of more or less complete separation by a full cadence.

112. Some of these irregularities have already been intimated—in par. 87*e*, and 105*b*; but it is necessary, here, to enumerate them more specifically.

(a) Cases of UNDUE ISOLATION OR DISTINCTNESS OF PART II, caused by striking difference in style or thematic structure, or by complete detachment (at the cadence) from Part III, are exhibited in the following:

SCHUMANN, *Kreisleriana* (op. 16) No. 4; *Albumblätter* (op. 124) No. 3. CHOPIN, Nocturne 4 (op. 15, No. 1).—BRAHMS, op. 118, No. 5.

In BRAHMS, op. 117, No. 2, the Second Part is thematically almost identical with Part I, but radically different in style, through its entire length.

In BRAHMS, op. 116, No. 2, and GRIEG, op. 38, No. 1, the distinct Second Part is followed by quite an elaborate Retransition.

(b) A REPETITION OF THE SECOND PART ALONE often occurs in direct consequence of such distinctness of character. Compare par. 103; and par. 105*a*, last clause. For illustration, see:

BEETHOVEN, *Bagatelle* op. 33, No. 2; Pfte. Son. op. 14, No. 2, *Finale*, meas. 73–124 (Part II repeated and extended; followed by a Retransition).—Ex. 91 of this book.—CHOPIN, Mazurka No. 24.—SCHUMANN, op. 124, No. 4; op. 15, No. 6.—GRIEG, op. 38, No. 7.

An extraordinary example is found in BEETHOVEN, Pfte. Son. op. 90, *Finale*, first 32 measures; peculiar, not only because of the (apparently uncalled-for) repetition of Part II, but chiefly for its modulatory design; each of the three Parts,—*including Part II and its repetition,—closes with a perf. cadence in the principal key.* Such daring experiments as this are for the pupil's amazement, not for his imitation; he must defer them to the period of his most absolute maturity.—Compare par. 88.

113. Indirectly analogous to the Transposed Third Part (par. 110), is the SEQUENTIAL, OR TRANSPOSED, REPRODUCTION of one or another of the Parts,—a process which also militates against the stability of the structure. See:

BACH, Well-tempered Clavichord, Vol. II, Prelude No. 11 (F major); modified sequence of Part I, in meas. 17–32.

CHOPIN, Prel. op. 28, No. 24; sequential reproduction of First Part, in meas. 21–38. Nocturne 18 (op. 62, No. 2), meas. 32–57; Two-Part form, Part II sequentially reproduced (a third higher). Nocturne 10 (op. 32, No. 2) *più agitato;* Two-Part form, reproduced bodily a half-step higher.

SCHUBERT, Fantasie in G (op. 78) *Andante*, meas. 31–49; a 2-Part form with Codetta, followed, in the next 19 measures, by a slightly modified sequence.

BRAHMS, Pfte. Son. op. 1, *Finale*, second Subject (one-sharp signature); Third Part extended by elaborate transposed reproduction.

3. Group of Parts, developed, and extended.

114. The disintegration of the regular Song-form, of which the above paragraphs exhibit the incipient stages, becomes complete when *Part number Three* (unmistakably identified as such by its style, and by the foregoing cadence) does not in any sense correspond to the *First Part*. Comp. par. 81*a*. For such a series of three independent Parts, no other epithet than "Group" can properly be employed. Review 69*b*, and 70. See:

Haydn, Symphony No. 9 (Peters ed.), *Finale*, principal Theme. (Part I, 8-meas. Period; Part II, 8-meas. Period, with strong perf. cadence on original Tonic; Part III, 16-measure Double period,—suggestive of the foregoing Parts, but unquestionably independent of them).

Schumann, *Papillons* (op. 2) No. 9,—Parts II and III similar, each Part repeated.

115. Such examples of the Group-form as are thus limited to *three* Parts, are, however, very rare. It is far more usual, when this irregular design is adopted, to extend it to *four or more* Parts.

And, quite frequently, the specific principle of the tripartite forms is manifested by a "return to the beginning" (Part I), in one of the later Parts,—generally the last one. In this case, especially, the possibility, and occasional presence, of an *independent Coda* to the Group may be demonstrated. For illustrations, see:

Beethoven, *Bagatelle* op. 119, No. 3 (five Parts, each repeated, and Coda; Part V like I).—Schubert, *Momens musicals* op. 94, No. 3 (four Parts and Coda; Part IV like I).

Chopin, Nocturne 5 (op. 15, No. 2;—four Parts, and Codetta; Part IV like I). Nocturne 6,—four distinct Parts. Nocturne 9 (op. 32, No. 1; peculiar; Parts I to III regular,—III like I; followed by a Fourth Part which embraces a transposed recurrence of Part II, and is repeated; with Codetta-extension). —Mazurkas, Nos. 3, 7, 20 (five Parts, V like I); Mazurkas, Nos. 14, 19, 21, 39 and 41 (four Parts, IV like I); Mazurka No. 27 (five Parts, thus: I, II, III, II, I); Mazurka 34 (six Parts, VI like II; each Part repeated); Mazurka 35 (seven Parts; I repeated; VI like III; VII like I; VII reproduced, "dissolved" and extended; Coda).

Schumann, *Waldscenen* (op. 82), No. 6, represents an ostensible 5-Part form (Part III like I) with *omission of the final da capo* (Part V). Such deficiencies are usually made partly good in the Coda; but in this case there is no more than a trace (in the last measure) of such a compensation. Op. 82, No. 9, is almost precisely the same. In the *Papillons* (op. 2), No. 8, the form is ostensibly 3-Part, with introductory Part (four in all).

BRAHMS, *Capriccio*, op. 76, No. 5 (six Parts, III like I, V like II, VI like III, brief Coda; the form is quasi 5-Part, first stage,—par. 106*a*,—with *interpolated Part* after Part III).

EXERCISE 34.

A. An example of the 3-Part Song-form with transposed Third Part (par. 110). Choice of key optional; and the transposition may extend through the whole, or only a portion, of Part I. Apply par. 129, or 130. See par. 137.

B. One example of the Group of Parts, according to par. 115. Apply par. 133, or 131.

DIVISION THREE.

THE COMPOUND SONG-FORMS.

116. The last degree of enlargement and development possible within the domain of the homophonic forms, is achieved by *associating complete Song-forms*. See par. 69*c*.

The association is effected in general accordance with the rules governing the union of *Parts* in the 3-Part and 5-Part forms, but with less stringency. Thus, while the law of "Recurrence" must be respected, more latitude is permitted in regard to thematic and formative relation between the several Song-forms; and uninterrupted connection at the points of contact, is the exception, rather than the rule.

CHAPTER XVIII.

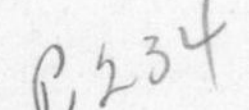

THE SONG-FORM WITH ONE "TRIO."

117. The most common of these Compound forms consists in the association of *two* Song-forms. The one which comes first is called the PRINCIPAL SONG (chiefly by virtue of its location, and its recurrence); the second one in the series is commonly called the "TRIO" (for reasons derived from a now obsolete custom), but the designation adopted in this book, in analogy with the terminology of all Higher forms, is "SUBORDINATE SONG."

After the latter, the Prin. Song recurs, as a "DA CAPO," conformably with the ruling principle of all tripartite designs. Thus, the Song-form with one "Trio" is perceived to be a broader exposition of the 3-Part Song-form, in which each "Part" has expanded into a complete "Song-form." Compare par. 77; 81*a*; 91.

Besides the popular term "Trio," many others are employed by different composers to indicate the Subord. Song in their Compound Song-forms; e. g., "Alternativo," "Intermezzo," "Musette" (in the Gavotte), "Fris" or "Friska" (after the "Lassân" in the Hungarian Czardas). In older compositions, the successive Song-forms were sometimes simply numbered:

Menuet I, Menuet II; Passepied I, Passepied II, etc. (BACH, 2nd English Suite). Sometimes the terms "Minore" and "Maggiore" are used, indicating at the same time the corresponding change of *mode* for the Subordinate Song; and frequently, for a similar reason, the sign of altered *tempo* or character ("più lento," "meno mosso," etc.) serves to denote the second Song-form. Finally, all external indication is often omitted, save perhaps a change of signature. The derivation of the term "Trio" is illustrated in BACH, 3rd French Suite, *Menuet* (Prin. Song for two melodic parts, Subord. Song for *three*, hence a "Trio").

The details of the SONG-FORM WITH "TRIO" are as follows:

THE PRINCIPAL SONG.

118a. The PRINCIPAL SONG may be of any character, and is constructed most frequently in the 3-Part Song-form, with all repetitions; possibly with a brief Codetta. As a rule, it closes with a strong perfect cadence in its own key, sufficient to constitute absolute independence of form.

See: BEETHOVEN, Pfte. Son. op. 2, No. 1, *Menuetto*, first Song (40 measures); 3-Part form, all repetitions.—Pfte. Son. op. 2, No. 2, *Scherzo* (ditto).—In HAYDN, Pfte. Son. No. 6 (Cotta ed.), first movement, the Principal Song is repeated entire, as Variation, before the Subord. Song appears.

(b) A Prin. Song in 2-Part Song-form is very unusual; and still more rarely is the One-Part form chosen. In the latter case, the *Subord.* Song must be at least 2- or 3-Part form, and very distinct in character.

See: CHOPIN, Mazurka No. 50, first 32 measures (2-Part form, each Part separately repeated).—BEETHOVEN, Pfte. Son. op. 31, No. 3, *Menuetto* (ditto); Pfte. Son. op. 110, second movement, first signature (2-Part form).—BRAHMS, op. 116, No. 3, first 34 meas. (Prin. Song only One-Part form,—ext. Double period; but the following Subord. Song is 3-Part form and distinct). Op. 116, No. 7 (similar).—Hungarian Dances, No. 1 (Prin. Song 2-Part form, each Part repeated); Nos. 5, 6, 9, similar.—CHOPIN, Nocturne No. 1 (Prin. Song, One-Part).

(c) In some comparatively rare cases, a very brief TRANSITION intervenes between the Prin. Song and the following "Trio." It serves as a mediating link between the different styles and keys of the two Songs, and becomes more necessary, and more extended, in proportion to the degree of their differentiation. It need not impair the independence of the Prin. Song, for the complete cadence of the latter may precede the transitional passage; though sometimes this cadence is so modified or concealed that the Transition may emerge from it.

See: BEETHOVEN, Pfte. Son. op. 14, No. 1, second movement (Prin. Song, 3-Part form with Codetta; one measure of Transition).—HAYDN, Symphony No. 3 (Peters ed.), *Menuetto* (2 meas. of Transition precede the "Trio").—CHOPIN, Prelude op. 28, No. 15 (Prin. Song 3-Part form, cadence evaded—measure 27—by resting on Dominant).—SCHUMANN, *Waldscenen* (op. 82), No. 8; Prin. Song 3-Part form, long Codetta; the cadence-measure transitionally bridged.

THE SUBORDINATE SONG, OR "TRIO."

119. The SUBORDINATE SONG, or "Trio," should contrast quite positively in general character with its Principal Song, though radical or extreme difference of style, to the utter exclusion of organic interdependence, consistency, and congruity, must be avoided. In some examples, especially older Dances, there is scarcely any recognizable diversity between the two Songs; but in more modern composition, *contrast and separation* are the laws of the Subord. Song.

In BEETHOVEN, Pfte. Son. op. 2, No. 1, *Menuetto*, the Prin. Song is rhythmically marked, and somewhat dramatic; the "Trio" is smooth and more lyric; but the organic harmony between them is perfect. In the next Sonata, op. 2, No. 2, *Scherzo*, the contrast is more striking; and in the 3rd movement of the next (op. 2, No. 3) it is still more emphatic; but in both, admirable consistency is preserved.

Thematic relation of the Subord. Song to its Prin. Song is uncommon, and, when it appears, it must be counteracted by more complete contrast in *style*.

See: HAYDN, Pfte. Son. No. 6 (Cotta ed.), first movement; the first figure of the Subord. Song corresponds closely to that of the Prin. Song; the rest is thematically independent, but similar in style.—In the next Son. (No. 7), *Finale*, the Prin. Song is in 2-Part form; the Subord. Song resembles it, for a time, so closely that it appears to be no more than a Variation of the former; but it is in 3-Part form, and in the opposite mode.—In BRAHMS, op. 116, No. 3, and op. 119, No. 2, the thematic material of the two Songs is identical, but the change in style almost radical, especially in the latter example.

But the entire perplexing question of analogy (consistency, inner and outer harmony) between the two Songs in this Compound form, depends more largely upon the correlation of Time, Key and Tempo. These establish the requisite *external* conformity without encroaching upon the conditions of contrast and separation; while thematic coincidence may only ensure the more vague and (in homophonic forms) comparatively unessential *inner* affinity.

(a) The Time of the Subord. Song is almost invariably the same as that of its Prin. Song; i. e., *both* are either in duple, or triple, measure. Exceptions:

In Chopin, *G♭*-major Impromptu, and Nocturne No. 10, C or ₵ and $\frac{12}{8}$ time are interchanged. In Nocturne 14 (op. 48, No. 2) the Prin. Song is in $\frac{4}{4}$ time, and the "Trio" (*molto più lento*) in $\frac{3}{4}$.—In Brahms, op. 116, No. 7, the time changes from $\frac{2}{4}$ to $\frac{6}{8}$.—Beethoven, Symphony No. 6, third movement; change from $\frac{3}{4}$ to $\frac{2}{4}$.—It must be emphasized, that this is exceedingly uncommon.

(b) The Key of the Subord. Song is always related, in some degree, to that of the Prin. Song, though unlimited option prevails in the choice of relationship (near or remote). In the oldest, and in some modern, examples, the *selfsame* key is retained; in which case the separation of the Songs, and their respective completeness of form, is more strongly marked:

Haydn, Symphonies (Peters ed.), Nos. 1, 4, 5, 6, 7, 8, 10, 11, 12,—third movement of each. Beethoven, Symphonies, Nos. 1, 2, 3, 4, 6, 8,—third movement of each.

The next step to this, in the early history of the "Trio," appears to have been the choice of the *Opposite Mode* of the same Tonic:

Beethoven, Symphony No. 5, third movement (*c*-minor and *C*-major); Pfte. Sonatas, op. 2, No. 1; op. 2, No. 2; op. 7,—third movement of each.

Brahms, op. 119, No. 2.—Chopin, Polonaise No. 1.

The *Relative* (major or minor) key is found in:

Beethoven, Pfte. Sonatas, op. 2, No. 3, third movement (*C*-major and *a*-minor); op. 22, op. 28, third movement of each.

Next to these in popularity is the choice of the *Subdominant* key (or its Relative) for the "Trio"; this, in the modern March and in many Dances, has become a usage almost equivalent to a rule. It is notably appropriate in the homophonic domain of musical architecture, because the inclination to relax toward the lower (Subdom.) keynotes,—in distinction to the aspiring impression conveyed by the upper (Dominant) ones,—*is characteristic of the inferior range of forms.* This point, which is of vital moment in the Complex forms, will be reverted to in connection with the Rondo- and Sonata-forms, in a subsequent Volume.

The Subdom. key appears in BEETHOVEN, Pfte. Son. op. 10, No. 3, third movement, (*D*-major and *G*-major); and in Pfte. Son. op. 101, second movement (March).—The Relative of the Subdom. in BEETHOVEN, Pfte. Son. op. 10, No. 2, second movement (*f*-minor and *D*♭-major); also op. 14, No. 1; and op. 27, No. 1, second movement of each.

See also: CHOPIN, Polonaises, No. 2, No. 3, No. 4.

Other possibilities of key-relation between the Prin. and Subord. Songs are exhibited in the following:

BEETHOVEN. Symphony No. 7, third movement (Mediant-Dominant relation,—*F*-major and *D*-major,—the Mediant of the key of the Prin. Song is the Dominant of the "Trio"). The same relation obtains in HAYDN, Symphony No. 3 (Peters ed.), third movement.—In HAYDN, Symphony No. 2, third movement, the keys are *D* and *B*♭-major (Tonic-Mediant relation).—The same in CHOPIN, Polonaise No. 6.—BRAHMS, op. 116, No. 6 (Dominant-Relative key). SCHUBERT, *Impromptu* op. 90, No. 2 (*E*♭-major and *b*-minor).

(c) The TEMPO of the Subord. Song is very often, perhaps usually, a little more tranquil than that of the Prin. Song; though it may be the reverse of this, and, sometimes, it remains unchanged. This is dictated by the consideration of *contrast*, which prevails, *mildly*, in this respect also. See:

BEETHOVEN, Symphony No. 4, *Menuetto* ("Trio"—*un poco meno Allegro*); Sym. No. 7, third movement ("Trio"—*Presto meno assai*).—BRAHMS, op. 116, No. 3 (Subord. Song—*un poco meno Allegro*).—CHOPIN, Nocturne 13 (*poco più lento*).

MENDELSSOHN, Pfte. Son. op. 6, second movement ("Trio"—*più vivace*).

GRIEG, op. 38, No. 8 (*più mosso, ma tranquillo*).

In BEETHOVEN, Pfte. Son. op. 26, second movement,—as in the majority of cases,—no tempo-mark is given for the "Trio"; but it is manifestly more tranquil in character than the Prin. Song, and will almost certainly suggest a slight relaxation of speed,—to a thoughtful and susceptible performer.

(d) The FORM of the "Trio" is generally Three-Part; occasionally only Two-Part. The One-Part form is very uncommon, and can be chosen only when the Subord. Song is very distinct in character, and when its Prin. Song contains at least two Parts,—compare par. 118*b*. See:

BEETHOVEN, Pfte. Son. op. 2, No. 1, *Menuetto* ("Trio" 3-Part Song-form); op. 10, No. 2, second movement (Subord. Song in 3-Part form, with modified repetitions).

BEETHOVEN, Pfte. Son. op. 26, second and third movements ("Trio" in each case 2-Part form); the same in op. 27, No. 1, second movement, and op. 27, No. 2, second movement.

CHOPIN, Mazurka 10 (Prin. Song 3-Part; Subord. Song *only One-Part form*, but distinct); Mazurkas 45 and 46 ("Trio" One-Part form); Mazurka 51

("Trio" one *large* Part).—SCHUMANN, *Waldscenen*, op. 82, No. 7 (Prin. Song Two-Part form with Codetta; Subord. Song, one Part).—BEETHOVEN, *Bagatelle*, op. 33, No. 4 (Subord. Song, one Part); Pfte. Son. op. 10, No. 3, *Menuetto* (ditto).—BRAHMS, op. 116, No. 6, and op. 117, No. 1, the same.

(e) While the Subord. Song, like the Principal one, is expected to terminate with a complete perfect cadence,—as implied in par. 116,—it is by no means uncommon to introduce a brief RETRANSITION after the Subord. Song, serving to lead smoothly back into the recurrence of the Prin. Song, or "Da capo." Comp. par. 90*c*. It is more necessary than the Transition into the Subord. Song (par. 118*c*), because, the form having once been expanded by the addition of a Subord. Song, the "Da capo" is inevitable.

The Retransition may be independent of the Subord. Song,—following after the complete cadence of the latter; or it may be evolved by dissolution and modification of the cadence-member. The details may be apprehended from the following examples:

BEETHOVEN, Pfte. Son. op. 7, third movement, end of "Minore" (two measures of Re-transition); op. 10, No. 2, second movement (6 meas. of independent Re-transition); op. 26, *Scherzo* (4 meas. of Re-transition); op. 2, No. 3, *Scherzo* (the "Trio" is in 3-Part form; Parts II and III are repeated, and the latter is so modified,—dissolved,—at its end, as to lead away from its own Tonic, into the Dominant of the Prin. Song, which follows as "Da capo"); op. 10, No. 3, *Menuetto* (similarly, the "Trio" ends on the Dom. of the Prin. Song); op. 14, No. 1, second movement (the same).—BEETHOVEN, Symphony No. 3, and No. 5, third movement of each.—HAYDN, Symphony No. 2 (Peters ed.), and No. 3, third movement of each.—BRAHMS, op. 116, No. 7 (elaborate independent Re-transition, after the Subord. Song); op. 117, No. 3 (the same).

THE "DA CAPO."

120. The recurrence of the Prin. Song, or the so-called "DA CAPO," after the Subordinate Song, is, as a rule, *literal* When such is the case, it being unnecessary to write out the entire Prin. Song again, its reproduction is merely indicated by the words *da capo* (i. e., "from the beginning"), or simply the letters *D. C.*; or *dal segno* (i. e., "from the sign"—𝄋—) in case the first few tones or measures are so involved in the Re-transition as to be excepted from the recurrence.

It is a rule, however,—with no other foundation than tradition,—that such repetitions of the Parts as may have occurred at first, are to be omitted in the "Da capo"; hence the directions often encountered: *D. C. ma senza ripetizione.*

See: BEETHOVEN, Pfte. Son. op. 2, No. 1, third movement, end of "Trio"; op. 10, No. 3, *Menuetto*, end of "Trio"; op. 22, *Menuetto;* and op. 26, *Scherzo*, end of "Trio."—CHOPIN, Polonaise I; Mazurka 6, 12, etc.

The "Da capo," as a *literal* reproduction of the Prin. Song, is, as implied above, the species which characterizes the genuine Song-form with "Trio."

But slight modifications or variations of the "Da capo," *as long as they remain thoroughly unessential*, are permissible. In such cases the recurrence of the Prin. Song (Menuetto, Scherzo, or whatever it be) is, of course, written out.

N. B. It must be strictly borne in mind, that, as the modifications of the "Da capo" become more and more elaborate, the design diverges in the same ratio from the specifically *homophonic Compound Song-form*, and approaches the spirit and detail of the *Rondo form*.

See BEETHOVEN, Pfte. Son. op. 31, No. 3, *Menuetto;* the "Da capo" is written out, but not a tone is altered, excepting the final chord. Writing out the *literal* reproduction of the Prin. Song appears whimsical, but it is often involved by the Coda, and may be done purely for the convenience of the player.

CHOPIN, Mazurka No. 23 (literal); No. 47 (literal, excepting repetitions); *Impromptu*, op. 29 (*A*♭-major), literal; *Impromptu*, op. 66 (*c*♯-minor), literal, excepting introduction.—SCHUBERT, *Momens musicals*, op. 94, Nos. 1 and 4.

The "Da capo" is slightly variated in CHOPIN, Nocturnes No. 11, No. 10, No. 1.—BRAHMS, op. 116, No. 3; op. 117, No. 1; op. 117, No. 3 (repetitions also omitted); op. 119, No. 2.

Somewhat more elaborate variation occurs in the "Da capo" of CHOPIN, Nocturne No. 13; BEETHOVEN, Pfte. Son. op. 27, No. 1, second movement; and BEETHOVEN, *Bagatelle* op. 33, No. 4.

In CHOPIN, Mazurka No. 36, the first 14 measures of the "Da capo" are transposed (a half-step lower).

Alterations of the *design* of the Prin. Song, in the "Da capo," affect the genuineness of this class of forms more seriously than simple variation of detail, because they are of a more essential nature. The most natural, justifiable and common practice, is to *abbreviate* the "Da capo";—especially by reducing the recurrence of the 3-Part (or 2-Part) Song-form, to its First Part alone. Such a contracted "Da capo" may, subsequently, be extended, or otherwise modified. See N. B. above.

See BEETHOVEN, *Bagatelle* op. 33, No. 2.—Also, Symphony No. 5, *Scherzo*.

CHOPIN, Mazurkas 17 and 31; Mazurka 25 (Prin. Song, broad 2-Part form, with complete repetition; "Da capo" abbreviated to First Part, slightly expanded). Polonaise No. 4; Polonaise No. 6 (Prin. Song, 3-Part form, broad First Part; "Trio," 2-Part form, Part I repeated, Part II dissolved into elaborate Re-transition; "Da capo" contracted to one-half of Part I). *Impromptu* in *G*♭-major, op. 51, ("Da capo" abbreviated, and modified by extension); the same in Nocturnes 3 and 14, Prelude, op. 28, No. 15, and Mazurka 38.

BRAHMS, op. 116, No. 6; op. 118, No. 4. ("Da capo" abbreviated and modified.)

An *extension* of the "Da capo" takes place in:

CHOPIN, Mazurkas 32 and 36; and BRAHMS, op. 116, No. 7.

THE CODA.

121. The addition of a CODA to the entire Compound form is not only possible, but desirable and necessary, apparently in proportion to the importance attached to the "Da capo," and the extent of its elaboration. Hence, while a Coda very rarely follows the simple forms of the Song with "Trio" as employed in older Dances (with *literal* D. C.), it is rarely, if ever, absent after a "Da capo" that has been modified, and often it is quite extensive and self-assertive. See par. 98*a*.

The Coda may be derived from *any* anterior motive or member; or it may (rarely) introduce new motives. And it may conform in style and melodic contents either to the Prin. Song or the Subord. Song (chiefly the former); or, possibly, to both in turn. See:

BEETHOVEN, Pfte. Sonatas, op. 2, No. 1; op. 2, No. 2; op. 7, etc., third movement of each,—*no Coda.*

BEETHOVEN, Pfte. Son. op. 2, No. 3, *Scherzo* (Coda derived from Prin. Song); Pfte. Son. op. 14, No. 1, *Allegretto* (Coda taken from Subord. Song, "Maggiore"); Pfte. Son. op. 26, third movement ("Funeral march"), last 7 measures; Pfte. Son. op. 27, No. 1, second movement, last 12 measures (Coda simply an extension of the "Da capo").—CHOPIN, Mazurka No. 32 (elaborate Coda); No. 38 (Coda from Part II of Subord. Song).—SCHUBERT, *Impromptu*, op. 90, No. 2 (Coda from "Trio"); MENDELSSOHN, Symphony No. 4 ("Italian," op. 90), third movement,—Coda utilizes ingeniously a motive of the "Trio."—BRAHMS, op. 116, No. 6, last 7 measures (from Subord. Song); op. 118, No. 4, last 23 measures; op. 119, No. 2, last 5 measures (from Subord. Song).

MISCELLANEOUS EXAMPLES OF THE SONG-FORM WITH ONE "TRIO."

SCHUBERT, Pfte. Sonatas, Nos. 1, 2, 4, 6, 8, 9, 10,—third movement of each. —*Impromptu*, op. 142, No. 2.

MOZART, Symphonies (Litolff ed.), Nos. 2, 3, 4, 5, 6, 11, 12, 13, third movement of each.

BRAHMS, Pfte. Son. op. 1, *Scherzo ;* Pfte. Son. op. 2, *Scherzo ;* Pfte. Son. op. 5, *Scherzo ;* Pfte. Balladen, op. 10, No. 1; Intermezzo, op. 76, No. 7 (Prin. Song, One-Part form); Symphony No. 3, third movement

The String-quartets of HAYDN, MOZART, BEETHOVEN and other classic writers, *Menuetto* or *Scherzo* (as a rule, the third movement of each).

122. A confusing trait of resemblance between the Song with one "Trio" and the simple 5-Part Song-form, is exhibited in certain diminutive examples of the former, where the Subord. Song is only One-Part form, and the "Da capo" abbreviated.

This is seen in CHOPIN, Mazurka 13 (Prin. Song 3-Part form; Subord. Song only one Part, but very distinct in character and mode; "Da capo" contracted to *one* of the original three Parts). Precisely the same conditions prevail in GRIEG, Lyric Pieces, op. 12, No. 3.—These are both examples of the 5-Part Song-form, stage 5, cited in par. 106*e*; but they are extreme specimens, owing to the *unusual independence and diversity of the Fourth Part*,—which, for this reason, assumes the rank and characteristics of a "Trio." Were the "Da capo" not reduced to one Part, the identity of such a Subord. Song would be beyond question.

In CHOPIN, Mazurka 42, again only five Parts are represented,—the Prin. Song being in *two* Parts, and the Subord. Song in *one ;* but here the "Da capo" is not abbreviated (save by omission of repetitions).

EXERCISE 35.

A. An example of the Song-form with one "Trio," in major; both Songs in 3-Part form; "Da capo" literal; no Transition or Re-transition.—Apply par. 136.

B. An example of the same form, in minor; design of Songs optional; "Da capo" literal.—Apply par. 134, or par. 135.

C. Same form; design of Songs optional; Re-transition; "Da capo" unessentially modified.—Apply par. 136.

D. Same form; "Da capo" abbreviated; Coda.—Apply par. 135. See par. 137.

CHAPTER XIX.

EXTENSIONS OF THE "SONG WITH TRIO."

123. The simplest method of extension is, here again, that of Repetition. It is applied, not infrequently, to the Subord. Song and the "Da capo" *together*, precisely as in the 3-Part Song-form with repeated Second and Third Parts. See par. 105*a*.

The repetition may be exact or modified,—generally the former, though it is natural to *abbreviate the last "Da capo,"*—more rarely the first one. A Coda may follow.

See BEETHOVEN, Symphony No. 4, third movement (Prin. Song—"Minuetto"—3-Part form with all repetitions, and Codetta; "Trio" 3-Part form; Re-transition; 1st "Da capo" literal, excepting repetitions; "Trio" again, exactly as before; second "Da capo" contracted to Third Part; Coda of 3 measures).—In BEETHOVEN, Symphony No. 7, third movement, the same repetition occurs, in the original score; a Coda is added, reverting very briefly to the motive of the Subord. Song. (In some modern editions, and modern performances, this extensive repetition is omitted.)—BEETHOVEN, *Bagatelle* op. 33, No. 7, (both "Songs" in concise 2-Part form, with repetitions; both "Da capos" complete, but variated; Coda).—BEETHOVEN, Pfte. Son. op. 54, first movement (the Subord. Song is at first an extended Period, with *transposed* and enlarged reproduction, and Re-transition; when it recurs, after the first "Da capo," it is abbreviated to the length of a simple Period; the two "Da capos" are variated, in progressive degrees; Coda).

In HAYDN, Pfte. Son. No. 7 (Cotta ed.), *Finale*, the Subord. Song and "Da capo" are repeated with considerable, but probably unessential, modification (Prin. Song, 2-Part form; Subord. Song, 3-Part; no Coda). Pfte. Son. No. 8, *Scherzando* (very similar; brief Coda). Pfte. Son. No. 12, first movement, the same.

In SCHUMANN, Symphony No. 4 (*d*-minor, op. 120), *Scherzo*, the "Trio" recurs, similarly, after the "Da capo," but is linked with the Transition which leads into the *Finale*; in other words, the second "Da capo" is omitted.

THE SONG-FORM WITH TWO "TRIOS."

124. When such an enlargement of the form is contemplated, it is, however, much better and more customary to avoid the monotony attendant upon so extensive a repetition, by inventing a *new* (*second*) "*Trio*," instead of the recurrence of the first one. This design corresponds to that of the fully developed 5-Part Song-form (par. 106*e*), of which it is a broader exposition. Compare par. 117, second clause.

The two "Trios" should stand in quite marked contrast with each other; one of them generally maintaining closer agreement, in character and style, with the Prin. Song, while the other diverges more emphatically. Consequently, it is not unusual for the Subord. Songs to differ from each other in *Time*, as well as in tempo and key; though this is more commonly the case in modern examples.

After each Subord. Song, the Prin. Song recurs, as "Da capo," sometimes literally (excepting the repetitions), but more frequently abbreviated, or otherwise modified. A Coda may be added.

See JOHANN LUDWIG KREBS, Partita II, "*Menuets*" (three, numbered I, II, III,—No. I recurring as "Da capo" after each of the others). [To be found in "Les Maîtres du clavecin" (Litolff ed.), Vol. I, p. 73.]

MOZART, Symphony No. 8 (Litolff ed.), *fourth* movement,—Menuetto with two "Trios" (not to be confounded with the second movement of the Symphony).

MENDELSSOHN, *Wedding-March* from music to "Midsummer-Night's Dream."

SCHUMANN, Symphony No. 1, *Scherzo* (Prin. Song 3-Part form; "Trio I" very divergent in character, time, and tempo; broad form, with modified repetitions; first "Da capo" without repetitions; "Trio II" resembles Prin. Song; 3-Part form, with Codetta from Second Part; second "Da capo" abbreviated; Coda contains reminiscences of "Trio I").—Symphony No. 2, *Scherzo*.—Pfte. Quintet, op. 44, *Scherzo*.—Pfte. Quartet, op. 47, *Scherzo*.—Pfte. Trio, No. 3, op. 110, third movement.

BRAHMS, Pfte. Scherzo, op. 4.—Symphony No. 2, third movement (Prin. Song $\frac{3}{4}$ time, *Allegretto*, 3-Part form; First Subord. Song, same key, $\frac{2}{4}$ time, *Presto*, 3-Part form; first "Da capo" abbreviated and modified; Second Subord. Song, $\frac{3}{8}$ time, *Presto*; second "Da capo" complete, but transposed during the first Part; Coda). In this unique example, the two "Trios" represent, essentially, *two similar extreme Variations of the Prin. Song*.

THE GROUP OF SONG-FORMS.

125. The process of group-formation, beginning with the Phrase-group (par. 57) and passing on through the Group of Periods (par. 59), the Large Phrase-group (par. 104) and the Group of Parts (par. 114, 115), culminates, in the homophonic forms, in the Group of *entire Song-forms*. It is distinguished from the regular Compound forms, explained above, by the absence, or irregular disposition, of the "*Da capo*," whereby the condition of "Return, after Departure," is not fully or correctly satisfied (par. 81*a*). See par. 69*c*.

See BEETHOVEN, Pfte. Son. op. 106, *Scherzo* (First,—or Principal,—Song, 2 Parts, each repeated; Second Song, ditto; Third Song, change of time and tempo, 3 Parts; Fourth Song like First, variated; Coda. The form is quasi "Song with *two Trios in succession*").

CHOPIN, Polonaise No. V, the same; (the Third Song,—or 2nd "Trio,"—is in Two-Part form, very broad, and with complete *transposed reproduction*).

BRAHMS, Pfte. Ballade op. 10, No. 2, the same design. Rhapsody, op. 119, No. 4, (design: Prin. Song—"Trio I"—"Trio II"—"Trio I"—Prin. Song, Coda). Pfte. Ballade op. 10, No. 4, (design: Prin. Song—"Trio I"—Prin. Song—"Trio II"—Coda, consisting in a portion of the First Subord. Song, interwoven with the first motive of the Prin. Song. The final "Da capo" is omitted).

SCHUMANN, *Nachtstücke*, op. 23, No. 2, (design: Prin. Song—"Trio I" 7-Part form—Re-transition—Prin. Song, abbreviated—"Trio II"—"Trio I"—Prin. Song).—Symphony No. 3 *Scherzo*, (design: Prin. Song—Song II—Song III—Song IV, transposition of Prin. Song—Song V—Song VI, "Da capo" of Prin. Song—Coda).

CHOPIN, Waltz No. 1 (Group of 5 Songs, V like I).

These represent the last degree of enlargement, the broadest proportions attainable within the sphere of the Homophonic Forms.

EXERCISE 36.

A. An example of the Song with two "Trios," in major, first "Da capo" abbreviated.—Apply par. 133 (*Scherzo*).

B. The same, in minor. Apply par. 136.

DIVISION FOUR.

CONVENTIONAL STYLES OF COMPOSITION.

126. An extremely large proportion of all music written, belongs to the Homophonic domain of composition. The entire range of musical products within this domain may be approximately divided into *three general classes* or styles of composition, distinguished by the respective predominance of one of the three essential factors of the art: Melody, Harmony and Rhythm. (Carefully review par. 97, recollecting, however, that the distinctions there defined constitute a different classification from the one under present consideration.)

(a) The first, or LYRIC, class, in which the element of MELODY predominates, is characterized chiefly by the Song (with or without words), and embraces also the Air or Aria, Lied, Canzone, Cavatina, Idyll, Barcarolle or Gondellied, Romanza, Reverie, Nocturne, Serenade, "Melody," Chanson, Lyric Piece, Ballade, Elegy, Berceuse or Cradle-song, Pastorale,—and many other compositions of similar character but with more or less arbitrary and specific titles. All of these may be *either vocal or instrumental* in conception and setting. To this class belong also the sacred Hymn, Psalm-tune, Chorale, Chant, the simpler church Anthems, the secular Terzetto, Quartet, Chorus, Glee, Madrigal, etc., all of *vocal* conception.

(b) The second, or ÉTUDE-, class, in which the most prominent element is that of the HARMONY, is characterized chiefly by the Étude, and includes also the various kinds of Studies and Exercises; the Toccata; certain varieties of the Prelude; generally also the Caprice or Capriccio, Scherzo, Scherzando, Impromptu, Intermezzo,—though the character of these latter is indefinite and variable. The compositions of this class are almost invariably *instrumental* in conception and setting.

(c) The third, or DANCE-, class, distinguished by the prevalence of the element of RHYTHM, embraces all Dances, old and modern, and the March. Conspicuous among these are the Minuet, Gavotte, Courante, Sarabande, Gigue or Jig, Waltz, Polka, Galop, Mazurka, Tarantella, Saltarello, Siciliano, Ländler, Bolero, Quadrilles, Polonaise, Marches of varied character (Wedding-M., Funeral-M., Festival-M., etc.), and many other species of a more or less kindred nature. This class of compositions is very generally, though not always, *instrumental* in conception and setting.

(d) It must be remembered that this is only an *approximate* classification, and that, while some of the conventional styles enumerated have become distinctly typical, others again are so indefinite and arbitrary as to defy exact classification. Hence, it is often impracticable and unwise to apply these class-distinctions rigorously. It is perfectly just to impart a conspicuously melodic character to a Dance-form, as long as the rhythmic element maintains its preëminence; or to an Étude,—though, in the latter case, it would transfer the composition to the lyric class, and the reasons for calling it an "Étude" would have to be sought in other, technical, peculiarities of the piece. This accounts for the apparently careless or erroneous choice of title in certain examples; many a Nocturne or Waltz, so-called, belongs properly to the Étude-class,—and *vice versa*.

As a rule, however, the student should exercise judgment in naming his compositions. It is best never to use descriptive titles (almost utterly senseless when applied to music—e. g. "Among the roses,"—"Shower of pearls," etc.), but only such conventional titles as the above, which indicate the *general or typical musical* characteristics of the piece. A very important lesson is conveyed to the young composer by BRAHMS, in his almost exclusive use of the terms Capriccio, Intermezzo, Fantasie, for his pianoforte-pieces; and in the choice of the simple *tempo* designations: "Allegretto," "Andante," etc., adopted as sole title by many serious composers.

127. A description of each of these conventional species of composition may be found in standard dictionaries of music, and in such books as the "Musical Forms" by E. PAUER. All that need be added, here, is a purely technical definition of such structural traits as concern the present student, who is expected to write an example of each, or at least of the most important, of the typical varieties noted.

CHAPTER XX.

THE LYRIC CLASS.

1. The Song, with Words.

128a. As concerns the first, and apparently difficult, consideration of choosing the TEXT for a Song, the student will find the richest and most trustworthy fund of suitable words in the volumes of Songs already written and published. From these he can choose, studiously ignoring the musical setting before him. Or he may take a Psalm, or some other Bible passage; or may adopt a poem from books of standard poetry, though this is the least advisable course for the beginner to pursue.

The text should first be thoroughly memorized, and mentally repeated, until it begins to suggest consistent musical setting. This will facilitate the choice of general characteristics, i. e., between duple and triple Time, major and minor mode, brisk or deliberate tempo, bold or graceful style.

(b) In the SETTING, the rhythmic distinctions of the musical meter must coincide quite accurately with the prosody of the text. *Important words and accented syllables* should be placed against the *accented*, *or higher*, *or longer*, *tones;* and lower, shorter or unaccented tones should accompany unemphatic words and syllables.

This important rule operates, however, mainly by comparison: an unaccented word or syllable may be set to an accented tone, if the accent is *subordinate;* or to a higher tone, if it occupies a *light beat*. For illustration:

*1) Good, because the accent at *c* is subordinate to that at *g*, and at the following *b*.—*2) Doubtful, because of the emphasis attached to a *comparatively* very high tone.—*3) Better, because the high tone is unaccented.—*4) Eccentric.—*5) Objectionable.—*6) Better.—*7) Such an accent as this, upon a light final syllable, is permissible at any *cadence*.

Furthermore, this rule must always be applied with sufficient latitude to ensure *perfectly unconstrained melodious* conduct of the vocal part. The words are to be regarded and treated, constantly, as the *subordinate element* of a Song.

(c) In writing for the human voice, it is necessary to regard the average compass of the part in question:

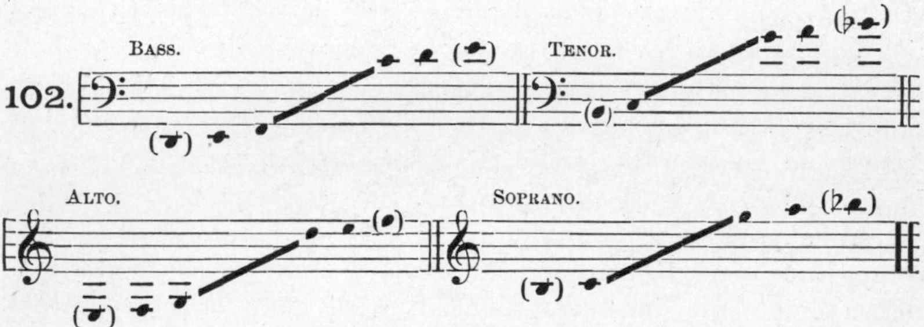

The range of Baritone is between Bass and Tenor; that of Mezzo-Soprano, between Alto and Soprano.

Care must be taken to avoid maintaining, persistently, either a comparatively high, or low, range of the chosen voice. This consideration will influence the choice of key.

(d) The student should endeavor to reflect the character of the text in the mood of the music. He must determine the dynamic and declamatory design, according to the dramatic undulations of the text; *but must avoid exaggerated minuteness in this respect.* The effort to "illustrate" each single suggestive word leads to unevenness of structure, and hampers the essentially *musical* conception. This is the gravest error that can attach itself to a vocal composition; *for a Song must be first, and always, good, melodious, and self-sufficient music.*

(e) In the NOTATION of the vocal part, the notes which accompany separate words or syllables must be detached; two or more notes to the same word or syllable must be connected, either by beams, ties, or slurs:

(f) The FORM of the Song will depend largely upon that of the text, which may demand almost any of the forms explained in chapters VI to XVII of this book, from the large (or repeated) Period, up to the 3- or 5-Part form, or Group of Parts. But preference should be given to the Two- and *Three-Part* Song-forms, and an effort be made to adapt the text to such a design, before commencing the composition.

When the text is divided (or divisible) into stanzas, the composition may be strophic, i. e., music may be set to the first stanza only, and simply reproduced, with more or less essential change, for the following ones. See:

SCHUBERT, "Müller-Lieder" (op. 25), Nos. 1, 7, 8, 9, 10, 13, etc.

BEETHOVEN, "An die ferne Geliebte" (op. 98), sections *a*, *b*, *c*, *d*, *e*; (section *f* is in 3-Part form; the final section is a Coda, compounded out of the first section). This cycle of Songs ranks among the most beautiful and impressive in all musical literature. The student is to examine it thoughtfully. Its design is, of course, the Group of Song-forms (par. 125).

SCHUMANN, "Liederkreis" (op. 24), Nos. 4, 7.

Or the composition may be progressive, i. e., the words may be set to music consecutively, throughout,—with, probably, a *da capo* at the end, as in some of the Group-forms. In this case, the 3 Part or 5-Part Song, or the Group of Parts,—possibly Song with "Trio,"—may be chosen as structural design. See:

SCHUBERT, "Müller-Lieder," No. 2,—Song with "Trio"; (Prin. Song, 3-Part Period; Subord. Song, 3-Part Song-form; "Da capo," a compound of both foregoing Songs; Coda). No. 3,—Group of four Parts; (I, a Period; II, a Phrase, repeated; III, an extended Phrase; IV, two repeated Phrases). No. 4,—quasi 3 strophes. No. 5,—Song with "Trio."

SCHUMANN, "Liederkreis" (op. 24), Nos. 1, 2 (almost strophic), No. 3 (Three-Part form), No. 5 (Five-Part form); "The two Grenadiers," op. 49 No. 1 (partly strophic).

(g) The primary objects of the instrumental ACCOMPANIMENT to a Song are, first, to *support*, and secondly, to *complement*, the vocal part. It should not disturb or overpower the latter, and therefore the danger of *too much* accompaniment must be recognized and avoided.

The simple rhythmic enunciation of the chords, as in SCHUBERT, "Haidenröslein" (op. 3, No. 3) is antiquated, but often very appropriate. The method adopted by SCHUMANN in the "Lotosblume" (op. 25, No. 7), in which the vocal melody is from time to time reinforced by the pianoforte, is more artistic.

But the student must guard against the impression that the vocal part should be duplicated throughout in the accompaniment (as in SCHUMANN, op. 25, Nos. 1, 2, 9, etc.). This tends to obscure, more than to support, the vocal part; and, while it is often necessary, it is better, as a rule, for the accompaniment to limit itself to general harmonic figuration,—which is at once less obtrusive, and more individualized. See SCHUMANN, op. 25, Nos. 3, 11, 25. SCHUBERT, "Müller-Lieder" (op. 25), Nos. 1, 2, 3, 4, 5, 9, 11, etc.—A duplication of the vocal melody, as found in SCHUBERT, "Winterreise" (op. 89), No. 15; or in SCHUMANN, op. 25, No. 10; and op. 27, No. 4,—is very effective.

But it is permissible, and common, to assign to the instrumental accompaniment the task of reflecting and emphasizing the poetic, epic, or dramatic contents of the text; and, in so doing, it will become more or less characteristic, and assume a degree of independence, which, *at times*, may even exceed that of the vocal part itself.

See SCHUBERT, "Müller-Lieder" No. 3 (Bass part), No. 12; "Winterreise," Nos. 2, 4, 9, 17. SCHUMANN, op. 24, No. 6; op. 27, No. 3; op. 30, No. 1; "Löwenbraut," op. 31, No. 1; "Frauenliebe und -leben," op. 42, No. 6; "Dichterliebe," op. 48, Nos. 4, 6, 9, 13, 16.

This will give rise most naturally to the prelude, interludes and postlude in the accompaniment (during the pauses of the vocal part); though the necessity of *occasional interludes*,—not too frequent or long,—both for the relief of the singer and the benefit of the structural design, is sufficiently imperative, in itself.

See SCHUBERT, "Winterreise," Nos. 2, 6, 14, 19, 24 (especially).

SCHUMANN, op. 25, No. 3; op. 24, Nos. 5, 6 (elaborate postludes). "Dichterliebe," Nos. 5, 6, 9, 10, 11, 12, 15, 16 (elaborate postludes).

Additional examples for reference and study:

Other Songs of SCHUBERT, BEETHOVEN and SCHUMANN, not referred to above.

The Songs of MENDELSSOHN, BRAHMS, ROBERT FRANZ; RUBINSTEIN, GRIEG, JENSEN, TAUBERT; Song-albums (Schirmer ed.).

2. The instrumental Duo.

129. The instruments most frequently chosen for the *duo* are the Pianoforte and Violin, or Pfte. and Violoncello.

The rules for the conception and treatment of this style of music conform in general to those of the Song (excepting those bearing upon the text), but with such additional liberty, or modifications, as are conditioned by

The wider compass,
greater technical facilities and resources, and
specific peculiarities of the "solo"-instrument.

The absence of words leaves the composer without a certain quality of melodic stimulus and suggestion, but, at the same time, at liberty to develop his musical conception and purpose without embarrassment. Some theoretical guides to his natural musical impulses are recorded in par. 94, 95, 96, 97, which are to be reviewed. See also par. 137.

The student, if unfamiliar with the Violin and Violoncello, should not undertake to write for them until he has consulted some expert performer, and obtained from him sufficient information concerning the tone, specific tone-effects, compass, and the various technical characteristics of the instrument. The same law applies to the use of the Flute, Clarinet, Cornet, Horn, etc.

The species of composition for the instrumental *duo* is to be selected from the list given in the next paragraph (or par. 126 *a*).

Examples for reference: *

Violin and Pianoforte: Raff, Cavatine.—Svendsen, Romance, op. 26.—H. Wieniawski, Légende, op. 17.—F. Ries, Romance from Suite II; Gondoliera from Suite III.—Max Bruch, Swedish Dances, op. 63 (essentially lyric); Romanze.—Jadassohn, Serenade op. 108*b*, Nos. 1, 2, 3, 4.—Spohr, Barcarolle.—Bazzini, Élégie.—Joachim, Romanza.—Dvořák, Notturno, op. 40.—Ernst, Élégie.—Vieuxtemps, Reverie.

Violoncello and Pianoforte: Mendelssohn, Song without Words *for 'Cello* (*D*-major, op. 109).—Dvořák, "Waldesruhe."—Popper, op. 3, Nos. 2, 6; Nocturne, op. 22.—Goltermann, Cantilena in *E*.—H. Sitt, Romanza and Serenata.—Davidoff, Romance sans paroles, op. 23; Lied, op. 16, No. 2.

3. The Song without Words, etc.

130a. The conception of this class of instrumental compositions, most commonly set for the Pianoforte, or as *duo*

* See Preface, section II.

(par. 129), is invariably the same as that of the vocal Song, viz.: a continuous, coherent, tuneful melodic thread,—*cantilena*,—as distinctly predominating element; with a more or less characteristic and elaborate equipment in the accompanying parts. Each specific variety of conventional style embraced under this heading,—Romanza, Nocturne, Barcarolle, etc. (par. 126*a*),—will call forth its own peculiar modifications, in the *execution* of this aim; but the ruling principle is identical in them all. These modifications, dictated by the special character and purpose of the chosen variety, may be inferred from the self-explaining titles, and need no exposition here. See GROVE's dictionary, or BAKER's "Dictionary of Musical Terms." Any form may be employed, from 2-Part Song up to Song with one "Trio." See par. 137.

Examples, from pianoforte literature, for reference:

CHOPIN, Nocturnes (especially Nos. 1, 2, 4, 5, 7, 8, 11, 13, 15, 16, 17, 18, 19).—FIELD, Nocturnes (Nos. 1, 2, 4, 5, 6, 7, 9, 10, 11, 13, 14, 16, 18).—MENDELSSOHN, "Songs without Words" (especially Nos. 1, 6, 7, 12, 18, 19, 22, 25, 29, 30, 31, 36, 37, 40, 43, 46).—SCHUBERT, Impromptu op. 90, No. 3; *Momens musicals*, op. 94, No. 2.—BEETHOVEN, Pfte. Son. op. 27, No. 1, *Adagio*; op. 27, No. 2, first movement; op. 79, *Andante;* op. 109, third movement, *Theme;* op. 110, third movement, *Arioso dolente*.—SCHUMANN, "Kinderscenen" (op. 15), Nos. 1, 4, 5, 7, 12; "Fantasiestücke" (op. 12), Nos. 1, 3; Pfte. Son. op. 22, *Andantino;* Romanzas (op. 28), Nos. 1, 2; op. 82, No. 9.—W. BARGIEL, Élégie, op. 31, No. 2.—DVOŘÁK, Silhouettes, op. 8, Nos. 6, 10, 11.—GADE, Idyls, op. 34, Nos. 2, 4.—GRIEG, op. 12, Nos. 1 and 7; op. 38, Nos. 1, 3, 6; op. 43, No. 6; op. 47, Nos. 3, 7; op. 54, No. 4; op. 62, No. 5.—LISZT, 3 Notturnos ("Liebesträume"); Gondoliera and Canzone from "Venezia e Napoli"; Consolations.—MOSZKOWSKI, op. 31, No. 1; op. 36, No. 2.—RAFF, 2 Élégies, op. 149.—RUBINSTEIN, 2 melodies, op. 3; Barcarolle, op. 50, No. 3 (*g*-minor); also Barcarolles in *a*-minor, *f*-minor, and *G*-major.—PADEREWSKI, Mélodie, op. 8. No. 3.—ST.-SAËNS, Chanson, op. 72, No. 5.—TSCHAIKOWSKY, Chanson, op. 40, No. 2.; Romance, op. 51, No. 5.

(b) The *Ballade* belongs, properly, also to this class, but its character is indefinite and variable. It is usually more elaborate, longer, and more dramatic than the Romanza, and constructed in Group-form. It implies a more or less ideal narrative.

See CHOPIN, 4 Ballades.—BRAHMS, op. 10, Nos. 1, 2, 4.—REINECKE, Ballade, op. 20.

4. THE HYMN, ANTHEM, GLEE, ETC.

131a. It may appear that these species of composition, commonly known as "PART-SONGS," belong to the second class (par. 126*b*), characterized by predominance of the Harmony; and, indeed, this fallacious view has been often confirmed by writers not sufficiently scrupulous in regard to artistic distinctions. But it is nevertheless strictly true that, in those examples of the "Part-Song" which fall within the domain of the homophonic forms, *the lyric element must prevail.* One of the parts, usually the Soprano, must consist in a distinctly melodious, coherent and continuous *cantilena*, which the other parts chiefly serve to accompany and support.

(b) For the Sacred Hymn, Chorale, Anthem, etc., words may be chosen from a church hymn-book, the Psalms and other parts of the Bible, or from the ritual of any denominational service. The use of *Latin* sentences from the Roman Catholic liturgy is strongly commended.

(c) The *ensemble* most commonly adopted for the setting, is the mixed quartet (Soprano, Alto, Tenor, Bass); but the female trio (more rarely female quartet), the male trio or quartet, the mixed trio, and the duet (the association of any two voices), are all equally practicable and often very effective. In any case, excepting perhaps the duet, the "parts" may be rendered by solo singers, or by a chorus; and either with instrumental accompaniment (Pfte. or Organ), or without—("*a cappella*").

(d) The choice of *secular*, instead of sacred, text, will influence the character of the musical conception, but none of the above details. The dignity and seriousness which should distinguish all music designed for religious use and association, is more or less thoroughly supplanted, in secular music, by such brightness, gaiety, grace, dramatic fervor, pathos or brilliancy, as befits the character of the words selected.

(e) The structural design will depend largely upon the text. For the Hymn, the Double-period form, or *simple* 2-Part Song-form, is best. For the Anthem, or the secular "Part-Song," the 3-Part form should be used, if possible; though the "Group of Parts" is often more convenient, and affords excellent opportunity for characteristic and interesting formal designs, in which, for instance, the several Parts of the Group may be differently treated (as solo, duet, quartet or chorus, perhaps in different varieties of time, tempo and character). The conditions of the instrumental accompaniment are similar to those explained in connection with the "Song" (par. 128*g*), though, as a rule, less elaborate and independent. For more specific definitions, see GROVE's dictionary.

See also: MENDELSSOHN, female Terzetto from *Elijah;* Duet from *St. Paul* (No. 31); also Chorales (Nos. 3, 9, 16), and Choruses (Nos. 26, 33) from *St. Paul.*

The vocal duets of MENDELSSOHN, RUBINSTEIN, SCHUMANN, and BRAHMS.

BRAHMS, "Ave Maria"; 13th Psalm; Song from Ossian's Fingal.

Anthem-books for mixed voices (Schirmer ed.).—Reference may also be made to a *few* specimens of the "Part-Songs," sacred and secular, for various ensembles of male, female, or mixed voices, contained in great number in the 8vo collections of the edition of G. Schirmer; and similar collections of other publishers.

CHAPTER XXI.

THE ÉTUDE-CLASS.

1. THE ÉTUDE, OR STUDY.

132. In the genuine representatives of this class of composition, the melodic element (as sustained *cantilena*), though never totally absent, is so vague, imperfect and fragmentary, or so disguised and obscured, as to recede into the background, while the chords, i. e., the Harmonies, both individually and collectively, stand out in proportionately greater prominence.

In the ÉTUDE proper, the harmonies are not, as a rule, thus prominent in unbroken bulk, but in some figurated form (as shown in Ex. 4 and context). For this figuration of the harmony, a motive is adopted with a view to some *technical* purpose; hence the titles: Étude, Study, or Exercise. But, for the simple reason that the aim of a "study" is not always a purely *technical* one, these species may, without inconsistency, sometimes assume a distinctly lyric character. See par. 126*d*.

The design of the Étude is usually one of the Song-forms,—possibly, though rarely, with "Trio."

See CHOPIN, Études, op. 10 (especially Nos. 1, 2, 5, 7, 8, 10, 11, 12); Études, op. 25 (especially Nos. 2, 3, 4, 5, 6, 8, 9, 10, 11, 12). Op. 10, Nos. 3, 6, 9, and op. 25 No. 7, are lyric.—AD. HENSELT, Études, op. 5, No. 1, (both lyric and étude-class), Nos. 2, 3, 7, 9, 12 (10 and 11, lyric).—See also a *few* Études of CLEMENTI, CRAMER and CZERNY.—LISZT, three Concert-études; *Études transcendentales*.—MENDELSSOHN, Études op. 104, Nos. 1, 3.—MOSCHELES, Studies, op. 70.—RAFF, "La fileuse," op. 157, No. 2.—SCHUMANN, op. 3.—RUBINSTEIN, op. 23, and op. 81.—TSCHAIKOWSKY, op. 40, No. 1.—

2. THE TOCCATA, CAPRICCIO, SCHERZO, ETC.

133a. When the motive or figure, upon which the "figuration" or dissolution of the harmony is to be based, assumes more of a *thematic* character, and thus enters more essentially into the *structure* of the composition than is the case with the chiefly technical figures of the Study, the style is usually designated Toccata (especially when the figure is small), or Caprice, and Prelude. Review par. 126*b*.

In the latter species, and also in the Impromptu, Intermezzo, etc., the harmony frequently appears in unbroken, or but partially broken, bulk.

(b) The Scherzo was originally nearly identical with the "Caprice." Later it was substituted for the Minuet in the Symphony, Sonata, and Quartet, and adopted the time ($\frac{3}{4}$) of that Dance. Finally, it superseded the latter, appearing in duple as well as triple time, and often as an independent piece, without reference to the Symphony.

(c) In all of these species of composition the element of Melody, it must be remembered, is necessarily *always present in a more or less apparent and assertive degree*, but neither as conspicuously, nor as continuously, as in the lyric class. Certain sections of an Étude, Toccata, etc., or of a Dance-form (e. g., the "Trio"), may be purely lyric; and, as already stated, the distinctions of style, especially among the étude-species, are quite vague,—often scarcely perceptible. Review par. 126*d*.

(d) These species are usually, though by no means always, written in the homophonic forms. In this case, the designs chosen are the Song-forms,—rarely with "Trio," excepting in the Scherzo, which sometimes has two "Trios."

Examples for reference:

Toccata-species, and **Prelude:** BACH, Well-tempered Clavichord, Vol. I, Preludes 1, 2, 5, 6, 15, 21; Vol. II, Preludes 3 (1st section), 12, 15; Partita No. 1, "Gigue."—BARGIEL, Étude and Toccata, op. 45.—SCHUBERT, Momens musicals, op. 94, Nos. 4, 5.—SCHUMANN, Arabesque, op. 18; op. 21, No. 2.—

HELLER, Præludien, op. 81.—CHOPIN, Preludes, op. 28; op. 45.—ST.-SAËNS, Toccata, op. 72, No. 3.—MENDELSSOHN, "Songs without Words," Nos. 8, 24, 34, 38.—RUBINSTEIN, Preludes, op. 24, Nos. 1, 4.

Caprice, Impromptu, etc.: CHOPIN, Impromptus, op. 29, op. 51, op. 66.—GADE, Aquarelles, op. 57, Nos. 1, 3, 5; Fantasies, op. 41, Nos. 2, 3.—GRIEG, op. 43, Nos. 1, 4; op. 62, No. 4.—MOSZKOWSKI, op. 7, No. 2; op. 36, No. 6.—SCHUBERT, Impromptu, op. 90, No. 4.—RUBINSTEIN, Caprices, op. 21.—TSCHAIKOWSKY, Capriccio, op. 8.—SCHUMANN, Intermezzi, op. 4; op. 12, Nos. 2, 5, 6, 7, 8.

Scherzo: BEETHOVEN, Pfte. Son. op. 2, No. 2, third movement; op. 26, second movement; op. 28, third movement.—CHOPIN, Pfte. Son. op. 35, second movement; Scherzos, op. 20, 31, 39, 54.—GRIEG, op. 54, No. 5.—MENDELSSOHN, "Songs without Words," No. 45; op. 16, No. 2.—SCHUMANN, Pfte. Son. op. 14, second movement; op. 22, third movement; op. 12, No. 4; op. 21, Nos. 1, 3, 6; op. 26, No. 3; op. 32, No. 1.—SCHUBERT, Pfte. Sonatas Nos. 1 and 9 (Peters ed.) third movement of each.—HUMMEL, Pfte. Son. op. 106, second movement.—BRAHMS, op. 4.

CHAPTER XXII.

THE DANCE-CLASS.

1. OLD DANCE-SPECIES.

134. Very many of the older dances have fallen into disuse, and the corresponding musical species are therefore seldom written expressly for the purpose of dancing. But the old types, with their respective rhythmic peculiarities, are nevertheless often adopted, and invested with the characteristics and charms of modern musical setting.

For the list of old dance-forms, and their several details, reference must be made to GROVE's dictionary, or some standard book upon "Dances," old and modern. See par. 126*c*, and par. 127; and examine, carefully, the following examples of these dance-species as found, in their original condition (in older writings), and in the idealized expositions of more modern composers:

Allemande, Courante, Bourrée, Sarabande, Passepied: BACH, English Suites; French Suites; Partitas.—LES MAÎTRES DU CLAVECIN (Litolff ed.), Vol. I, pages 68, 69, 70, 82–86, 117–119, 166, 167, 189; Vol. II, pages 16, 46, 47, 109, 110, 174 (*Tambourin*), 178, 221 (*Galliardo*).

Gavotte: BACH, Engl. Suites, Nos. 3, 6; French Suites, Nos. 5, 6 (Ex. 75 of this book).—LES MAÎTRES DU CLAVECIN, Vol. I, pages 50, 191; Vol. II, p. 28.

Gigue: Les Maîtres du Clavecin, Vol. I, p. 58, 74, 93, 132, 178, 192; Vol. II, p. 48, 50, 111, 142, 144, 189.

Minuet: Bach, Engl. Suite, No. 4; French Suites, Nos. 1, 2, 3, 6; Partitas, Nos. 1, 4.—Les Maîtres du Clavecin, Vol. I, p. 128, 143; Vol. II, p. 150, 187, 196, 200, 208.—Haydn, Pfte. Son. No. 1 (Cotta ed.), second movement; Symphonies and String-quartets.—Mozart, Pfte. Son. No. 9 (Cotta ed.), second movement; No. 12, third movement; Symphonies and String-quartets.—Beethoven, Pfte. Son. op. 10, No. 3, third movement; op. 22, ditto; op. 31, No. 3, ditto.—Schubert, Pfte. Sonatas, Nos. 4, 8, third movement of each.—Mendelssohn, Son. op. 6, second movement.—Grieg, op. 57, No. 1.—Paderewski, op. 14, No. 1.

Further: Bargiel, Suite of old Dances, op. 7.—Rubinstein, ditto, op. 38.—Moszkowski, Bourrée, op. 38, No. 1.—Raff, Tambourin, op. 204, No. 6.—Silas, Gavotte in *e*-minor.

2. Modern Dance-species.

135. The most prominent place among modern dances with musical setting is assigned to the Waltz, Mazurka, Polonaise, Polka, Tarantella, Quadrille, and a few others of national, rather than universal, importance. Their musical exposition is sometimes brief and simple; but more commonly they are idealized, or elaborated into "Concert-pieces" of considerable length and freedom of form, without neglect, however, of the distinctive rhythmic peculiarities of the respective species. Information concerning the latter may be obtained from the authorities already cited, and from careful inspection of the following examples:

Chopin, Waltzes; Mazurkas (especially Nos. 1, 5, 6, 12, 13, 14, 17, 18, 20, 22, 24, 25, 26, 32, 36, 41, 47); Polonaises (especially Nos. 1, 2, 3, 4, 6, 8, 9, 10); Tarantella, op. 43; Bolero, op. 19.—Johann Strauss, a *few* Waltzes and other Dances (Schirmer ed.).—Brahms, Waltzes for 4 hands, op. 39; Hungarian Dances, for 2 or 4 hands.—Dvořák, Waltzes, op. 54; Slavonian Dances, for 2 or 4 hands, op. 46, op. 72.—Grieg, op. 12, Nos. 2, 5, 6; op. 38, Nos. 4, 5; op. 47, Nos. 1, 6; op. 62, No. 1.—Liszt, Polonaise in E major; Tarantella ("Venezia e Napoli").—Moszkowski, Waltzes, op. 8; op. 46, No. 1.—Rubinstein, "Le Bal," op. 14.—St.-Saëns, Waltzes, op. 72, No. 4; op. 104.—Tschaikowsky, Mazurka, op. 9, No. 3.—Weber, "Invitation to the Dance" (Waltz).

3. The March.

136. Though not a "Dance," in the specific sense of the term, the March belongs in the foremost rank of that class of musical compositions in which marked *rhythm* is the ruling trait and purpose.

To a certain extent this is also true of the Polonaise and Minuet (each of which might be defined as a "March in triple time"), the Quadrilles, and some of the stately old dances (Pavana, Passamezzo, etc.).

The March is written in duple time ($\frac{4}{4}$), and usually in the form of a Song with "Trio" (rarely without "Trio"). Its character is generally vigorous, though the special type depends upon the nature of the procession which the March is to accompany and regulate,—hence the distinctions: Wedding-March, Funeral-M., Festival-M., Military-M., Quickstep, etc.

See Beethoven, Pfte. Son. op. 26, third movement; op. 101, second movement.—Chopin, Pfte. Son. op. 35, third movement.—Mendelssohn, "Wedding-March"; Priests' March from *Athalia*, op. 74.—Schubert, Marches for 4 hands (Peters ed.), including "Characteristic Marches" ($\frac{6}{8}$ time) op. 121.—Schumann, Marches, op. 76; op. 99, Nos. 11, 14.—Tschaikowsky, Funeral-March, op. 40, No. 3.—Bargiel, "Marcia fantastica," op. 31, No. 3 ($\frac{3}{4}$ and $\frac{2}{4}$ time).—Brahms, "German Requiem," second number, first section ($\frac{3}{4}$ time).

The student is also urged to examine the works of *leading* American and English composers in the homophonic forms, among which many exquisite examples of the conventional styles will be found, worthy of imitation.

Conclusion: Criticism.

137. In his judgment of his own compositions, or those of other writers, the conscientious composer or critic must reason from the following vital considerations, testing each question in turn with the utmost objectiveness and fullness:

(1) **Is the work sufficiently *melodious;* and is its melodic delineation striking, agreeable, and ingenious?**

(2) **Is the *Formal Design* rational and clear?**

(3) **Is its *Rhythmic Structure* distinct and effective?**

(4) **Does it contain sufficient *harmonic* and *modulatory* fullness and charm?**

(5) **Is the demand of *Contrast* adequately respected; and the bane of *Monotony* avoided?**

(6) **Is it written conveniently and sensibly, with regard to the *technique* of the instrument for which it is designed?**

(7) **Is its *title* appropriate?**

(8) **Does it *sound* as well as it looks upon the paper?**

There are many other considerations of minor importance. But if the young composer can honestly affirm each of these main questions, he may confidently defer all other details until he shall have secured the resources of contrapuntal technique, by faithful study and exercise of the

POLYPHONIC FORMS OF COMPOSITION.

THE END.